Ethiopia, Great Britain,
and the United States, 1941–1974

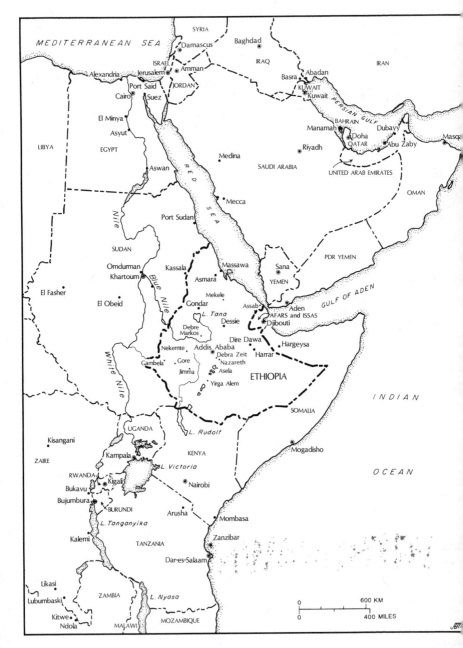

Map 1. Ethiopia in geographical context.

Ethiopia, Great Britain, and the United States, 1941–1974

The Politics of Empire

Harold G. Marcus

University of California Press

Berkeley / Los Angeles / London

University of California Press
Berkeley and Los Angeles, California

University of California Press, Ltd.
London, England

Printed in the United States of America

1 2 3 4 5 6 7 8 9

Library of Congress Cataloging in Publication Data

Marcus, Harold G.
    Ethiopia, Great Britain, and the United States, 1941–1974.

    Bibliography: p.
    Includes index.
    1. Ethiopia—Politics and government—1889–1974.
2. Ethiopia—Foreign relations—1889–1974. 3. Ethiopia
—Relations—United States. 4. United States—Relations—
Ethiopia. 5. Ethiopia—Relations—Great Britain.
6. Great Britain—Relations—Ethiopia. 7. Ethiopia
—History—Coup d'etat, 1960. I. Title.
DT387.9.M37 1983   327.63   82-8522
ISBN 0-520-04613-7   AACR2

For Susan
who deserves dedication

Contents

Preface

The idea for this book germinated in Ethiopia during 1961, when social life in Addis Ababa was dominated by reminiscences of the abortive coup of 1960 against Haile Sellassie. Most people were convinced that U.S. intervention had guaranteed the loyalist victory and the emperor's return to power. None could substantiate their charges, but all knowingly discussed the intricacies of American paramountcy in Ethiopia and the primacy of Washington's need to retain important military facilities in Eritrea. Indeed, it was an easily observable fact that the U.S. Embassy in Addis Ababa wielded enormous influence over its host government, and I grew fascinated by the visibility of American power in the Horn of Africa. I decided that one day I would investigate and write about United States involvement in postwar Ethiopia, in the 1960 coup, and thereafter.

Periodic research commenced after my return to the United States in 1963, and became a preoccupation after 1976, when the State Department's Freedom of Information Office made embassy files on the coup of 1960 available. Although I had begun to draft the book in 1977, research continued until January 1982: by then, I had worked through a new transfusion of documents released in 1980-81 by the State Department, the Department of Defense, and the National Security Council, and had read the Foreign Office Archives for 1950 and 1951, the years when the British Military Mission in Ethiopia, and therefore London's primacy there, were being dismantled. My research has been as thorough as possible, although, given the way the Freedom of Information Act works, my data remain incomplete. I apologize to those who will find that my scholarship fails to conform to the terminology of their disciplines or to the ideology of their politics. I also regret that I have been unable to provide a comparative analysis, an inadequacy that stems from the limitations of my craft and interest. I leave it to subsequent writers, therefore, to find more data, to reify my study in language more appropriate to their concerns, and to supply the comparative perspectives lacking here.

I now realize that one day, when more information is available, I shall return to the period of the sixties in Ethiopia, to write about AID, the Peace Corps, and the many other activities which brought thousands of Americans to Addis Ababa and elsewhere in Haile Sellassie's empire. Their work originated in Washington's effort to retain the emperor on his throne but led directly and indirectly to his overthrow—the ultimate irony. The present book is inevitably a preface to the American decade in Ethiopia and, as such, concentrates on geopolitics, strategies of empire and state, and the military. Since this is not the last word on the subject, but very close to the first, I welcome all criticisms, emendations, and amendments.

I want to thank Donald Levine, John Cohen, Patrick Gilkes, Richard Greenfield, David Robinson, Christopher Clapham, Tekeste Negash, James McCann, Alberto Sbacchi, Richard Pankhurst, and Jon Edwards for their advice and criticism. I am grateful to the staffs of the following organizations for their unfailing courtesy and cooperation: the National Archives in Washington, the Public Record Office in London, the Institute of Ethiopian Studies in Addis Ababa, and the Freedom of Information Offices in the Departments of Defense and State and the National Security Council. I am indebted in particular to my friend Robert Caldwell of the State Department who helped to declassify so many necessary documents and then delivered them to my home in East Lansing en route to his daughter's graduation from a western university. Out of many typists, the names of Christine Russell, lately of MSU's Department of History, and Kay Irish of the African Studies Center should be printed here in recognition of their vital role in making this book possible. Last, I record my deep gratitude to the Social Science Research Council for helping to support some necessary overseas research and to Michigan State University whose liberal leave and financial aid policies stimulate scholarship.

Harold G. Marcus

Bailly, France
18 February 1982

Terms and Abbreviations

Ethiopian titles of honor and respect

Ato	Literally "sir" in Amharic; now "Mr."
Blatta	A title associated with the lesser nobility in Ethiopia
Dejazmatch or Dej.	A title roughly equivalent to earl
Negus	Literally "king"; often used to refer to the Emperor of Ethiopia, or King of Kings
Ras	Literally "head" in Amharic; a title equivalent to duke

Abbreviations used in text and sources

AID	Agency for International Development
BMME	British Military Mission in Ethiopia
EAL	Ethiopian Airlines
E.C.	Ethiopian Calendar (which follows the Julian prototype)
ENC	Ethiopian National Corporation
FO	Foreign Office (Great Britain)
FY	Fiscal Year
HMG	His (or Her) Majesty's Government (Great Britain)
IBG	Imperial Bodyguard
IEG	Imperial Ethiopian Government
JCS	Joint Chiefs of Staff (United States)
MAAG	Military Assistance Advisory Group
MAP	Military Assistance Program
MDAP	Mutual Defense Assistance Pact
MESC	Middle East Supply Center (a Cairo-based, British-controlled, trade authority)

NDC	No decimal classification
NEA	Near Eastern and African Bureau (of the U.S. State Department)
NSC	National Security Council (United States)
SD	(United States) State Department
SYL	Somali Youth League
UKCC	United Kingdom Commercial Corporation
USAF	United States Air Force
USNA	United States National Archives
WO	War Office (Great Britain)

Introduction

The abortive coup of December 1960 was an important episode in late modern Ethiopian history. For the first time, the potential power of the modern military revealed itself in Addis Ababa, if not nationwide. Furthermore, an inchoate but nonetheless recognizable radical-left program and set of ideas was publicly enunciated. It was a time of mayhem, warfare, and death, forecasting some of the events of the Ethiopian revolution of 1974, if none of its achievements. Then, as now, the students supported the revolutionaries, and then, as now, had to yield to the power of the military. Finally, various elites sought and obtained the support of a superpower.

United States intervention, it has been alleged, determined the internal struggle in favor of Haile Sellassie's loyalists. As Richard Greenfield put it:

> American interest was natural and inevitable considering their . . . base in Asmara, their agreements with Haile Selassie, their influence at the air force base and the presence of their military mission (not to mention their fear that in Gimmame Neway they had educated a communist). Their involvement was obvious and unconcealed—an American colonel later rode in an open jeep in front of Haile Selassie's vehicle when after subsequent fighting the latter re-entered the stricken capital—and it has been discussed, even criticised, by several American political writers.[1]

As I investigated the history of the coup, it indeed became obvious that by 1960 Washington's only real interests in Ethiopia were the continued existence of U.S. military facilities and the retention of a leader who supported America's geopolitics in the Red Sea–Indian Ocean area.

The bases of U.S. policy had narrowed considerably since 1941–42, when the State Department reopened relations with Ethi-

---

1. Richard Greenfield, *Ethiopia, A New Political History* (London, 1965), pp. 412–13.

opia. Then, Washington could proudly broadcast its commitment to self-determination, stress its traditional anticolonialism, demonstrate to Afro-Americans that the government was fighting their war, too, and reveal to the world that the White House was as much concerned with the rehabilitation and reconstruction of Axis-occupied countries as with winning the war. The State Department could also quietly ensure that American products would find new, postwar markets and could obtain landing rights for U.S. airlines. Implicit in the last two objectives was the destruction of London's hegemony in the Middle East, an aim which Haile Sellassie explicitly sought for Ethiopia.

In 1941-42, he perceived a British threat to Solomonic sovereignty and began to court the United States to counter Britain's weight in East Africa. By 1944, he had been successful enough to interpose the threat of American intervention into vitally important Anglo-Ethiopian negotiations. Of course, the monarch could not know that in 1942, London had rejected various plans to incorporate Ethiopia into British East Africa and had opted for the country's independence as a "native state." Haile Sellassie also failed to realize that the British Empire's will to dominate and rule was by then a matter of history, based as it was on economic strength long since dissipated. Prime Minister Churchill may have closed his eyes to Britain's eroding world position, but Anthony Eden and his lieutenants at the Foreign Office observed the process on a daily basis. For them, one remedy—unpalatable though it certainly was—was to use the wealth and power of the United States to brace the British Empire, particularly where Anglo-American interests corresponded, and especially on the semiautonomous periphery of British hegemony, in such places as Saudi Arabia and Ethiopia.

The Ethiopian case is therefore one example of the historic shift in world power from the United Kingdom to the United States which began even before World War II and ended only in the 1960s. The process was often regarded as great power competition between London and Washington or seen, mostly by uncomprehending British expatriates and empire loyalists, as crass American opportunism. In Arabia and Ethiopia, however, it was an arrangement of convenience, considered, sponsored, and even orchestrated by Whitehall. My analysis gratefully follows the conclusions of W.

Roger Louis and Christopher Thorne, who suggest that the global struggle forced the United States and Great Britain into an uneasy cooperation.[2] I add, however, that the need to order the postwar world compelled policy coordination to continue, a point underscored by the Suez crisis of 1956.

However begrudgingly, London was willing to hand over its authority to the United States because the two nations shared basically similar economic and strategic aims. Nowhere was the mutuality of these interests better revealed than in the need for Middle Eastern oil. In 1948, Admiral of the Fleet William D. Leahy, then chairman of the Joint Chiefs of Staff, observed that American policy in the Red Sea area should consider not only "our over-all requirements within the framework of our global strategy" but "also the security interests of our potential allies, particularly Great Britain." The concerns of London and Washington in the region were "so interrelated that they must be considered as a whole."[3]

As rapidly as America had become involved in the business of world hegemony, so had Ethiopia become part of the world economy. The process of linkage had actually commenced in the twenties and thirties, when the general incorporation of Africa into the world economy was happening swiftly because of the postwar consolidation of colonialism.[4] Neither historic Abyssinia nor its empire were immune from this global process: during those two decades Haile Sellassie was busily modernizing and centralizing government and reforming and reequipping his military. He needed to purchase expertise, technology, and weapons from advanced nations, and the necessary revenues could come only from the sale of Ethiopia's primary products, particularly coffee. The emperor, his close associates, and the government bureaucracy composed an oligarchy which, in cooperation with foreign merchants and traders, exploited the Ethiopian economy to meet the demands of the world commodities market. Haile Sellassie's policy provided enough revenues to permit the preliminary modernization of the military, the

2. W. H. Louis, *Imperialism at Bay* (Oxford, 1977), p. 7; Christopher Thorne, *Allies of a Kind* (New York, 1978), p. 699.

3. Leahy to Secretary of Defense, Washington, 5 Aug. 1948, U.S. National Archives, National Security Council, "Disposition of the Former Italian Colonies in Africa," *A Report to the National Security Council*, n. 19 (1948).

4. Catherine Coquery-Vidrovitch, "La Mise en Dépendance de l'Afrique noire: essai de periodisation, 1800–1970," *Cahiers d'études Africaines* 16 (1976):36.

government, the infrastructure of the state, and Addis Ababa, which became the imperial showcase.[5]

Upon returning to Ethiopia in 1941 with the combined Ethiopian-Commonwealth forces that ended the Italian occupation, the emperor and a cadre of surviving and newly incorporated oligarchs immediately reverted to the political economy that had functioned so well. Given the ongoing war, demand was high for all primary products, but particularly for wheat and other cereals in short supply in the Middle East. Under the colonial regime, the agribusiness sectors of the economy had expanded in response to demands from settlers, the metropole, and greater Italian East Africa. The fascists had laid down thousands of kilometers of all-weather roads so as to more efficiently administer and exploit the country; the restored Addis Ababa government used those roads to tap the empire's richest agricultural areas in order to meet the needs of the Middle East. Furthermore, the Italians had left behind tens of thousands of Ethiopians oriented to a consuming and money-using economy. Thus, the oligarchy had the means and the manpower to facilitate production quickly; it established trading corporations and trucking concerns to capture every bit of profit, and presided over the sale of such high-demand imports as cotton goods, many of which entered the country through lend-lease. Although a few American officials complained about the obvious venality and corruption, Washington followed a pro-Haile Sellassie policy, provided some weapons, a few airplanes, a number of new trucks, and even facilitated a summit meeting with President Roosevelt in early 1943.

For Haile Sellassie, such recognition was not enough, and his government hatched ambitious plans and programs, based largely upon the findings of the American Technical Mission which had studied Ethiopia's economy in 1944–45. Washington responded in a piecemeal fashion, coming up with just enough aid, particularly for Ethiopian Airlines, to frustrate Addis Ababa. The emperor grew disillusioned about ever obtaining enough economic and military assistance to facilitate his programs; he turned to the Eastern bloc and, in 1948, successfully negotiated with Czechoslovakia an arms deal which sent a shiver of apprehension through Washington's geopoliticians. By then, American planners were concerned about

5. H. G. Marcus, "The Infrastructure of the Italo-Ethiopian Crisis: Haile Sellassie, The Solomonic Empire, and the World Economy, 1916–1936," *Proceedings of the Fifth International Conference on Ethiopian Studies,* part B (Chicago, 1979).

Great Britain's withdrawal from the Ogaden, an event ironically spurred by the activities of the Sinclair Oil Company of New York. Meanwhile, the Pentagon and the National Security Council became nervous about the imminent British evacuation of Eritrea and increasingly came to appreciate that only Ethiopian sovereignty there would guarantee U.S. control over what was becoming a strategically important signals facility in Asmara (Kagnew Station) and a convenient supply and oil depot in Massawa.

This determination helped Addis Ababa to obtain control over Eritrea, an overriding foreign policy objective since 1941. A grateful Haile Sellassie demonstrated his continuing commitment to the Western idea of collective security by sending Ethiopian soldiers to police and die in Korea. This gesture, and the continuous pro-Western statements emanating from Addis Ababa, led John Foster Dulles to include Ethiopia in his southern tier strategy for keeping the Middle East free of Soviet influence. The primary role on the African side of the Red Sea had been assigned to Egypt, but Nasser balked at the State Department's obvious attempt to control Arab oil and destiny. Washington turned, therefore, to Haile Sellassie, and in 1952 the new relationship yielded an agreement to provide technical assistance (under the Point Four Program established during the Truman Administration), followed in May 1953 by a military assistance pact and a treaty governing the use of U.S. facilities in Asmara and Massawa until 1978. Even so, it was not until the Suez crisis of 1956 that the United States finally provided Ethiopia with the type, if not the amount, of American assistance the emperor really wanted.

From 1957 on, Washington contributed sparingly to Ethiopia's military program and tended to promote economic projects that would assist the defense effort; simultaneously, the dynamics of the Ethiopian economy tied the country increasingly to international commodities exchanges. Meanwhile, a new group of Ethiopians, many of them trained or educated in the United States, entered the army and the government. They were dismayed by the sordid improprieties at the highest levels of government and by the squalid exploitation of the masses by local and provincial administrators. They became increasingly frustrated as their plans to reform and modernize Ethiopia were thwarted by the entrenched oligarchy and its bureaucratic allies. They became embittered when African colonies, which supposedly had suffered under the yoke of European

domination, emerged into independence with more modern economies and infrastructures than Ethiopia enjoyed. Although the political dissidents did not then identify Ethiopia's domestic problems
with the American connection—indeed they looked to the United
States as an ideal—they quickly concluded that Haile Sellassie and
his myrmidons would have to be removed before the country could
advance.

The conspirators, although a very small group, represented
Ethiopia's emergent military and bureaucratic intelligentsia. They
were left-of-center reformers, who believed in the efficacy of their
own Western educations as a vehicle of modernization. Their considerations included a fervid desire to improve the Ethiopian standard of living by reducing corruption and venality in government.
They were so certain of the support of all right-thinking Ethiopians
that they failed to apprise their colleagues in the army and the air
force of their plans. By using the small imperial bodyguard as the
sole lever of change, the cabal created suspicion and distrust of its
motives and goals. Moreover, the coup was so ridden with mistakes,
oversights, and absurdities that the attempt rapidly dissipated into
failure.

Its miscarriage was almost exclusively an Ethiopian affair. The
U.S. Embassy remained neutral until it became clear that the loyalists would win, and only then offered important staff and telecommunications support to the emperor's men. The mission's response was based upon the intelligence gathered by Lt. Col. W. H.
Crosson, Jr., the army attaché, who crisscrossed Addis Ababa many
times during the coup, observing, talking, evaluating. His strong
personality and opinions influenced policy in an embassy which had
no predetermined principles and rules to guide officials in cases of
a coup or an attempted coup, and where the ambassador was
new to his job. Thus, the mission delivered its support according to
circumstance and opportunity, and its major interest was not the
Ethiopian political situation but the protection of America's military facilities in Eritrea.

So long as these were guaranteed, it was unlikely that Washington
would impinge upon the established order in Ethiopia, even though
embassy officials fully understood the rot and reaction of the
emperor's regime. In fact, they informed Washington that Addis
Ababa was doing little or nothing to address the causes of the
attempted coup, and, as a matter of record, they foresaw the revo-

lution of 1974. Their prediction received short shrift in a Washington attentive only to the larger geopolitical struggle between East and West. Thus, the Department of State reflexively pushed for increased U.S. activities and programs in Ethiopia, and the sixties saw thousands of Americans working in the government, advising the military, and teaching throughout the country. Ethiopian radicals correctly assumed that Washington's support fostered Haile Sellassie's corrupt government.

As the radicals became more militant in the late sixties, their criticism of the United States became more Leninist in terminology and tone. Their identification of Washington as the center of world imperialism, reaction, and exploitation made it necessary to break not only the power of Haile Sellassie's regime but also the control of the United States. Although Washington was fully aware of this logic, it offered nothing to counter it; Washington was concerned neither with Ethiopia nor its peoples, but with strategic realities, which, in the end, undermined relationships marginal to the struggle for world hegemony.

The Vietnam War drained the U.S. treasury of money, and its people of morale and concern with strange and remote places. Moreover, in the late sixties, space-borne satellites rendered Kagnew Station superfluous, thus removing an important reason for American involvement. Nasser's death in 1970, and the changing politics of the Middle East, led to a more pro-Western Egyptian regime which ejected the Soviets and permitted Washington to acquire its long-coveted strategic ally in the eastern Mediterranean on the African side of the Red Sea. Finally Addis Ababa's continuing demands for an army with offensive capabilities went beyond American policy determinations. Thus, when the Eritrean insurrection and the Somali infiltration into the Ogaden combined with Haile Sellassie's senility and an economic crisis to bring about the Revolution of 1974, the United States abandoned its primacy and left Ethiopia to work out its own destiny. Washington nevertheless watches from positions along the periphery of the Ethiopian state, awaiting its chance to return on the cheap to a position of importance in the center of northeast Africa, when the new regime solves its internal problems and decides it needs to counterbalance the Soviets.

1. A Tale of Two Lions, 1941–1943

After four years of Italian occupation (1936–40), Ethiopia's supplications were answered by a suddenly solicitous Albion, which, upon Rome's entry into World War II, saw an opportunity to secure the Suez Canal's Red Sea flank from the Axis. Haile Sellassie, a lion at bay in Bath, was evoked by his British hosts to return to his conquering ways. His resurrection was, however, incomplete; London merely sought to use him as a cat's-paw to divert Italian strength away from the main British Commonwealth forces entering Ethiopia from Kenya in the south and from Sudan in the north, early in 1941. Beyond such immediate utility, the emperor, with the cooperation—nay, with the fealty—of the idiosyncratic Orde Wingate, trained a ragtag force of Ethiopian exiles, European misfits and eccentrics, and the dross of the Sudanese Army to invade Ethiopia via Gojjam province, there to join up with strong guerrilla forces and to defeat the enemy. To everyone's surprise, the last goal was fairly easy to attain, thanks to Ethiopian freedom fighters whose four-year struggle had undermined Italian morale. Wherever and whenever "Gideon force" and the guerrillas campaigned, the fascists seemed eager to surrender, to march out of their redoubts, to stack their weapons, and to enter into the safety of being prisoners, rather than prosecutors, of war. Throughout the process, the emperor was received enthusiastically by even the most cynical guerrilla leaders and tumultuously by the rank and file. He was an emperor among his people, but he was not yet ruler in Addis Ababa, occupied in April 1941 by the British, who had immediately established a military government for what they considered occupied enemy territory.

A frustrated and brooding Haile Sellassie had to wait until 5 May, five years after Marshall Badoglio had taken Addis Ababa, before entering his capital. It was a bittersweet moment: he was home, an emperor in a palace, but he was neither authoritative nor apparent sovereign. The British were everywhere and acting as if Ethiopia were a colony. Moreover, General Sir Philip Mitchell, an archimperialist and ex-colonial governor, had been charged with directing an "Occupied Enemy Territory Administration" (OETA) over what Haile Sellassie refused to acknowledge as anything but free territory.[1] As vigorously as the Ethiopian argued that his return to the throne restored the nation's sovereignty, the Englishman energetically sought to maintain the country as a quasi-protectorate. He protested that Addis Ababa was incapable of administration,[2] and appealed to Britain's civilizing mission.[3] The old shibboleth, however, contained no magic for the embattled London Government. The War Office, for example, could not afford to garrison Ethiopia with troops desperately needed elsewhere,[4] and advised a "native" administration with no formal British suzerainty.

The emperor, of course, was guided by his own political needs. As soon as he set foot in Ethiopia in February 1941, he started to restore loyal provincial and local governments and was so successful that by late July it could be remarked that "apart from the few areas actually occupied by [British] troops the only effective authority is that of the Emperor."[5] He also triumphed in repairing the central government. On 11 May, just a few days after his return to Addis Ababa, Haile Sellassie announced to an irate Mitchell that he had named seven ministers.[6] Bluster though he might about the emperor's impetuous action, correctly seen as a symbolic exercise of sovereignty, the military governor was forced to use Haile Sellassie's government, and reported that "much of our administrative action in the past five months has been taken as a matter of convenience through these Ministries."[7]

---

1. Sir Philip Mitchell, *African Afterthoughts* (London, 1954), p. 202.
2. Eden to Margesson, Foreign Office (hereafter FO), 10 Oct. 1941, FO 371/27514.
3. Margesson to Eden, War Office (hereafter WO), 9 Oct. 1941, ibid.
4. Memo of standing interdepartmental committee on administration of occupied enemy territory, administration of Ethiopia vis-à-vis the Emperor, O.E.T.A. (41) 11, 5 May 1941, FO 371/27518.
5. MacKereth memo on the Ethiopian problem, FO, 21 July 1941, FO 371/27520.
6. Mitchell, *Afterthoughts*, p. 204.
7. GOC, EA, to WO, 24 Nov. 1941, FO 371/27524.

In truth, at this crucial time, Britain could not afford to take on new responsibilities, so full were its hands and so bare its larder. Mitchell's idea of a much enlarged East African dependency therefore countered tactical needs and strategic realities. Even Churchill conceded that "Ethiopia should be handed over to its rulers as a native state and we should not concern ourselves unduly how it is governed."[8] This conclusion directly contradicted Mitchell's bumptious efforts to force Haile Sellassie to agree that Addis Ababa should undertake "to be guided in all important matters, internal and external, touching the Government of Ethiopia by the advice tendered by the representative of His Majesty's Government [hereafter HMG]." The Englishman even wanted London to control all taxation and public expenditure, to have justice administered by British officers, and to keep the Ethiopian army subject to War Office command. Mitchell also sought to retain specified areas, particularly the Ogaden, under military rule, blandly observing, "His Britannic Majesty's Government are aware that His Majesty has claims to this territory." In return for the concessions, Ethiopia would receive generous financial aid, advisers, a military mission, a British-led police force, and what "would amount to *de facto* recognition of His Majesty as the authority administering Ethiopia."[9]

Haile Sellassie diplomatically found some "generosity" in Mitchell's proposals, but his response generally underscored his determination to sustain his position and Ethiopia's sovereignty. For example, while he was willing to permit a short-term British military administration for the Ogaden, he wanted to circulate a proclamation clarifying his acceptance of the occupation only for the duration of the war. Similarly, he evinced satisfaction at Britain's proffered assistance in restoring Ethiopia's government, but declined guidance "in all important matters [as] not consistent with the re-establishment of a free and independent state," although he admitted the necessity of advisers, who would, however, be responsible to the Ethiopian Government and not to HMG's representative in Addis Ababa.

The latter would be a diplomatic agent similar to the plenipotentiary assigned to London by the emperor as the *de jure* sovereign of Ethiopia, a status never abandoned during exile. Haile Sellassie argued that while *de facto* recognition would meet "practical re-

8. Note for the Secretary of State for War, 16 Oct. 1941, WO 32/9641.
9. Mitchell to Haile Sellassie, Addis Ababa, 30 June 1941, FO 371/31597.

quirements," full acknowledgement was morally warranted "as the first fruits of Great Britain's crusade of Liberation." Denial of *de jure* status "would denote an attitude of reserve . . . which could not fail to be misinterpreted by the watchful nations of the world and not least by the Ethiopian patriots and people." His country, the emperor concluded, had fought for its independence twice in the last fifty years, and he therefore would "not be true to himself or to the pledges he made at his coronation and would . . . fail . . . in his duty to his people if he entered into any agreements which in an essential manner surrendered his own sovereignty or curtailed the independence of his people."[10]

The response from Brig. Maurice S. Lush, Mitchell's deputy, was testy and impatient, as if he were admonishing a naughty and irresponsible child. Making no effort to explain his rebukes, Lush merely asserted and repeated Mitchell's positions. He brushed aside the emperor's request that Britain's continued Ogaden occupation be explained: "it would be unwise in present conditions for administrative reasons to promulgate a proclamation by His Majesty among the Somali tribes of the Ogaden." Then, in a perfect exercise of illogic, Lush claimed an inability "to agree . . . that it would be derogatory to national sovereignty or inconsistent with the establishment of a free and independent state, to give an undertaking to be guided in all *important* matters by . . . the representative of His Britannic Majesty's Government."[11] The emperor did not have to waste too much time considering whether Lush was merely confused or intoxicated with power because on 26 September 1941, Anthony Eden, the foreign minister, and Lord Moyne, the minister of state resident in Cairo, agreed that Ethiopia "should be treated . . . as an independent state, subject to necessary safeguards and provisions."[12] Notwithstanding the disavowal of his policy, Mitchell was directed to negotiate a treaty with sovereign Ethiopia.

Signed in Addis Ababa on 31 January 1942, the Anglo-Ethiopian Agreement was a significant victory for Haile Sellassie, whose nation was acknowledged as "a free and independent State." London and Addis Ababa would exchange plenipotentiaries, although the emperor conceded the British minister "precedence over any other foreign representative." This slight derogation of sovereignty was

---

10. Aide memoire for Sir Philip Mitchell, Addis Ababa, 11 June 1941, ibid.
11. Lush to Haile Sellassie, Addis Ababa, 17 July 1941, ibid.
12. Note for the Secretary of State for War, 16 Oct. 1941, WO 32/9641.

more than balanced by HMG's admission that Ethiopian civil administration should replace British military government "as soon as possible." The emperor, however, yielded significant freedom in economic matters in return for a four-year subvention of £3,250,000, and also agreed "that there should be the closest cooperation between Ethiopian authorities and British advisers. . . . " On the other hand, he did not capitulate on the matter of Ethiopian administration of justice, although he acknowledged that cases concerning foreigners could be heard in Addis Ababa before the High Court, with at least one British judge sitting. To obtain a military training mission, the emperor gave up little by promising to forego external operations without the approval of the Nairobi command, but surrendered a great deal by agreeing to London's continued administration of the Ogaden, certain reserved areas along international frontiers, and the railway zone, including Dire Dawa. Finally, the emperor had to grant a British airline a monopoly over services to and from Ethiopia. The Anglo-Ethiopian agreement was valid for two years, after which termination was possible upon three months' notice.[13]

Though Ethiopia had gained important treaty recognition and assistance, Haile Sellassie was inherently dissatisfied with the agreement's demeaning tone, the British presence on Ethiopian territory, and with London's control over finance. Consequently, when the Americans appeared on the scene, the emperor appealed to Washington's traditional anti-colonialism by complaining bitterly that the British had suborned Ethiopia's sovereignty. Ironically, U.S. military personnel had entered Eritrea at London's behest to investigate the colony's possibilities as an assembly point and distribution center for lend-lease equipment. By August 1942, Eritrea was the scene of a major American effort: 77 U.S. officers and 259 enlisted men directed projects that employed 2,829 U.S. civilians, 5,611 Italians, 7,384 Eritreans, and 22 Arabs, for a total of 16,182 persons.[14]

After U.S. efforts were well under way, E. Talbot Smith, Washington's new consul in Asmara, visited Addis Ababa, where he found an emperor unhappy with the terms of the 1942 agreement, irritated that his mail had been monitored until June 1942, and

13. Margery Perham, *The Government of Ethiopia* (New York, 1948), pp. 418ff.
14. Gaudin to Secretary of State, Asmara, 21 Aug. and 23 Sept. 1942, State Department Decimal Files (hereafter SD) 884.20/63 and 65.

annoyed about foreign influence in government operations. The American also learned that the British controlled trade through "essentially colonial" import and export restrictions. Neither Smith nor his Ethiopian informants had much sense of British war needs, and the diplomat accepted the testimony of one of the emperor's officials who claimed to have witnessed what he described as the looting of Addis Ababa by Commonwealth forces. He complained bitterly that it would take years for Ethiopia to regain the industrial capacity, the weapons, the transport, and the technology shipped to Nairobi and elsewhere.[15] Even with all the liabilities, Smith found that Haile Sellassie "can and does control" his country and that Ethiopian forces functioned "as an excellent factor of internal peace."[16]

Nevertheless, the consul complained, the country's independence was tainted by London's control over currency and foreign exchange and exports and imports which had to be authorized by the Cairo-based Middle East Supply Centre (hereafter MESC). He also pointed out that Ethiopia was surrounded by British-controlled territories; that London-appointed ministerial advisers exerted considerable authority under the terms of the 1942 agreement; and that British personnel controlled the railway from Jibuti to Addis Ababa as well as Ethiopian access to shipping. The indignant Mr. Smith continued that even if the British alone had conquered Ethiopia, "I do not believe it follows that they may do with it as they wish. This is Nazi theory, but certainly is not the theory inspiring the Atlantic Charter and other United Nations pronouncements." Although he grudgingly conceded British rights "based on military necessity . . . I fail to see any military necessity in the complete economic, financial, and industrial control of the country," which he believed made Ethiopia virtually "a British Colony." Good American anti-colonialist that he was, Smith inveighed against the "sham and hypocrisy" of Britain's pose "as the high-minded liberator of conquered peoples."[17]

15. There was considerable truth in these charges. For information about the appropriation, dismantling, and shipment of Italian property and other movables, see WO 230/99.

16. The British minister agreed: "As regards public security, the Emperor's authority in the country generally appears to be stronger and wider than I expected to find." Howe to MacKereth, Addis Ababa, 27 Feb. 1942, FO 371/31602.

17. E. Talbot Smith memo on "Conditions in Ethiopia, September 1942," Asmara, 8 Oct. 1942, SD 865D.01.

The consul's suspicions about Britain were also shared by Sumner Welles, undersecretary of state and one of Roosevelt's confidants. In July, he strongly advocated a substantial presidential response to various communications sent by Haile Sellassie. Welles was "delighted" by Roosevelt's agreement, since "there have been various indications that the British Government intended to seize the present opportunity for establishing what would be tantamount to a protectorate over Abyssinia."[18] The moment for a letter came in late July, when Haile Sellassie, in his ceaseless quest for recognition of Ethiopia's sovereign status, wrote Roosevelt that:

> My Government and people are anxious to assume the obligations of the United Nations Pact. We the first nation to regain its freedom and independence wish to place the military and economic resources of our country at the disposal of those nations who gladly sacrifice all for liberty and justice.[19]

The president's response was balm:

> It is a source of much satisfaction to me and to the people of the United States that your country, which fought so courageously against a ruthless enemy has regained its independence and self-government. The steadfast friendship of the American people and their sympathy with you in your period of trial will continue to be manifested during the days of reconstruction now facing your country.[20]

Behind Welles's anticolonialism and Roosevelt's concern were sophisticated political and economic considerations. American activities in Ethiopia "would indicate in a concrete way the interest of the United States in the stake which Negroes have in the war," as would declaring the Solomonic Empire an ally. Ethiopia would then qualify for lend-lease, not only advertising Washington's interest in the rehabilitation of liberated countries, but also facilitating "a resumption of trade between the United States and Ethiopia [and] opening the way for American interests to share in the development of the resources of Ethiopia after the war." Finally, permitting Ethiopia to join the United Nations was considered by the State Department to be "a friendly gesture [which] might prove a valuable asset after the war to American airlines desiring to operate

18. Wells to Roosevelt, 24 July 1942, SD 884.001 Selassie.
19. Haile Sellassie to Roosevelt, Addis Ababa, 28 July 1942, ibid.
20. Roosevelt to Haile Sellassie, Washington, 4 Aug. 1942, ibid. Yet, Washington had denied the emperor the right to visit the United States while he was in exile.

across Ethiopia which lies in the path of probable air-routes to India
and the Far East."[21]

The State Department was needlessly concerned about American
prospects. By late 1942, Britain realized its inability to supply the
Middle East's civilian population with consumer goods and "began
to advise importers to shift to American sources of supply wherever
possible—despite the ominous meaning of such action for Britain's
postwar trade." The Red Sea was reopened to American merchant
ships, and U.S. exports quickly soared to twice the 1938 figure,
moving "into a commanding lead over British trade." Washington's
obvious economic strength made it, ipso facto, an active political
force in the Middle East, where nationalists and others quickly
moved to solicit American assistance against British domination.

The White House and State Department were not immune to such
blandishments, and "as a consequence, Allied solidarity was often
breached in the Middle East, particularly where preordained or
preconceived anti-British prejudices of long standing affected the
vision of the men involved." Such a judgement is certainly true in
the Ethiopian case, and Washington's forward policy was well underway, at least in its rationale, before mid-1943, the date which
may be assigned to the beginning of an independent American foreign policy in the Middle East.[22] Moreover, official British and
American records "amply reveal," to use W. Roger Louis's words,
"that the sense of historic antagonism between Britain and the
United States continued to exist along with the spirit of cooperation engendered by the war."[23]

The friction was roiled by an American idealism which bordered
on naiveté, present in a highly developed form in another of
E. Talbot Smith's reports about Ethiopia. The consul fulminated, in
early 1943, that the British had betrayed their trust to the United
Nations by not undertaking an extensive rehabilitation program
and by picking the country clean of the Italian-built modern sector.

Happily the Axis propaganda experts do not know this, for if they did,
they would be shouting it to the heavens, and could make out a fine case
proving that Allied promises to rehabilitate countries the subject of

21. Wallace Murray memo to Berle, Acheson, Welles, et al., Washington, 20 Nov.
1942, SD 884.24/89.
22. Martin W. Wilmington, *The Middle East Supply Centre* (Albany, N.Y.,
1971), pp. 1, 4, 75, 79, 164.
23. W. H. Louis, *Imperialism at Bay* (Oxford, 1977), p. 7.

aggression were pure hypocrisy. Goebbels could now point to Ethiopia and say to the people of Norway, Belgium, Holland, France, Poland, and Greece, 'If the United Nations win, they will treat your country as enemy territory, just as Great Britain treated Ethiopia. Look at Ethiopia and be warned! When the British got through with it, what was left?'

He therefore recommended that Ethiopia be developed as an outstanding example of United Nations concern and assistance. Very little aid would be needed, he considered, to create a propaganda vehicle which would stimulate occupied peoples to eject the Axis. Moreover, Ethiopia would be a useful "experimental station" for relief and rehabilitation operations.

> Send out a committee to study at first hand what the nation needs to put it on its feet. Send out agronomists, timber experts, agricultural experts in general, for Ethiopia is not sufficiently advanced to be an industrial country. So let this organization try out different forms of organization on Ethiopia, so that, when the time comes, it will know what the best form of organization will be for us to use in the conquered countries of Europe when they are freed.[24]

Smith's proposals accurately reflected American officialdom's passionate faith in Yankee ingenuity and Washington's sense of the future, if a confusion about goals and methods. The situation was ideal for Haile Sellassie, whose ambitions for Ethiopia's continued independence were exceeded only by his diplomatic skills. He cajoled and finally wheedled Washington into reopening its legation in Addis Ababa, and when a preliminary mission was dispatched to see to the details the emperor took the opportunity to transmit an aide-mémoire defining his problems and aspirations. American assistance played a key role in Haile Sellassie's reflections, and the British were cast into a secondary, even antagonistic, position.

The aide-mémoire commenced by suggesting, fancifully, that Ethiopia continued to suffer "much more than the countries which are taking part in the actual fighting." Then, ignoring the continuing British outlay of men and money, the document baldly observed that the country would "suffer still further owing to the fact that she has none [sic] at her side to assist her in the peaceful administration of her Empire. . . ." In an obvious reference to the inadequacy of London's aid, the memo generally chastised those who had reneged on promised assistance because they "are engaged in the pros-

24. Smith to Secretary of State, Asmara, 18 Feb. 1943, SD 884.24/112 1/2.

ecution of the war." This excuse already had served, the memo clarified acidly, to justify the British command's removal of so-called enemy property. Among the booty were almost all the Italian weapons, leaving nothing for defense, let alone "for the maintenance of internal security."

British military and diplomatic archives indicate a deep reluctance to transfer captured enemy weapons to the Ethiopian government or even to permit Italian technicians to remain in place to operate the modern infrastructure developed during the occupation. Haile Sellassie and his close associates interpreted HMG's general behavior—however well argued in terms of the war effort—as threatening Ethiopia's ability to govern itself. This conclusion was reinforced by London's failure to find spare parts for vitally needed radio transmitters, to maintain Italian-built roads in good repair, and to restore any of the thousands of Italian trucks confiscated by the East African command. So serious was the transportation shortage that the Ethiopian government had trouble moving troops from one province to another. This problem was exacerbated by the British refusal to supply aircraft, which before the war the emperor had used effectively to assert central government authority. "If a few aeroplanes were available they would contribute to a considerable extent towards the maintenance of internal security."[25] Indeed, though almost all Ethiopian memoranda of 1943–44 began with complaints about the British, they invariably ended with requests for weapons and other military goods for reasons of internal security, a continuing refrain in Ethio-American relations.

The emperor always couched his requests in terms of consolidating his government and of pressing the war effort, and American officials were perfectly willing to justify supplying small arms and ammunition in similar language: "Once law and order is restored . . . it may be possible for Ethiopia to make a greater contribution to the war effort, in such ways as the furnishing of food-

25. Aide memoire, the Imperial Palace, Addis Ababa, 10 Feb. 1943, in ibid. For the prevailing British military attitude about supplying captured war material to the Ethiopian army, see Platt to CIGS, Nairobi, 28 Oct. 1942, WO 193/879. For insights into the deeply embedded prejudices of a certain type of British official, see Mitchell, note for the Secretary of State for War, for use at War Cabinet meeting of 16 Oct. 1941, WO 32/9641; Howe to Peterson, Addis Ababa, 1 May 1942, FO 371/31602; and MacKereth Minute J1173, 10 March 1943, FO 371/35603. London's reasons for evacuating Italian technicians are fully exposed in FO 371/31593. Finally, the Ethiopian interpretation of British policy is well presented in Howe to Eden, Addis Ababa, 1 Oct. 1943, FO 371/35634.

stuffs to British and American armed forces operating in the Near Eastern area."[26] Since guns and butter were linked in the American mind, Haile Sellassie sent Lij Yilma Deressa, a trusted official, to the United States, ostensibly to participate in an international conference on food, but in reality to negotiate a lend-lease agreement. In discussions with State Department officials in June 1943, Yilma pointed out that the rehabilitation of Ethiopia accorded "with the declared policy of the United Nations. It is implied in the Atlantic charter." He stressed, however, that peace and order would permit an "increase in agricultural products which will contribute substantially to the feeding of the United Nations army in the Middle East and elsewhere." As a bonus, Ethiopia's proximity to operations would release shipping space elsewhere for other duties.

> To state the problem simply, we have an abundance of labor, land and tractors. These are all ready to go to work to produce food for the United Nations. To release this energy, we must guarantee to the producer safety in the pursuit of his labors. The Government's power to carry out the plan in view will depend almost entirely upon the degree of internal security it can provide. It is, therefore, hoped that the request by my Government for the supply of arms and ammunition will be favorably examined.

It always came down to weapons, but it would be cynical merely to see this fixation as another manifestation of the emperor's devotion to political survival. The monarch and his government did have security problems: large areas of Ethiopia's south and southwest remained disaffected and outside of Addis Ababa's authority; London controlled the Ogaden and various reserved areas; there was trouble brewing in the north; and the imperial army was thoroughly dependent, as was the emperor, on a small British military mission for supplies and leadership. Above all, Haile Sellassie's obsession with weapons was rooted in experience. As Yilma Deressa put it: "If Ethiopia had even a minimum armament in 1935 the occupation of the country would not have been so easily accomplished." After indirectly drawing attention to British encirclement of his nation, the vice-minister defined his request for armaments as inconsequential for the United States, "but for Ethiopia's armed force it will be a source of moral and material strength in the event of threat of invasion."

26. Alling to Wilson, Washington, 24 March 1943, SD 884.24/110.

Then Yilma invited a peaceful American attack on Ethiopia's many problems, asking more of Washington than Great Britain was able to provide, more indeed than Addis Ababa had ever solicited of another power. He sought a technical mission including agricultural specialists to train his compatriots in the use of abandoned Italian farming machinery, to increase yields "at least ten fold during the coming years," to advise on the improvement of existing crops and methods of marketing, and to establish an agricultural institute emphasizing animal husbandry, cereals and cotton cultivation, and equipment maintenance. "A relatively small number of [experts] can tap the resources of 320,000 square miles of territory and [the] manpower of a population of 13,000,000." Since these people needed a competent public health service, the Imperial Government wanted a medical mission to study and improve the current system, which was short of staff, equipment, and medicine and overwhelmed by such war-related diseases as typhus, dysentery, and the like. "Attached to the mission should be a group of doctors and [nurses] to remain in Ethiopia and train native midwives, male and female nurses."

Beyond the human scene, the physical environment required an investigation of mineral resources. Experts were needed to increase output in gold and platinum mines and to exploit a recently discovered gold lode in southeastern Ethiopia. Production, Yilma asserted, was 4,000 ounces monthly, "and it is believed that the goal of 10,000 oz. per month can be attained easily by improved methods and organization." The Ethiopian Government offered American business a "partnership" in the mineral industry: "We sincerely believe that the field for the investment of American Capital and the employment of American technicians and experts after the war will prove to be tremendous."

Then Yilma turned to his country's critical shortages in the field of communications and transportation, "not only an economic problem but . . . also an administrative problem." Ethiopia therefore requested transport, telecommunications, and printing equipment. Next, the country sought the ability to semifinish raw hides and skins, which, because of the shortage of shipping, were deteriorating and going to waste. Again stressing the future, Yilma suggested that Ethiopia's leathers would find a great postwar market. Altogether, the Ethiopian official asked for a total of 286 experts and technicians, among them doctors, teachers, nurses, and engineers, and fifty-four master blacksmiths, tanners, carpenters, masons, plumbers, and shoemakers to train Ethiopian youth in needed trades.[27] Behind this request lurked the larger goal of recruiting America's support for the emperor's pursuit of independence.

On 13 July, during a White House appointment, Yilma recapitulated Ethiopia's unhappiness with London's domination, implying that Haile Sellassie was determined to rid the country of British personnel and influence. One American official analyzed Ethiopian policy as seeking Washington's "diplomatic cooperation . . . in [the] drafting and negotiation of a new Anglo-Ethiopian Treaty . . . more satisfactory to the Ethiopians." This aim was not regarded as damaging Anglo-Ethiopian relations, and "possibly an expression of our interest in this matter might have a healthy effect." Moreover, Yilma's reference to Ethiopia's need for an outlet to the sea was also heard with equanimity: "It is our opinion that a fairly strong case could be made in support of the Ethiopian contention that Eritrea, or a part of it, should be incorporated into Ethiopia."[28]

When Haile Sellassie realized in 1940 that Britain soon would sponsor his return to Ethiopia, he had begun a campaign to have Eritrea placed under Addis Ababa's sovereignty. While not unresponsive to the idea, London took the official stance "that this matter can only be properly considered at the peace settlement."[29] The immediate and obvious American sympathy probably derived as much from Washington's chronic suspicions about the British Empire as from the attitudes assumed by U.S. personnel in Eritrea. One individual even wrote the president in strong support of postwar unity: "It is incontestable that vast practical problems exist in such a program, but that undeniable moral, political, and ideological reasons exist for Abyssinian-Eritrean independence and unity is equally clear." Eritrea, he commented, "is not economically a self-contained state. It is a small portion of a larger picture, which is Abyssinia plus Eritrea." Any sources of distrust which existed between the two polities were "mainly superficial and have been fostered by Italian domination of Eritrea." Racially and culturally,

27. Yilma Deressa memo to Secretary of State, Washington, 24 June 1943, SD 884.24/111.

28. Wallace Murray memo for Secretary of State, 20 July 1943, SD 884.014/7-2043.

29. Eden to Howe, 27 June 1942, FO 371/31608.

the populations of southern Eritrea and northern Ethiopia "are as similar as the people of Nebraska and Kansas."[30]

Given the developing U.S. attitude on the Eritrean question, Haile Sellassie must have been delighted to learn that Washington had agreed to accord lend-lease coverage to Ethiopia: "to supply such articles, services, and information as we may be in a position to furnish for the defense of Ethiopia, and, through other means as may be possible, to render all practical assistance in the rehabilitation of your country."[31] Signed on 9 August 1943,[32] the "Mutual Aid Agreement" represented a watershed in Ethiopian diplomatic, social, and economic history, and was planned in Addis Ababa, agreed to by Washington, and condoned by London.

The Second World War continued to take its toll on Great Britain's human and industrial treasure. The resources of the British Empire were not adequate to the effort, and HMG itself was a grateful recipient of American aid. Indeed, originally conceived to succor an embattled United Kingdom, lend-lease may have permitted Whitehall the means to retain its empire intact, policed, and united in pursuit of the Axis-enemy. With American assistance, London maintained hegemony through such all-inclusive paragovernmental organizations as the MESC, in which the United States began participating in July 1942. Indeed, while London remained the apparent political leader in the Middle East, Washington quickly became the obvious economic power, a theme I have already generalized.

Now, however, I wish to expose the specific Ethiopian case, since I believe that it established precedents later applied piecemeal, as Britain lost its empire and as America attempted to establish its world order. In 1943, very few ranking British officials realized that London's weakness was not circumstantial but chronic and long term. Most continued to view the empire as substantial and capable of future growth; just as Churchill, they would be forced to witness and also preside over its deterioration and dismemberment.

30. Harold Courlander to Roosevelt, Gura, 22 March 1943, SD 865D.01/608.
31. Roosevelt to Haile Sellassie, 11 June 1943, SD 884.24/112.
32. Mutual Aid Agreement of 9 August 1943, and appended letters, SD 884.24/128.

2. The Anglo-Ethiopian Agreement of 1944: America Intervenes

In early 1943, Robert Howe, the British minister in Addis Ababa reminded London that the 1942 agreement could be terminated after 31 January 1944. He defined British interests in terms of water resources for the Sudan via a projected Lake Tana dam, trade, and tranquility along the frontiers. He favored Ethiopian independence, of course, but considered that London should seek "the maintenance of . . . British influence in Ethiopia," perhaps through a post-war "adviser" system. He suggested that HMG attend to favorable rectification of the Sudan borders and "disposal of Eritrea and ex-Italian Somaliland in such a way as to safe-guard our imperial interests." He favored a united Somalia which, "to my mind, offers the best if not the only prospect of political and economic stability."[1]

In Cairo, a committee on Ethiopia, chaired by Lord Moyne, recommended that negotiations with Addis Ababa should commence soon since "there are signs that the Ethiopians are seeking political support in other than British quarters." It also suggested the following bases for the talks: (1) Ethiopia to receive southern Eritrea, but the whole of Christian Tigre on either side of the frontier to be united in a greater Tigre under British protection; (2) Ethiopia to concede a united Somaliland, certain wells to Kenya, and the Baro salient to Sudan.[2] A few months later, Moyne revealed further ignorance about Ethiopia and its ruler: "It is evident that the Emperor is not playing. British Advisers and Military Mission are the sole props of civilised administration in Ethiopia and, if this

1. Howe to Eden, Addis Ababa, 4 March 1943, FO 371/35633.
2. Committee on Ethiopia, Report on Future Policy Towards Ethiopia, Cairo, 18 May 1943, ibid.

structure is destroyed, it will be impossible to rebuild." He reckoned that London ought to try for a new agreement "providing for our long-term objectives with maximum possible control." He wanted Washington's cooperation—"Control could be exercised by an Anglo-American board"—and its resources—"The American might be induced to share the burdens of finance and provision of administrative man-power."[3]

Eden did not think the scenario would play in Washington, and he also considered that Ethiopian failure to undertake administrative reform or even to heed British advisers had not damaged London's strategic position in the Middle East. He therefore would not be able "to recommend to the Cabinet a reversal of policy, viz. the imposition of what would be tantamount to a protectorate over Ethiopia, the financial burden of which would have to be borne by the United Kingdom."[4] Moyne rejoined that he could not understand how it could be "a matter of indifference to His Majesty's Government whether Ethiopia is well or ill governed." He argued that "we have a moral duty to see that the people of the country are not oppressed and enslaved. When we are fighting for freedom in Europe how can we restore Gallas and other subject races to Amharic tyranny?" If Ethiopia returned to disorder and injustice, "the results of our conquest will be sharply contrasted with the law and order and material improvements achieved by the Italians." The crucial issue was between "good government and no government at all," and without a "good" Ethiopian administration, Great Britain should not return the Ogaden and should obtain control over greater Tigre. Moyne's echoes of Mitchell and Mussolini horrified the Foreign Office,[5] and from Addis Ababa, Howe explained with brilliant insight:

> To me clearly the issue is not between good government and no government but between good government and government as the Ethiopians knew it before 1936. This was the government the Ethiopians wanted and to which they had been accustomed for centuries, a government for which they were prepared to fight.[6]

Taking a slightly different tack, Howe's oriental counsellor, E. A. Chapman-Andrews, commented: "[the] Occupied Enemy Territory

3. Moyne to Eden, Cairo, 4 July 1943, ibid.
4. Eden to Moyne, (?) July 1943, ibid.
5. See minutes attached to Moyne to Eden, Cairo, 13 July 1943, ibid.
6. Howe to Eden, Addis Ababa, 17 July 1943, ibid.

Administration are at present doing all they can to restrain the strong affection the Eritreans are showing for the Emperor (styled 'tyranny and maladministration') in preference to the good British military administration."[7] The War Cabinet sensibly followed Eden's view that London was under no obligation to ensure "good government" in Ethiopia and his recommendation that current policy be retained.[8]

Even though Howe basically agreed that Ethiopia should "return as speedily as possible to its condition as a native state under its own ruler," he thought any new pact should retain various perquisites that accompanied London's privileged position under the terms of the 1942 agreement: special rights in the Ogaden, control over the reserved areas, the prerogative to send troops into the country, the operation of a military mission, extra-territorial jurisdiction, and management of the railway.[9] The British advisers, closer to reality and therefore better informed about Ethiopian grievances, disagreed; they argued that only abandonment of all special rights and negotiation of a simple treaty of commerce and friendship, thus confirming Ethiopia's sovereignty, would establish good relations.[10] One advisor believed that the 1942 agreement and "the fairy promise of 'Lend-Lease'" had bemused Haile Sellassie into believing that he could play off the Americans against the British "and cash in with both hands."[11] Gordon MacKereth, the officer at the Foreign Office with primary responsibility for Ethiopia, dryly commented that the man would "seem to have acquired no knowledge of the Ethiopian needs and ambitions."[12]

In September 1943, Lord Moyne returned to the fray. He memorialized the War Cabinet to the effect that Ethiopia was maladministered, that the advisory system was not functioning well, that justice was corrupt, and that road communications were being neglected. He argued strongly that Haile Sellassie must be made to heed the advice of appointed specialists—in other words that Ethiopia should become less than a sovereign state.[13] In November, the

7. Oriental counsellor to Howe, Addis Ababa, Aug. 1943, ibid.
8. Extract from War Cabinet Conclusions 101 (43), 19 July 1943, ibid.
9. Howe to Eden, Addis Ababa, 6 August 1943, FO 371/35634.
10. Advisers' memo on a new Anglo-Ethiopian agreement, Addis Ababa, 14 July 1943, ibid.
11. Bethel memo in Bethel to Howe, 21 August 1943, ibid.
12. Minute J4267, 18 Oct. 1943, ibid.
13. War Cabinet, Ethiopia, memo by the Deputy Minister of State Resident in the Middle East, London, Oct. 1943, ibid.

War Cabinet again met to consider the Ethiopian problem, and Winston Churchill demonstrated that he was not among those who realized that Empire was on the wane or even that the United States was on the rise in the Middle East. He assumed Moyne's tack that HMG "could not afford that our liberation of Ethiopia should be stultified by allowing the country to lapse into a barbarism which compared most unfavourably with its condition during the period of Italian control." Any backsliding "would be a reproach to H. M. Government and an injustice to the troops from this country . . . and the Dominions who had driven the Italians out of Ethiopia." He therefore directed that the Ethiopian situation be studied further, as might the question of possible U.S. participation in any new arrangement. The War Cabinet thereupon decided to establish a subcommittee to review the utility and limits of policy toward Ethiopia "in the light of the changes which had taken place in the general world situation since 1941."[14]

One of those developments was the increased American involvement in the Middle East, which was to become obvious in Ethiopia because of Addis Ababa's increasing sensitivity to continued British hegemony. The emperor was particularly embarrassed by London's control over the Ethiopian economy, which also meant less profit to him and the ruling oligarchy. John Spencer, the American foreign affairs adviser—his own appointment by Haile Sellassie an act of defiance against the British—summed up the bases of the Imperial Government's case:

> Specifically, their grievances relate to exchange control, the attempt to force . . . sterling . . . upon the country, the refusal to allow the minting of coins or the printing of currency and the requirement that all dollar exchange be converted before being brought into Ethiopia. It is felt that such policies impose an entirely unwarranted restriction upon Ethiopia's economy and industry.[15]

Addis Ababa therefore decided to erode HMG's curbs by introducing a national currency after the expiration of the 1942 agreement. Upon request, the Ethiopian government easily obtained a stabilization loan from the United States and an advance of silver for minting, under lend-lease terms, because it was U.S. policy, "approved by the President," to assist in the rehabilitation of Ethi-

14. Extract from War Cabinet conclusions 151 (43), 8 Nov. 1943, ibid.
15. Spencer to Alling, Addis Ababa, 30 Oct. 1943, SD 884.01A/56.

opia and the maintenance of its political independence.[16] Meanwhile, the British War Cabinet subcommittee was drafting instructions for a commission that revealed London's policy as neither the rehabilitation of Ethiopia nor the maintenance of its political independence.

The projected British study group was directed to report on conditions prevailing in Ethiopia and the degree of success attained "in establishing a reasonably satisfactory state of administration." This objective, although probably distasteful to Addis Ababa, was not unjustified, given the terms of the 1942 agreement. Grossly unreasonable, senseless, ignorant, and perhaps escapist, was the statement that "it is for consideration whether Ethiopia can continue to be governed on a centralised system or whether the traditional system of government through Rases should be restored."[17] As if Britain had the power to turn the clock back to the nineteenth century! Howe tried to return the War Cabinet to twentieth-century realities by gently clarifying the uncertainty of Britain's position in Ethiopia and the developing American role.

The diplomat first recommended that Haile Sellassie be permitted officially to raise the matter of the new treaty. Second, the minister urged London to come to "an understanding" with Washington before embarking upon negotiations with Addis Ababa. "We have evidence already in the Lend-Lease silver transaction of their desire and/or intention to share the burden of helping this country and at the same time their complete failure . . . to consult with us." He believed that American cooperation during foreseeably difficult negotiations "could only be of help to us." He recommended, therefore, that the United States be invited to participate in the proposed mission—fully appreciating that Washington's inclusion would drastically alter the terms of reference—"with a view to sharing the burden of development of Ethiopia and depriving the Emperor of any grounds on which he could play the Americans off against us." Finally, the minister chided London for presuming that a visiting commission could easily establish data from which to derive valid

16. Memo for Mr. Feis, 28 July 1943, SD 884.51/7-2843, and McGuire memo on proposed Import-Export Bank loan for Ethiopia, 29 July 1944, SD 884.51/7-2944. The United States made available 5,830,000 ounces of silver; see White to Lindsay, Washington, 18 Oct. 1943, SD 884.515/34d.

17. War Cabinet, Ethiopia, draft for a memo by the Chancellor of the Exchequer, n.d., in Extract from War Cabinet Conclusions 167 (43), 8 Dec. 1943, FO 371/35634.

conclusions: "Of all countries this is perhaps the least subject to analysis and accurate judgment by a short visit, especially in its present extraordinary conditions."[18]

In his very next cable, Howe directly reproached the War Cabinet's decision. He could not with "clear conscience" approach the emperor to gain acceptance of the mission as defined. He would not lie, and if it became known that Britain intended to involve itself in internal politics, then the effort "will meet every kind of obstruction."[19] Given Howe's persuasive logic, the War Cabinet decided to limit the mission to studying the effectiveness of the 1942 agreement, prefatory to negotiating a new arrangement. Churchill and associates, however, took a dim view of American involvement at a stage when HMG was merely collecting information about the functioning "of an agreement to which the USA is not a party."[20] The decision hardly mattered; the Foreign Office knew that Washington was watching. As Lord Halifax cabled Eden, "Unilateral action by us might therefore be resented in the Department, and public opinion generally would be likely to regard such intervention as further evidence of unregenerative British imperialism."[21]

Moreover, acting on Yilma Deressa's request of June 1943, the United States was about to send a technical mission composed of experts in transportation, agriculture, public health, animal husbandry, mining, and engineering. While not exactly a task force, the American invasion symbolized a modernizing potential far beyond Ethiopia's experience. Furthermore, the group was sponsored by the Foreign Economic Administration (a precursor of the Agency for International Development) and the Department of State, demonstrating Washington's interest and commitment. Finally, while the undertaking was "exploratory in character . . . it is anticipated that a considerable amount of actual work will be undertaken and concrete results obtained."[22] Meanwhile, further evidence of American interest in Ethiopia had arrived in Addis Ababa in the guise of five Afro-American teachers, one of whom, William Steen, later replaced a British subject as Director of the English Section of the Press and Propaganda Department of the Ministry of Pen, as

18. Howe to MacKereth, Addis Ababa, 17 Dec. 1943, ibid.
19. Howe to FO, Addis Ababa, 17 Dec. 1943, ibid.
20. FO to Howe, London, 29 Dec. 1943, ibid.
21. Halifax to Eden, Washington, 6 Dec. 1943, FO 371/41448.
22. Alling to W. G. Hayter, First Secretary, British Embassy, Washington, 31 Dec. 1943, SD 884.01A/62.

editor of the *Ethiopian Herald,* and as supervisor of English-language broadcasting.[23]

It was hardly surprising, therefore, that the Ethiopian government rejected the proposed British mission, even with its limited goals, particularly since on 13 January 1944, the Foreign Ministry had transmitted a proposed treaty which had nothing in common with London's thinking.[24] The draft closely adhered to a document drawn up by Prof. Norman Bentwich, one of the emperor's durable English partisans. His close consultations with emperor and cabinet had yielded nothing more than a treaty of friendship and commerce, with addenda to place the British Military Mission under the control of the Ethiopian Ministry of War, to ensure evacuation of the Ogaden by 8 April 1944, and to "restore" the railway to Ethiopian management.[25]

Upon reflection, Howe concluded that the draft was not anti-British but intended "to restore Ethiopia to full sovereignty."

> This is what His Majesty has been aiming at since his restoration. . . . The Emperor has flatly rejected the assumption that we have a responsibility moral or otherwise for good government in Ethiopia or for any other kind of government here. He will not have it and will only let us in on his uniform terms.[26]

When Moyne pointed to Ethiopia's "obvious inconsistency" in accepting an American mission but rejecting the British group, Howe vigorously rejoined, "Inconsistency disappears if strong Ethiopian desire for outward signs of independence is remembered. While Ethiopians object to British *political* mission of 'inquiry' they accept ostensibly disinterested United States *technical* mission."[27]

A ranking official in the Foreign Office explained the diplomatic rebuff and the opening to the United States in terms of HMG's weakness and lack of commitment to Ethiopia's future:

> So far the facts only indicate that he [Haile Sellassie] has gone to the United States for help we have denied him i.e. over silver for his currency, motor vehicles, and a technical mission to recommend vast development schemes. The first two were beyond our means and the last we were

23. Caldwell to Secretary of State, Addis Ababa, 28 Dec. 1943, SD 884.01A/72.
24. Howe to FO, Addis Ababa, 13 Jan. 1944, FO 371/41448.
25. Howe to Eden, Addis Ababa, 19 Jan. 1944, ibid.
26. Howe to FO, Addis Ababa, 1 Feb. 1944, ibid.
27. Moyne to FO, Cairo, 23 Feb. 1944; Howe to Moyne, Addis Ababa, 28 Feb. 1944, FO 371/41449.

unwilling to provide because it might have implied heavy financial assistance (for which he asked at the same time) to carry out the projects the mission might have recommended. In this the Emperor has acted quite reasonably. . . .[28]

This realism was retained for conversations with Wallace S. Murray, the director of the State Department's Office of Near Eastern and African Affairs, and a ranking member of the Stettinius mission which came to London in April 1944, for a general discussion of foreign relations.

The American was told that British policy had aimed at resurrecting Ethiopia "as an independent native state, to continue its natural progress, which had been interrupted by the Italian occupation in 1935." British advisers had therefore performed as "servants of the Ethiopian government. We have been scrupulous in not giving them directions." HMG welcomed American cooperation in Ethiopia, "in the task which the war has thrust upon us," but it would "deprecate direct action by the United States particularly in the absence of any American responsibility." Murray's responses revealed "The Americans [to be] clearly anxious to see the [1942] agreement, which they regard as discriminatory against themselves, replaced by something less restrictive (an anxiety fully shared by the Emperor!) but they were given no encouragement to suppose that we were going to be hustled in that direction."[29]

During 1943–45, Washington sought generally to secure America's postwar economic primacy. Foreign Service officers worked "for prestige and power overseas for the American government, and for profitable business opportunities for American private interests." The State Department assumed "that nationalism and the sovereignty issue would promote the dissolution of the spheres of influences of its economic competitors, albeit wartime allies, Britain and France."[30]

These considerations were reflected in America's foreign policy toward Ethiopia, even in as minor a matter as supplying radio equipment to Addis Ababa.

I would like to say on behalf of the Department that the lack of an external communication system in Ethiopia is a matter of concern to our

28. MacKereth minute, J912, 15 March 1944, ibid.
29. Scrivener minute, J1120, 4 April 1944, ibid.
30. Philip H. Baram, *The Department of State in the Middle East, 1919–1945* (Philadelphia, 1978), pp. 157, 320, 329.

Government. In the broad aspects of international communications, the United States Government maintains its position for equal opportunity of facilities. The present case of Ethiopia, therefore, offers an opportunity for the Government to put into effect, in a measure, its declared international policy as well as to implement its policy of aid to Ethiopia.[31]

Yet, American interests in Ethiopia were more potential than actual. In a discussion with Treasury Department officials about Ethiopia's difficulty in obtaining dollars from the British, Cass Timberlake observed that:

> We did not have at the present time a major interest in Ethiopia nor were we likely to have major interest in the foreseeable future. We do, however, have a general interest in preserving legitimate American rights to participate in commerce in Ethiopia as elsewhere and might, if development occurs in that country, have an increased interest in the future.

Timberlake nevertheless considered that the current level of American involvement should at least elicit fair treatment for U.S. trade. Besides, Washington's participation in MESC was in effect a subsidy for the British economy, in recognition of which Whitehall ought to permit Addis Ababa to retain its dollar earnings so that American business can obtain a "reasonable share" of Ethiopia's trade. Nevertheless, "our political interests and our commercial interest in Ethiopia are minor."[32]

This conclusion was not reflected in the outcome of the discussions between Murray and various Foreign Office officials. An agreed minute "established that there was a general community of aims and outlook between the Foreign Office and the State Department on Middle Eastern Questions." Both sides foresaw "even closer cooperation between British and American policy in the territories concerned." It was of course understood that Britain's administrative and security responsibilities would inevitably influence its actions, but "it was recognized that the United States Government, like His Majesty's Government, have economic interests in the Middle East which are bound to affect their policy." Since these interests did not conflict, Anglo-American relations "should be conducted on a basis of co-operation and of mutual frankness." As for Ethiopia,

31. A. A. Berle to Leo T. Crowley, 4 May 1944, SD 884.24/179A.
32. Memo of conversation by Timberlake on "Monetary Problems Involved in American Supplies to Ethiopia," 6 June 1944, SD 884.24/6-644.

both governments recognized the advisability of reestablishing "a stable independent government" and pledged "close consultation and co-operation between them for this purpose."[33] Neither side lived up to its promise.

On 11 July 1944, the War Cabinet's committee on Ethiopia approved negotiation of a new treaty based on Addis Ababa's draft but directed the American State Department's exclusion from the negotiations, even on matters of common concern. Washington would be asked, however, to cooperate in "a joint policy in regard to capital developments, to be worked out after the agreement was concluded."[34] The limitation on the State Department's participation galled the Foreign Office: "the more we get the Americans into Abyssinia the better we should be pleased. I cannot imagine any part of the world in which we ought to be more satisfied to see an introduction and expansion of American influence, political as well as economic."[35] The diplomats were hardly impressed with Eden's hard-won concession that if "the Americans press for our views on aspects of the Emperor's proposals, of which they have cognisance, we should not withhold them."[36] Maurice Peterson commented wryly: "Abyssinia is about the one and only place where American intervention can do us no harm and may do us some good. . . ."[37]

From the embassy in Washington came the advisory that the arrangements explicit in the Murray Agreement had led authorities to wonder whether HMG was considering a plan for Ethiopia similar to the Saudi Arabian scheme, "i.e., a joint sharing of the responsibility. . . ." If so, "now is the opportune moment to come forward with such [a] proposal," since "it will remove lingering doubts and misunderstanding about our motives in Ethiopia. . . . It will help to convince the Americans that Saudi Arabia is not an isolated and fortuitous instance of co-operation but that we are really in earnest in following a joint policy of co-operation with the United States in the Middle East." To "cold-shoulder" the Americans in Ethiopia might jeopardize "our general policy of enlisting

33. Text of agreed minute, 28 April 1944, FO 371/41450.
34. War Cabinet, Committee on Policy in Ethiopia, minutes of the meeting of 11 July 1944, EA (44), Meeting One, FO 371/41452.
35. Minute J2620/g, 18 July 1944, ibid.
36. War Cabinet, Committee on Policy in Ethiopia, draft report, 20 July 1944, ibid.
37. Pencil comment, 2 Aug. 1944, ibid.

United States collaboration and assumption of responsibility in the Middle East."[38]

Although its hands were tied by the War Cabinet, the Foreign Office responded as forthrightly as possible that it welcomed U.S. initiatives about Ethiopia, that it would answer Washington's queries, but that "more far-reaching collaboration" depended upon how the State Department viewed London's responses.[39] In other words, the Foreign Office would only react to American initiatives, hardly behavior calculated to win U.S. confidence. The ensuing suspicion permitted Haile Sellassie to take a harder negotiating position than would have been possible in face of Anglo-American unity.

On 11 August, Howe was instructed to inform the emperor that, "in consequence of His Imperial Majesty's proposals," London was willing to commence negotiations, during which HMG assumed that the 1942 agreement would not be denounced.[40] A few days later, however, Howe was informed officially that the Ethiopian Government would terminate the old treaty on 25 August, when Addis Ababa expected to resume control over the Ogaden, the reserved areas, and that portion of the Franco-Ethiopian railway located in Ethiopia. When the Englishman complained that the government was "rather rushing matters," the vice-minister for foreign affairs remarked that the note merely underlined the legal position and that "a delay of a month or two would, he was sure, be acceptable to [his] Government."[41] London reacted sharply, instructing Howe to warn the emperor immediately that movement of Ethiopian troops into the reserved areas might cause incidents.[42] On 25 August, the diplomat managed to interview the vacationing monarch in Harar, and elicited a royal promise not to act until back in the capital, by when, Haile Sellassie observed, Howe doubtlessly would know the British delegation's date of arrival.[43]

Keeping up the pressure, the Ethiopian Foreign Ministry officially refused to suspend the notice of termination, explaining that if London had not taken over four months to reply to its draft pro-

38. Law to Eden, Washington, 22 July 1944, ibid.
39. FO to Campbell, 11 Aug. 1944, ibid.
40. FO to Howe, 11 Aug. 1944, ibid.
41. Howe to FO, Addis Ababa, 16 Aug. 1944, ibid.
42. FO to Howe, 18 Aug. 1944, ibid.
43. Howe to FO, Harar, 25 Aug. 1944, in GOC in C, EA, to WO, 26 Aug. 1944, ibid.

posals, negotiations could have begun "while [the] status quo existed." Nevertheless, "in a spirit of mutual accommodation," Addis Ababa would delay action for two months, although if no agreement were reached by 25 October, it would, "while still disposed to continue negotiations, assume [its] rights of jurisdiction and administration."[44] Howe explained Ethiopia's strong assertions by referring to the 1941 negotiations, when various proposals, "subsequently abandoned, were strongly flavoured with the idea of a protectorate." In reaction, the emperor and government were striving "for what [the Ethiopians] call true collaboration which can be taken to mean collaboration on a basis of equality as between two sovereign states."[45] He was therefore pleased when London stopped fussing about the need for suspension *sine die* and cabled that Lord De La Warr had been appointed special plenipotentiary to negotiate the new agreement.[46]

Eden instructed Howe to do the impossible: impress the emperor with the importance of the relatively undistinguished aristocrat, since 1943 the director of home flax production in the Ministry of Supply. Lord De La Warr was nonetheless attractive to the Foreign Office: "He is probably available; he has political experience; he is unlikely to wish to turn Ethiopia into a colony; and he would, I think, accept our guidance."[47] His instructions would have been difficult for a Bismarck to fulfill. Lord De La Warr could concede everything except what the emperor most wanted—sympathetic consideration of Ethiopia's claim to Eritrea—since Churchill was adamant about the postwar disposition of Italy's colonies,[48] and the return of the Ogaden,[49] which various British policymakers long had sought.

The last problem had begun with Menilek II's defeat of the Italians on 1 March 1896, which rendered nugatory various Anglo-Italian frontier agreements in the Horn of Africa. Thereafter, the Ethiopians infiltrated well over half of what London considered its Somaliland protectorate. So obvious was Addis Ababa's presence in the Ogaden desert, immediately adjacent to Harraghe province, that

44. Text of Ethiopian Note, 31 Aug. 1944, FO 371/41453.

45. Howe to FO, Addis Ababa, 31 Aug. 1944, ibid.

46. FO to Howe, 4 September 1944, ibid.

47. Minute by Law for Eden, 29 Aug. 1944; FO to Howe, 5 September 1944, ibid.

48. Eden to De La Warr, 13 Sept. 1944, ibid.

49. Scrivener minute J3274, 3 Sept. 1944, ibid.

a British plenipotentiary was forced to concede the area in 1897. While many in Whitehall regarded the cession as "a slight loss," since it stopped Ethiopian encroachments, administrators in Somaliland were aghast that the December-to-March grazing lands of tens of thousands of British-protected Somalis were now located in Ethiopia.[50] From a governmental point of view, such an arrangement was not tidy, and thereafter colonial officialdom sought to restore the Ogaden to British rule. For example, in the early thirties, the protectorate establishment strongly supported exchanging the Port of Zeila for the coveted pasturage. Since, however, Addis Ababa was unwilling to give up so much, even for access to the sea, negotiations broke down.[51]

After the 1935-36 war, Rome integrated Somali-inhabited areas—and for seven heady months in 1940-41, even the British Protectorate—into the "Somalia" province of Italian East Africa. Thus, the fascists rationalized and substantiated the idea of "Greater Somaliland," and the British happily retained this tidy, if illegal, arrangement when they returned to power in 1941. No longer trifurcated administratively, and enjoying considerable political freedom under British rule, the Somalis developed the vital nationalism which led directly to the independence of Somalia in 1960. By then, of course, the Ogaden had reverted to Ethiopia, whose sovereignty over the area De La Warr had recognized in an agreement signed after very tough and lengthy negotiations.

He had finally arrived in Addis Ababa on 27 September 1944, and, three days later, commenced formal talks with an Ethiopian delegation consisting of seven cabinet-level officials. Almost immediately, questions arose concerning the Ogaden, the reserved areas, and Eritrea; the emperor even raised the last issue privately with De La Warr, who stated his opinion that London was well disposed toward Ethiopian aspirations there. Haile Sellassie thereupon thanked the Englishman for this assurance that he "would support [Ethiopian] claims at the peace conference," and De La Warr immediately countered that the emperor "was reading too much into my statement and that no formal considerations to such matters had as yet been given."[52]

50. H. G. Marcus, *The Life and Times of Menelik II: Ethiopia, 1844–1913* (Oxford, 1975), pp. 183–85; Memo by J. C. Ardagh, London, 30 July 1897, FO 403/255.

51. For details, see FO 371/16994.

52. De La Warr to FO, Addis Ababa, 3 Oct. 1944, FO 371/41454.

Concerning the Ogaden De La Warr made no headway whatsoever, since the Ethiopians saw no military reason for continued British occupation. Try as he might, the plenipotentiary could offer the Ethiopians no convincing explanation for London's policy.[53] In total frustration, De La Warr called for American intervention; he wanted Washington to instruct its minister to warn Addis Ababa that "America would view with disfavour any piecemeal adjustments in our frontiers or administration of boundaries which might prejudice [the] final peace settlement." At the Foreign Office, Mr. Cowley-Price considered that "this tel., in isolation, reads like a panic cry for help."[54]

The State Department, at any rate, would not have obliged. Officials there were so uneasy about London's stubbornly unreasonable position and its bullying of Ethiopia, that they informed the president about the situation. They cited the refusal by the British members of the Joint Munitions Assignments Board to approve shipment of five thousand rifles and some other military equipment to Ethiopia. The State Department was particularly irate since the arms request had been made "in anticipation of the increased responsibilities for maintaining internal security in Ethiopia which fell upon that country on August 25, 1944, with the termination of the Anglo-Ethiopian Agreement." The British claimed their veto on the basis of "'security' considerations," which the Americans considered a self-serving excuse to keep Ethiopia's central government weak and dependent upon London for support.[55]

This charge may have been well founded. In 1943–44, Addis Ababa was fighting a serious peasant uprising in Tigre that had been sparked by maladministration, excessive taxation, official corruption, and consequent brigandage. The Ethiopian government was forced ultimately to ask for British assistance, which, after much paperwork and discussion, was finally forthcoming. As the campaign against the rebels was ongoing both before and during De La Warr's mission,[56] British cooperation may be viewed as an effort

53. See his many anguished cables seeking clarification in FO 371/41454.
54. Minute attached to De La Warr to FO, Addis Ababa, 15 Oct. 1944, FO 371/41455.
55. Memo for the President, "Shipment of Arms to Ethiopia," 13 Sept. 1944, SD 884.24/9-1344.
56. Gebru Tareke, "Rural Protest in Ethiopia, 1941–1970: A Study of Three Rebellions" (Ph.D. diss., Syracuse University, 1977), pp. 128–47, 214–18. Although Dr. Gebru actually shows how little help the British provided, he cannot help asserting that "the rebellion was crushed primarily with British support," a fact which, however, obscures the truth.

to demonstrate the value of London's friendship; certainly Haile Sellassie was very lucky to be able to use British officers and to have important air support. Nevertheless, the suppression was largely an Ethiopian affair, and Whitehall's slow response strengthened Haile Sellassie's resolve to break his dependency upon the British.

The emperor's conclusion was echoed by the State Department in a memorandum to the president: "If they [the British] are able to convince the Emperor that they can block any attempt by him to obtain needed military supplies from other than British sources, the Emperor will be forced to rely upon the British for the means with which to guarantee the internal security of Ethiopia." London's policy was obviously aimed at the impending Anglo-Ethiopian negotiations: "The more convincing the British can be in showing the Ethiopian Government that they can deny the extension of aid to the Emperor by other powers, the better the terms they can presumably obtain from the Emperor." Washington should not allow Ethiopia to be browbeaten into submission, since "this government does wish to maintain a position of equality of opportunity in Ethiopia so that any future development of American interests would not be prevented by exclusive or preferential right obtained by Third Powers."[57] The president directed, therefore, that the British veto be ignored, and the arms shipment went forward, stimulating Haile Sellassie to attempt an American gambit to break London's resolve over the Ogaden.

To demonstrate the absurdity of HMG's position and to broaden the negotiations, Addis Ababa offered the territorial status quo against Washington's declaration that the war effort against Japan demanded the continued British occupation of the Ogaden. Then, the devolution of the country's sovereignty could be rationalized as an obligation of membership in the United Nations.[58] London testily attributed the ploy to John Spencer, the American foreign affairs adviser, who was well aware of Washington's anticolonialism. R. A. Butler, later to be foreign minister under Eden, was scandalized that the Ethiopian note had referred to "our American ally. . . . I have no doubt that the American adviser is responsible for the impertinent suggestion of reference to the U.S.G."[59] Whoever was the originator of the brilliant tactic, he put London on

57. See note 54 above.
58. De La Warr to FO, Addis Ababa, 5 Nov. 1944, FO 371/41457.
59. Various minutes, J3921, on above cable.

notice that it did not enjoy the same freedom of negotiation it had in 1942.

Haile Sellassie further narrowed Lord De La Warr's field of maneuver by offering all necessary safeguards to overcome British doubts about Ethiopia's ability to administer the Ogaden. He pledged to assign his best officials, to base his most efficient military and police units there, and even to hire a British advisor.[60] De La Warr cabled Eden that "this offer . . . is difficult to turn down without revealing our intentions concerning the future to a greater extent that I imagine you wish to do, but it is in fact a bid to prejudge the future by immediate reestablishment of an Ethiopian administration."[61] Meanwhile, the foreign secretary had concluded that retention of the Ogaden was not necessary, a position which contradicted Churchill's ideas about the future of the British Empire.

The Foreign Office had long doubted that any operational needs would be served by keeping the Ogaden. The protagonist was the Colonial Office, who "insist that [retention] is a matter of life and death, but nobody [here] really believes this." HMG nonetheless had decided that it would be wrong to return the Ogaden "without making an effort at the Peace Settlement to save [the Ogaden Somalis] from a fate which is generally regarded as being worse than death. The War Cabinet was definitely of the opinion that we must be tough with the blackamoor."[62] Eden so disliked the cabinet's "attitude" that he reopened the Ogaden question with Churchill.[63]

He warned the prime minister that Washington was watching the negotiations very closely and that the Ethiopians were clearly attempting to involve the United States, even if HMG "cannot accept American arbitration in such a matter or on such terms of reference." Eden argued that London had "no legal right" to the Ogaden, and that stubborn retention would appear to be "bullying a State by withholding parts of its territory without legal justification." If the emperor refused to see any advantages in a new agreement, then "Let there be no agreement and no ill will . . . I think that this would very likely bring the emperor to his senses although he might call our bluff and try to get help from the Americans." In other words, Eden wanted Haile Sellassie to realize that

60. De La Warr to Eden, Addis Ababa, 10 Nov. 1944, FO 371/41457.
61. Ibid.
62. Memo for Eden by Law, 6 Nov. 1944, ibid.
63. Eden note to Law, n.d., ibid.

no assistance would be forthcoming unless he yielded on the Ogaden. Churchill saw the sense of the move and agreed that the matter should be reconsidered by the War Cabinet.[64]

Meanwhile, Washington was totally confused about the negotiations in Addis Ababa. De La Warr had taken a dislike to the laconic American minister, John Caldwell, and told him very little about the proceedings. Caldwell had learned, however, of Haile Sellassie's American gambit and about the British counter that territorial issues ought to be left until the end of the war. The State Department wanted no part of the Addis Ababa negotiations, but a ranking officer did comment to Lord Halifax that Washington knew of no Allied agreement delaying territorial negotiations.[65] De La Warr again had blundered: first, his negotiating approach had permitted the Ethiopians to interject the illusion of American intervention, and then he had misrepresented Allied policy. London therefore sought to clarify the situation by briefing the State Department about the Addis Ababa deliberations.

R. A. Butler warned that "in doing so there is a risk of encouraging the Americans to intervene." Since, he caustically put forward, the "Americans are more impressed by Independence than Administration, [and] are incorrigibly suspicious of us," the British position on the Ogaden should be explained only partly in terms of responsibility for the Somalis. Rather, the argument should concentrate on the need to redraw East Africa's boundaries on a more rational basis and require that "the position of East African Somalis as a whole be taken into account." Butler warned, without explanation, that any return to "old-time boundaries," would complicate a postwar rearrangement.[66] Again and again, British comments clearly reveal that Ethiopian fears about London's intentions were well based; in sharp contrast, however, was Addis Ababa's naive belief that, in 1944, Washington would cooperate in forcing the evacuation of the Ogaden.

Of course, the emperor wanted to have his cake and eat it too. He coveted British money and support, while he sought to eliminate London's presence in the Ogaden. The State Department's rhetorical anticolonialism had obscured the emperor's perception of Lon-

64. Eden memo for the Prime Minister, "De La Warr's Negotiations with the Ethiopian Government," 9 Nov. 1944, ibid.
65. Halifax to FO, Washington, 12 Nov. 1944, ibid.
66. Butler minute J4050, 16 Nov. 1944, ibid.

don and Washington as major allies on the way to victory over the Axis. The two nations shared a common view of the world and probably of Ethiopia, and there was too much at risk elsewhere to permit a low-stakes game in Ethiopia to cause a rift. Churchill and Roosevelt therefore intervened with an agreement that robbed Haile Sellassie of his diplomatic leverage, even as it won him an important victory.

At the second Quebec Conference in September 1944, Roosevelt had handed Churchill a memorandum suggesting that all or a part of Eritrea be handed over to Addis Ababa. While the prime minister did not then commit his government, the U.S. demarche represented a major concession to Ethiopia, and the State Department probably felt it could not, however indirectly, sponsor the British evacuation of the Ogaden for risk of losing possible agreement over Eritrea. Furthermore, the Foreign Office deftly used the American rationale to support its Ogaden policy: If Eritrea is to be "handed over to the Ethiopian Government . . . there is a strong case in equity for [Addis Ababa] agreeing to some other regime for the Ogaden which, in contra-distinction to the greater part of Eritrea, is inhabited by peoples who have absolutely no cultural or racial affinities with the Amhara race."[67] Washington clearly acquiesced to this logic,[68] and on 24 November 1944, an embittered Haile Sellassie was forced to bow to Britain's terms for the Ogaden and the reserved areas, but even here he salvaged success. Article Seven of the Anglo-Ethiopian Agreement of 19 December 1944 specified that continuation of military administration was Ethiopia's contribution "to the effective prosecution of the war," and was volunteered "without prejudice to . . . underlying sovereignty."

The treaty generally was a triumph for Ethiopia. It proclaimed diplomatic equality between London and Addis Ababa, it provided no special relationship between British advisers and the Ethiopian government, and the head of the British Military Mission was placed under the authority of the Ethiopian minister of war. Moreover, HMG conceded control over the railway to the Imperial Government, as long as satisfactory arrangements were taken to ensure efficient operation and if British military needs received priority; it

---

67. Note on the Anglo-Ethiopian negotiations for the State Department, 22 Nov. 1944, ibid.

68. See De La Warr to FO, Addis Ababa, 18 Nov. 1944, ibid., about the noticeable change in attitude.

also promised to evacuate Dire Dawa and the area northwest of the railway, even before the line's transfer was accomplished.[69]

In light of London's forbearance and of its textual admission of Ethiopia's independence and sovereignty, even over the Ogaden and reserved areas, it is difficult to understand the emperor's expressed bitterness "at the necessity of so rigourous a settlement."[70] Nor can I agree with the conclusion that the negotiations represented "an unhappy and regretful chapter in the tale of Anglo-Ethiopian relations."[71] Given the determination of the Colonial Office and even Churchill to hold on to real estate, the Ethiopians obtained as much as they could, and were in good position to regain what they wished in a few years. Any pique merely reflected the emperor's failure to win his maximum demands and his inability to entice Washington's unequivocal and irrevocable support. Since the United States government removed its sustaining moral authority from the negotiations, Britain was able to obtain its minimal requirements, no matter how fraudulently or illegally based they were.

Upon reflection and for good reason, therefore, De La Warr judged the Ethiopian assignment his most difficult task. His interlocutors were not only tough negotiators but also deeply committed to safeguarding their patrimony. The Ethiopians were "under no illusions about our ultimate intention [but] they know their real dependence on us. They are surrounded by us, they want Eritrea, they need our financial mission . . . and they need and will have to have our financial help."[72] The last prediction was wrong because, shamed by the need to compromise Ethiopia's sovereignty, the emperor refused to accept financial assistance on London's terms. Given the magnitude of his concession, he believed that Ethiopia deserved an interest-free loan on lend-lease lines. Moreover, his council of ministers deemed the offered three million pounds "niggardly" and considered that a joint Anglo-Ethiopian allocations board gave HMG too much control over the monies. Lord De La Warr was wrong to conclude that rejection of the sterling

69. For a partial text, see Margery Perham, *The Government of Ethiopia* (New York, 1948), pp. 428ff. Otherwise see the complete treaty in FO 371/41457.

70. Aide memoire for HMG in De La Warr to FO, Addis Ababa, 24 Nov. 1944, FO 371/41457.

71. David Napier Hamilton, "Ethiopia's Frontiers: The Boundary Agreements and their Demarcations, 1896–1956," (Ph.D. diss., Trinity College, Oxford University, 1974), p. 140.

72. De La Warr to Eden, London, 3 Jan. 1945, FO 371/46052.

loan was based on "ignorance, bad advice, and illusory . . . national pride."[73]

73. De La Warr to FO, Addis Ababa, 6 Dec. 1944, ibid; cf. Caldwell to Secretary of State, Addis Ababa, 30 Dec. 1944, SD 884.51/12-3044.

3. British Decline, 1944–1950

Lord De La Warr was mistaken because he failed to realize that Addis Ababa had decided, quite soberly, finally to slip London's control; the preferred tool for this maneuver remained the United States, even if the American connection had not yielded anticipated results during the recent negotiations. Taking the long view, Haile Sellassie continued to elicit American interest in every aspect of Ethiopia's development, a process quickened by the arrival of the technical mission in May 1944. It was a quietly competent group that quickly went about the business of surveying and studying Ethiopia's problems. The emperor was delighted at its energy and drive and in September asked the Americans to assume supervision of the repair, maintenance, and construction of roads throughout the empire. Minister Caldwell considered that the mission as such could only examine and recommend, but did not interfere when four members resigned to take jobs with the Ethiopian Government.[1] The British minister ruefully admitted that London probably could not have recruited adequate candidates, given "our mobilization" and Ethiopia's low priority in terms of available manpower.[2] From Whitehall, Derek Riches offered a variation of the standard Foreign Office line: "anything the Americans achieve can only be to our advantage . . . while if they don't achieve anything or resign, or have rows with Ethiopians, at least Ethiopian resentment will not be directed against the British."[3]

At this time, however, ranking Ethiopians were grateful to the United States for inadvertently resurrecting the country's commerce, from which they reaped huge profits. The oligarchy, including Haile Sellassie and his family, controlled the economy through overarching holding companies which parcelled out scarce lend-

1. Caldwell to Secretary of State, Addis Ababa, 5 Dec. 1944, SD 884.154/12-544.
2. Howe to Scrivener, Addis Ababa, 22 Nov. 1944, FO 371/41491.
3. Minute J4352 on above, 14 Dec. 1944, ibid.

lease consumer goods through licensing arrangements and through the manipulation of foreign exchange. Such activity was hardly surprising since, "all trade should be seen as class trade, particularly in pre-capitalist social formations," where there is a direct "relationship of trade to the reproduction of the power of local ruling classes." For them, international trade was vitally important, since monopolies over "particular imports [or exports] were the key to the maintenance or expansion of their class power."[4] Thus, the imperial family was deeply involved in retail and wholesale businesses and transport,[5] and Haile Sellassie, as monarch, took a percentage of the revenues accruing from sales of Ethiopian gold in the inflated Bombay and Cairo markets.

For instance, the Ethiopian budget for 1945-46 (1938 E.C.) projected returns of £683,068 from gold sales, which "would seem to be a substantial underestimate for the probable yield of the gold mines, even allowing for the considerable proportion which probably disappears into the palace coffers."[6] An Ethiopian treasury official clarified, revealing that the current output of twelve thousand ounces per month would increase as a new vein near Adola came into production. Since gold sold in Cairo for £20/10/- per ounce, Ethiopia's output would yield £2,952,000 for the year.[7] The evidence of deficit financing in the Ethiopian government would seem to indicate that the emperor did not pocket the concealed revenues but used the funds to cover budgetary overruns, to purchase arms, and to dispense the largesse associated with the monarchy.

4. Adi Cooper et al., "Class, State and the World Economy: A Case Study of Ethiopia," paper delivered at the conference on "New Approaches to Trade" at Sussex University, 8-12 Sept. 1975, p. 1 (typescript). Trade has always been a catalyst to state and class formation in Africa. See, for example, the brilliant piece by Emmanuel Terray, "Long Distance Exchange and the Formation of the State: the Case of the Abron Kingdom of Gyaman," *Economy and Society* 3 (1974). Nevertheless, in the Ethiopian case, one must reject any notion of an African mode of production, and instead think in terms of the classic Asiatic mode. Compare Catherine Coquery-Vidrovitch, "Recherches sur une mode de Production Africain," *La Pensée* 144 (1969) with Cagler Keyder, "The Dissolution of the Asiatic Mode of Production," *Economy and Society* 5 (1976).

5. See Lyon to Minister, Harar, 3 Oct. 1946, FO 371/53462 about some of the Duke of Harar's commercial activities; *Addis Ababa Intelligence Report* n. 46, for August 1946, in FO 371/53461 for information concerning the "Imperial Motor Transport Co."; and *Addis Ababa Intelligence Report* n. 42, for April 1946, ibid., for insights into the crown prince's dealings.

6. Cook to Bevin, Addis Ababa, 9 April 1946, FO 371/53446.

7. Cook to Iliff, Addis Ababa, 29 March 1946, FO 371/53489.

Gold, of course, had been a vitally important trade item until after World War I, when the combined effect of the newly completed Addis Ababa–Jibuti Railway and the growing international commodities market brought Ethiopia into the orbit of the world economy. By the early thirties, coffee and hides had become the dominant Ethiopian commodities,[8] and modern financial mechanisms were functioning, and recovering a growing surplus. Haile Sellassie used the revenues to pay for arms and consumer goods, to modernize the capital, to finance social services, to create a centralized bureaucracy, military, and police force, and to educate necessary personnel.[9] The emperor believed in his prewar programs,[10] and upon return to Ethiopia in May 1941, he reverted to his earlier ideas about development and reliance on a bureaucratic class as a vehicle of control and change.

The Italian occupation seems to have augmented this group, although conventional wisdom continues to argue that the fascists destroyed the emperor's educated elite and sought to reduce the population to helotry. Yet, Christopher Clapham's evidence leads to the conclusion that many of the prewar educated survived,[11] and more recently John Cohen and Peter Koehn have inferred the connivance of a large group of Ethiopian officials in the Italian colonial administration. Therefore, the short colonial period must have increased the numbers of the bureaucratic bourgeoisie, just as it also caused significant and durable economic changes.[12]

The fascist government introduced money wages, and encouraged production of food crops to satisfy settler requirements. "Money consciousness and a money economy were thus spread widely in the interior." A protoconsuming society more or less emerged, particularly among those who had collaborated with the Italians in government and commerce. While traditional demand for cottons, salt, kerosene and the like strengthened, new needs

8. A. Zervos, *L'empire d'Ethiopie: Le Miroir de l'Ethiopie moderne* (Alexandria, 1935).

9. See H. G. Marcus, "The Infrastructure of the Italo-Ethiopian Crisis," in *Proceedings of the Fifth International Conference on Ethiopian Studies*, part B (Chicago, 1979).

10. Haile Sellassie I, *My Life and Ethiopia's Progress*, ed. and annot. by Edward Ullendorff (Oxford, 1976), p. 8.

11. Christopher Clapham, "Imperial Leadership in Ethiopia," *African Affairs* 68 (April 1969):119.

12. John Cohen and Peter Koehn, *Ethiopian Provincial and Municipal Government: Imperial Patterns and Post-Revolutionary Changes* (East Lansing, 1979).

appeared for tools, machinery, technical equipment, trucks, spare parts, and petroleum products. Generally, however, demand for capital goods was only characteristic of Ethiopia's few urban, political-administrative, market centers, whereas the countryside merely adopted modern money to fulfill traditional needs.[13] In other words, the Italians spurred Ethiopia's growth along lines already evident before their occupation. When the emperor and his followers returned, they found a familiar but more complex, larger, and better organized economy to exploit for the satisfaction of high wartime demand for Ethiopia's produce.

Confronted with British and Anglo-American governmental monopolies which transacted and transported goods in the eastern Mediterranean area, the Ethiopian oligarchy established its own import-export institutions. The most important monopoly, a private company, was housed in the Ministry of Agriculture and purchased grains for resale to the United Kingom Commercial Corporation (UKCC) which allocated foodstuffs throughout the Middle East. The grain monopoly was so successful in buying low and selling high, that the Foreign Office referred to grain purchases in Ethiopia as a form of subsidy.[14] The business was owned anonymously, and "it is impossible to ascertain the exact financial relationship of the company to the Government but profits do not appear as part of the budget."[15] The grain trade proved a lucrative venture for Ethiopian merchant-capitalists, who also benefitted from the high demand for the country's traditional exports.

Coffee, hides, and beeswax were finding quick markets, particularly in the adjacent Middle East. The elasticity of supply was high owing to the Italian-built road system. Even with worn-out transport, the exchange of goods between the interior and the capital "speeded up enormously." Anonymous backers financed newly reopened Indian and Arab firms, and everyone profited, including, for the first time, " a number of Ethiopians, many of the upper classes, who have now turned to trade."[16] These individuals had access to the highest levels of influence, and they offered to protect the inter-

13. Economic Report, Addis Ababa, 30 April 1946, in Cook to Bevin, Addis Ababa, 10 May 1946, FO 371/53461.

14. Scrivener to Howe, London, 29 Sept. 1944, FO 371/41465.

15. Information requested by Lord Moyne, in Howe to Moyne, Addis Ababa, 16 Sept. 1943, FO 371/36514.

16. A. D. Bethell, "Commerce in Ethiopia," Addis Ababa, 18 July 1944, in Howe to Eden, Addis Ababa, 2 Sept. 1944, FO 371/41463. See also Cooper et al., "A Case Study," p. 24.

ests of foreign colleagues for a price or a percentage of the profits.[17] And business was good, thanks to governmental controls, avarice, and a country-wide shortage of cotton goods. High demand and 4,800,000 yards of lend-lease textiles joined together to permit officials and merchants to profit heavily: the cotton goods, greatly overpriced, were used as currency to purchase grain for resale to UKCC at almost extortionate rates. A horrified American official, Hickman Price, learned about "The Textile Racket" and subsequently studied and reported the scarcely concealed workings of Haile Sellassie's oligopoly.

Consider, first, that textiles accounted for seventy percent of Ethiopia's imports throughout the 1940s; then, that the minister of commerce would license only those who promised to sell their goods, upon arrival, to the ministry at an unspecified but obviously low profit. The ministry, however, invariably waived its right of purchase and appointed "a private distributor," invariably the Ethiopian National Corporation (ENC).[18] Little was known about ENC's shareholders, but "circumstantial evidence clearly points to the ownership being vested very largely in the hands of the Minister of Commerce, or his nominees, and his friends." Furthermore, since the scale of business was so great, at an annual rate of £3,000,000 in 1944, the organization "must clearly meet with the approval of the highest powers."

The ENC sold its textiles at high prices to retailers who were stockholders and therefore benefitted doubly. In 1944, the corporation returned a profit of between £1,200,000 and £1,800,000, or twenty-five percent, approximately double the standard margin for most businesses in Ethiopia. "These figures may not seem large to you who are dealing in billions, but for this country it is colossal, reckoned by some to be an incredible 50% of GNP." In Hickman

17. David Molesworth, memo on progress or propaganda, Addis Ababa, 19 July 1943, FO 371/36527.

18. This organization succeeded a similarly profitable business established late in 1918, the "Société Ethiopienne de Commerce et d'Industrie" in which Haile Sellassie (then Ras Tafari) was not directly involved. He nevertheless decreed that "the Ethiopian Government will favor with all its power the operation of this business without ever becoming responsible financially if, despite its benevolent aid, the firm suffers losses in its commercial or industrial operations." The emperor's private secretary, Wolde Mariam, was one of SECI's stockholders, and he invariably acted as a surrogate for his master. In the thirties, SECI was reorganized, and the emperor and Blattengeta Herui, the foreign minister, openly invested considerable capital. Southard to Secretary of State, Addis Ababa, 16 Jan. 1932, SD 884.6363, Soc. Eth./3; Marcus, "Infrastructure," p. 565, n. 5.

Price's opinion, the profits came from a peasantry which was forced to pay excessively high prices for necessary goods.[19]

In essence, the countryside provided tribute for Addis Ababa's ruling "*camarilla*, which is riding with unparalleled recklessness down the highroad of new power to national suicide with the bit of personal aggrandizement clenched tightly in its teeth." In the provinces:

> a swarm of sycophants, all of whom have paid their price, rule in the name of the *camarilla*, exacting the highest taxes in the country, disbursing to the highest bidder the rights of distribution of imported goods (at, for practical purposes, their own prices), taking their toll of the population, dissipating for their own gain the not inconsiderable legacy of the Italians—from all of which a diluted but steady stream flows back to the coffers of the *camarilla* at Addis Ababa.

Price foresaw the oligarchy's demise "at the hands of the Ethiopian little man, inarticulate, driven beast that he is," although the final denouement was years away. "First the pendulum of unrestrained looting must swing its full course, and that pendulum is still in its early decline."[20]

Neither London nor Washington was eager to listen to such a refrain, nor indeed to similar themes and variations which had accompanied Haile Sellassie's movements since his regency in 1916. Government by venality was hardly unknown in the West, and remained general in the Middle East and Orient,[21] but it was ignored by European chanceries unless political profit stood to be made by denouncing it. Thus, the dissonant rumblings of foreign service officers were ignored in favor of harmony: the emperor was firmly in power and likely to remain in place for quite some time.

19. Hickman Price memo, "The Fundamental Welfare of Ethiopia: How Can it Be Achieved?": Part Two, "The Textile Racket," Addis Ababa, 18 Nov. 1944, SD 884.555/11-1844. In an interesting and innovative treatment, Siegfried Pausewang makes essentially the same point about the exploitation of the peasants and also applies more contemporary notions to his analysis. "Even if peasants had hardly any cash to spare, they proved to be a market for the traders . . . each little item [contributed] to a stream of resources flowing from the villages into the town, from there to the large centers, and finally to the export markets and big companies abroad." See S. Pausewang, *Peasants and Local Society in Ethiopia* (Bergen: The Chr. Michelsen Institute DERAP, 1978), special section on MAJETE, p. 31.

20. Hickman Price to MESC headquarters, Aden, 30 Oct. 1944, FO 371/41464.

21. James C. Scott develops the intriguing idea that a high level of corruption characterizes rapidly changing countries whose institutions can not keep pace with development. See "The Analysis of Corruption in Developing Nations," *Comparative Studies in Society and History* 2 (1969):328.

He was the hero of romantic liberals and even celebrated by the militant left. His was a world image: the tiny monarch standing before the globe's representatives and with tall dignity seeking fulfillment of the promise of collective security. His stature erased all reported blemishes and warts, particularly since the West, as always, talked often and loudly about morality in government, but did little to assure it in the world's various nooks and crannies. Liberal Western officials merely hoped that internal exigencies would convince corrupt governments to mend their ways and refrain from exploiting their people, particularly since, in 1944, the postwar modernization and Westernization of the world was anticipated. Surely such genuine heroes as Chiang Kai-shek and Haile Sellassie would grasp the moment and lead their nations to democracy and progress. It was therefore important to sustain these leaders in ways symbolic of their importance in a brave new world.

In late 1943, a very excited Blatta Ephrem Tewelde Medhen, the Ethiopian minister in Washington, told Cordell Hull that President Roosevelt had indicated that he wanted Haile Sellassie to visit the United States. The minister was eager to know the nature of the questions which the president wished to discuss, so that the emperor could prepare himself accordingly. In a memo to Roosevelt, a perplexed Hull noted that no urgent matters required review with the Ethiopian monarch and wondered what the president had in mind. As it turned out, Roosevelt had merely been expansive with Ephrem but instructed Hull to hold out the hope that a meeting might be arranged "possibly on the occasion of some future trip abroad."[22]

The eventuality materialized when the president was returning from the Yalta conference and decided to put into Egypt for a few days, there to interview Ibn Saud and Haile Sellassie and continue the business of shaping the world's future. The Middle East was an important part of America's posterity, and Roosevelt clearly wanted to accomplish a little personal molding. On 4 February 1945, Haile Sellassie learned that he was to meet with the president and was so pleased that Minister Caldwell reported that "for the first time in my experience [he] discussed an important matter of official business with me direct in English instead of through an interpreter."[23]

22. Cordell Hull, memos of conversation with Blatta Ephrem Tewelde Medhen, 28 Dec. 1943, and 19 Jan. 1944, SD 884.001/Selassie/400 and 403; Hull memo for the President, 1 Jan. 1944, ibid. /401a.

23. J. K. Caldwell Report, "Meetings of the Emperor of Ethiopia with the President and the Secretary of State," Addis Ababa, 27 Feb. 1945, SD 884.001 Selassie, Haile/2-2745 (hereafter cited as Caldwell Report).

Washington had not informed the British of the impending rendezvous, and London received the news from Jiddah.[24] After some tongue-in-cheek grumbling about American secrecy, the Foreign Office decided that the meeting was welcome and consistent with British policy.

> We cannot foresee what the President might promise in a moment of expansion. We need not be disturbed if he promises money on suitable conditions. *But it is to be hoped that, if Mr. Churchill meets the Emperor, he makes no commitment of any kind.*[25]

In fact, national prestige demanded equal time for the prime minister. The emperor, however, never raised the matter, and when Mr. Howe was instructed to arrange the summit, Haile Sellassie was too busy to receive the Englishman. Howe was awakened by the noise of an unusual takeoff from Addis Ababa airport at 5:00 AM on 12 February 1945. After learning that the emperor had departed on a USAAF DC-3, Howe telegraphed Churchill, arranged transport from Aden and trailed off after the Lion of Judah and his small troop of officials and advisers.[26]

En route, Haile Sellassie was in high spirits: he made the pilot circle Khartoum, to obtain "a view of the city from which he started his return to his own country in 1941"; and he directed a flight path which took the plane over the pyramids and the sphinx to Cairo's Payne Field, an American base, where emperor and entourage were housed. That evening, current Hollywood films were shown to a delighted movie-buff monarch and his minions. The next morning, 13 February, the Ethiopians inspected current American planes, among them two lend-lease Beechcrafts destined for the Imperial Air Force.

After lunch, the emperor and his party were flown to Great Bitter Lake, where they were escorted by Admiral William O. D. Leahy to the U.S.S. *Quincy*, where the president received them on deck at 5:00 PM. After a tour of the ship, Haile Sellassie, accompanied by Yilma Deressa and John Caldwell, met Roosevelt for tea. Social

24. Jordan to FO, Jiddah, 4 Feb. 1945, FO 371/46052.
25. Minute J584 by Coverely Price, 5 Feb. 1945, ibid. Italics added.
26. Howe to FO, Addis Ababa, 12 Feb. 1945, c61, ibid. John H. Spencer, *Ethiopia, the Horn of Africa, and U.S. Policy* (Cambridge, Mass., 1977), p. 11. The entourage included Ras Kassa, the president of the Crown Council; Aklilu Hapte Wolde, vice-minister of foreign affairs; Yilma Deressa, vice-minister of finance; Major Merid Mangesha, the emperor's aide-de-camp; John Spencer, foreign affairs adviser; and Kebede, the emperor's valet.

conversation was in French, but the formal meeting was in English and Amharic, with Yilma acting as interpreter. The official business took more than one hour, during most of which the emperor outlined Ethiopia's major concerns, substantially detailed in five memoranda handed to the president. During the last few minutes of the meeting, emperor and president talked alone, closing what was, according to Mr. Caldwell, "an exceptionally cordial and agreeable meeting."[27] Neither of the two major participants have left behind their impressions of the other, but one wonders whether the emperor sensed on 13 February, what Churchill appreciated two days later, the last time he saw Franklin Delano Roosevelt: "The President seemed placid and frail. I felt he had a slender contact with life."[28]

Slender contact or not, the president dutifully turned the memoranda over to Mr. Caldwell, who concluded that they did not require immediate action. The first reflected Ethiopia's continuing dismay with Paris's refusal in 1935–36, to permit arms to be shipped via the Franco-Ethiopian railway to Addis Ababa, "notwithstanding the fact that by virtue of Article 11 of the [railway] concession [of 30 January 1908] the Railway was to be placed in time of war at the disposal of the Ethiopian Government." This denial of rights "was clearly one of the most important factors leading to the defeat of May 1936" and amounted to abrogating the concession. At the peace settlement, Ethiopia therefore would seek its formal termination and demand ownership of the whole line, including that portion in French Somaliland. Addis Ababa desired a subcontractor to operate the railway, and asked Washington to facilitate a management agreement with an American firm. [29]

Even with complete control of the railroad, Ethiopia remained landlocked, a condition which the second memorandum sought to remedy. Addis Ababa explained that it had never recognized the validity of the nineteenth-century, inter-European treaties which had parcelled out Ethiopia's Red Sea littoral, even if forced to enter "certain bilateral agreements concerning these territories." Without its ports, Ethiopia had suffered indirect control by the adjacent colonial powers, the best case in point being France's refusal to

27. Caldwell Report.

28. Winston S. Churchill, *Triumph and Tragedy*, The Second World War, vol. 6 (Boston, 1953), p. 397.

29. Imperial Ethiopian Government, "The Franco-Ethiopian Railway," Addis Ababa, 9 Feb. 1945, SD 884.001 Selassie, Haile/2-945.

permit arms shipments from Jibuti. "Apart from the use of poison gas, it is clear that the immediate and most powerful cause for the defeat of . . . 1936 was the political control exercised over the Franco-Ethiopian Railway." Logically therefore, Ethiopia's isolation from the sea was the real antecedent of fascist occupation. Since all exports transitted French Jibuti for British Aden and ultimate disposition, Ethiopia was being deprived "of her U.S. Dollar exchange except in so far as the . . . Government in London chooses to make certain sums available." Merchants therefore could not buy or sell as they pleased, but had to deal exclusively with the sterling bloc, even if they wished to take advantage of American products and technical services. Such restraint was intolerable to a sovereign state and hindered the natural development of commerce and banking. Given the situation, businessmen in Aden exploited Ethiopia by charging excessive prices, which became even higher when goods were forwarded through Jibuti, where transit and other charges were levied. Ethiopia therefore sought its place on the sea and would "be eternally grateful for all assistance granted by the United States at the Peace Settlement to the realization of this vital aspiration. . . ."[30]

Eritrea encompassed the preferred access to the world, and in response to President Roosevelt's direct query, "the emperor said from a short term point of view Djibouti would be the best port because of the existing railway, but that a long term policy required a port in Eritrea."[31] The memorandum claiming the Italian colony was not "based solely upon the ground of necessity for economic reasons or for the equally pressing and vital need for access to the sea," but also on history: before recorded time, "Eritrea and its inhabitants have been an integral part of Ethiopia." This assertion was sustained by more or less spurious reasoning and appeals, of which one absurd example is enough: "it is as easy for the inhabitants of Addis Ababa to converse with the inhabitants of Asmara as with any peasants in the vicinity of Addis Ababa, for the inhabitants of both Addis Ababa and Asmara speak dialects of identical origin." Then came a curious twist of *post hoc* logic: "Yet another outward evidence of this basic truth [that Eritrea is an integral part of Ethiopia] is the fact that today, Ethiopia serves as the sole outlet for Eritrean intellectuals." The statement's accuracy depended more

30. Idem, "Access to the Sea," ibid.
31. Caldwell Report.

on the stupidity of Italian colonial racism and the contemporary economic malaise in Eritrea than on Ethiopia's absolute attractions.

More on the mark was an analysis which linked Eritrea's and Ethiopia's recent history. In July 1940, for example, the British had permitted Haile Sellassie to proclaim: "Whether on this side or the other side of the Mareb [the frontier] join in the struggle by the side of your Ethiopian brothers. Your destiny is bound up with the rest of Ethiopia." Moreover, Addis Ababa argued that Rome's callous attack in 1935–36 necessitated forfeiture of colonial rights and Eritrea's reversion "to its former and rightful owner." Cession would recognize "the existing historical, racial, cultural, economic and geographic ties which bind Eritrea integrally to Ethiopia and redress in part the injustices visited upon Ethiopia by the Fascist regime."[32]

The emperor's government also sought reparations for war crimes and damage, citing the "Graziani Massacres" of February 1937, the loss of the country's livestock, the use of poison gas in 1936, and the putative extermination of most of Ethiopia's modern-educated elite. The government asserted "that the hostilities which started in 1935 form an integral part of the war being waged today by the United Nations of which Ethiopia has been the first to be liberated." The country therefore sought membership on any War Crimes Commission, compensation for crimes committed against its citizens,[33] and arms to protect Ethiopia against potential aggression and civil insurrection. Above all, Ethiopia wanted small arms—even if they had to be purchased—as well as aircraft to enable emperor and agents to secure remote parts of the country, where usable landing fields outnumbered passable roads. Finally, the Ethiopians requested enough equipment for a forty-five-thousand-man army, including howitzers and other guns, thousands of rapid-fire weapons, armored cars, tanks, and trucks.[34]

American investment in the fledgling Ethiopian Airways and in oil exploration was also solicited.[35] When, however, U.S. donors were not forthcoming, others would suit. Sweden, like the United

32. Imperial Ethiopian Government, "Eritrea," Addis Ababa, 9 Feb. 1945, SD 884.001 Selassie, Haile/2-945.

33. Idem, "War Crimes and Reparations," ibid.

34. Idem, "Arms," ibid.

35. Memo of Conversation by Joseph Palmer, Washington, 17 Jan. 1945, SD 884.24/1-1745; Cole to Secretary of State, Addis Ababa, 2 April 1947, SD 884.6363/4-247.

States, was a noncolonial power, had survived the war with its infrastructure and industry intact, and knew of Ethiopia and its problems through a group of "Ethiopian-Swedes" who, before 1936, had served there as missionaries, advisers, and military instructors. It was therefore inevitable for Addis Ababa to turn to Stockholm for leverage and succor to circumvent the British. The effort was underway early in 1944, when Haile Sellassie's minister in Moscow handed his Swedish colleague a memo outlining Ethiopia's need for doctors, nurses, engineers, administrative experts, agronomists, and chemists. Stockholm was interested for humanitarian, political, and economic reasons, and in 1945-46 granted Ethiopia credits amounting to seven and a half million crowns to be used to pay for the travel and salaries of Swedish experts going to Ethiopia, and for any necessary equipment. By July 1946, Swedes were represented in almost every sphere of Ethiopian government and were training the Imperial Bodyguard and the air force.[36] While Ethiopians benefitted greatly from the Swedish presence, Haile Sellassie also was able again to assert his nation's independence, to throw off "the bonds of . . . British tutelage."[37]

The determination to be sovereign made diplomatic relations with Moscow especially welcome. As an avowedly antiimperialist power, Russia was perceived as a useful counterweight to Great Britain.[38] Felix Cole, the new American minister, insisted, however, that Haile Sellassie could be expected to block any serious penetration by the Soviets, but "at the same time hopes to string them along in order to have someone to play off, later, if he deems it advantageous, against all the western powers, including the United States." In a sentence full of words and concepts that could have been written by Ethiopian revolutionaries in the 1970s, Mr. Cole suggested that the emperor feared subversion against his "semi-Fascist, semi-feudal regime . . . the older noble classes, and the new, capitalistic, corrupt 'go-getters' of his bureaucracy."[39] Clearly, the processes which favored the development of the bu-

36. Viveca Halldin Norberg, *Swedes in Haile Selassie's Ethiopia, 1924-1952* (Uppsala, 1977), pp. 123, 169-78, 199, 229.

37. Norberg, "Swedes as a Pawn in Haile Selassie's Foreign Policy, 1924-1952," *L'Ethiopie moderne/Modern Ethiopia*, ed. J. Tubiana (Rotterdam, 1980).

38. "Ethiopia: Relations with Russia . . . ," *Intelligence Report,* Addis Ababa, Aug. 1944, U.S. National Archives, Record Group 226, OSS 99715.

39. Felix Cole to Secretary of State, Addis Ababa, 12 March 1947, SD 884.143/3-1247.

reaucratic bourgeoisie began long before the U.S. involvement of the 1950s.[40]

The period through 1945 had been profitable for Addis Ababa, and a considerable foreign exchange surplus had built up, particularly in sterling. Moreover, the introduction of the new Ethiopian dollar in 1945 and the retirement of the East African shilling greatly added to reserves, as did the demonetization and collection of millions of Maria Theresa thalers which were exported to Aden for resale. Thus, there was sufficient money to finance the administration without recourse to foreign assistance, a considerable achievement for a government that had depended on large British subventions in 1941–43.[41] Addis Ababa already had gone ahead with some projects, establishing a cotton and wool spinning center, an agricultural development bank, several schools, among them an industrial training center, and a produce exchange in the capital.[42]

The Ethiopian Government was more concerned about communications and transportation, however, and in 1945 worked up a loan request to the Import-Export Bank for U.S.$5,730,000 in order to purchase materials and services in the United States. The bank ultimately granted Addis Ababa a credit line of three million U.S. dollars, mostly to buy autos, trucks, spare parts, machinery and tires.[43] The war was soon over, and because Great Britain was able to supply more dollars, goods, and services, Ethiopia had used only $750,000 by 1948, when an extension was requested and granted. London, however, was not so generous with military assistance, and

40. Some analysts of recent Ethiopian history might want to reconsider their view that the United States was uniquely responsible for the growth and development of "the bureaucratic bourgeois state" in the 60s. As a matter of fact, that state was rooted in Ethiopian needs as perceived by Haile Sellassie and his governments of the 1930s and 1940s. Even the generally insightful Addis Hiwet distorts the sequence of events to favor the view of the American devil; he arranges and misconstrues facts to make Ethiopia dependent on outside events and not responsible for purely local phenomena. See Addis Hiwet, *From Autocracy to Bourgeois Dictatorship* (London ?, 1976), p. 41.

41. Cook to Bevin, Addis Ababa, 23 Jan. 1946, FO 371/53464; Cook to Pinset, Addis Ababa, 15 May 1946, FO 371/53446.

42. Speech of the Minister of Commerce, Industry, and Agriculture at the opening of the Chamber of Commerce of Addis Ababa, 25 Oct. 1945, in Cole to Secretary of State, Addis Ababa, 30 Oct. 1945, SD 884.50/10-3045; on education, see "Menelik School of Commerce Graduates Eleven," *Ethiopian Herald*, 3 Jan. 1945; and Department to Legation, 4 Oct. 1945, SD 884.42/10-445.

43. Department to Legation, 12 July 1946, and Cole to Secretary of State, Addis Ababa, 12 Dec. 1946, SD 884.51/7-646 and 12-1246.

during 1945–48, Ethiopia made numerous requests for arms and military hardware.

From the outset, the Ethiopian Government managed to reveal little about its forces, even when documenting its military requirements. One fact, however, was certain: Ethiopia's forces—army and bodyguard—needed everything. In early 1946, the "regular" army numbered about twenty-two thousand men, one half of whom had been integrated from the old territorial army. The latter had comprised the semiorganized patriots who fought the Italians and had become "a rag-tag and bob-tail agglomeration, differing but little in equipment and discipline from . . . 'shifta'—or bandits."[44] Surprisingly little was known about the bodyguard which, by 1947, reportedly comprised 4,500–5,000 men, an estimate which came from "an absolutely reliable and fully acquainted source but with difficulty and by a round-about method."[45]

Later that year, the American minister reminded Washington that the government wanted an army of four divisions and a headquarters company, totalling 45,000 men. Such a force was needed to reoccupy the Ogaden and to garrison the whole country, considerations little appreciated in London and Washington, which deemed Ethiopia's present army "far larger than needed for security."[46] Indeed, in December 1947, the touring Field Marshall Montgomery, then chief of the Imperial General Staff, deflected Haile Sellassie's request for more arms by stating "in direct and forceful language" that Addis Ababa's forces were "out of balance." He sensibly recommended that the army and bodyguard be reduced to a mobile force of ten thousand men, who, in cases of civil strife, would reinforce an enlarged gendarmerie, which the Englishman considered Ethiopia's real need. When Haile Sellassie raised the issue of external threats, the field marshal brushed them aside as inconsequential and mentioned that, given the many demands upon its resources, London could more easily meet the needs of a small and compact force.[47]

Montgomery probably wanted to do more for Ethiopia, since imperial strategy was then partly based on the use of Kenya as a staging area. A stable Ethiopia would relieve Nairobi's anxiety

44. Cole to Secretary of State, Addis Ababa, 5 Jan. 1946, SD 884.20/1-546.
45. Cole to Secretary of State, Addis Ababa, 15 Aug. 1947, SD 884.20/8-1547.
46. Cole to Secretary of State, 17 Sept. 1947, SD 884.20/9-1747.
47. Farquhar to FO, Addis Ababa, 15 Dec. 1947, FO 371/63160.

about a chronically troublesome frontier and also reduce the chances of interference with important lines of communication.[48] But London's cupboard was spare: the Labour Government's cradle-to-grave social security at home took precedence over the needs of imperial security abroad. In order to retain even the bare bones of its global strategy, the War Office was forced to abolish or reduce comparatively unessential programs such as the British Military Mission in Ethiopia (BMME) which cost a hundred thousand pounds annually. It is a mark of London's poverty at that time that defense officials could even contemplate considering "very carefully, whether in the present state of our finances we are justified in retaining the Mission at British Taxpayer expense." Nobody denied the BMME's contribution to regional stability and to good relations with Addis Ababa, but the military bureaucracy considered that such political benefits deserved a Foreign Office subvention of the training program.[49] The diplomats bluntly refused: "If you at the War Office can no longer afford [the BMME], that, in the final analysis, is because His Majesty's Government as a whole no longer can afford it."[50] The mission was therefore reduced to thirty-six officers and twenty-six men, a one-third cut, which, through some alchemy, saved fifty percent of the budget.[51]

Beyond this obvious sign of weakening commitment, the Ethiopians saw only British decline, even decadence. London no longer seemed capable of shipping military equipment as promised, British industry appeared unable to produce to specification, neither HMG nor the banks could decide about granting credit or arranging delayed payments, and delivered materials were often imperfect or arrived with parts missing.[52] Little wonder, therefore, that the emperor came to believe that the British were not so "efficient as [they] used to be," and began turning to "other powers in the world whose friendship might be more useful."[53]

During the second half of 1947, Ethiopia had, in fact, been "touting all over the world" for arms, had purchased sixteen used B-17 SAAB light bombers from Sweden, and, in Washington, Ras Imru, the Ethiopian minister, had transmitted a shopping list of

48. J. K. Petre, WO, to A. W. McEwing, Treasury, 14 Oct. 1947, FO 371/63141.
49. Morrison to Scott Fox, WO, 5 Nov. 1947, FO 371/63149.
50. Lascelles to Morrison, FO, 18 Dec. 1947, ibid.
51. Morrison to Scott Fox, WO, 23 Nov. 1947, ibid.
52. See FO 371/63144 for several cases in point.
53. Weld Forester to Lascelles, Addis Ababa, 24 Jan. 1948, FO 371/69299.

weapons "to be used for the purpose of strengthening the maintenance of law and order in the country."[54] There were reports of
deals with Belgium and Switzerland, and even a rumor that "the
Soviet Government has made a free offer of arms and munitions,
including heavy equipment and planes."[55] In face of such efforts, the
Foreign Office finally abandoned its pretense of military primacy in
Ethiopia and acknowledged its readiness not to object if Washington decided to supply "reasonable quantities of weapons and other
equipment."[56]

The United States was neither impressed with London's policy
shift nor with Addis Ababa's relentless quest for arms. Upon investigation, it found much of the Ethiopian activity "dispersed,
confused, inconsequential," as if Addis Ababa had constructed
straw men and purposely put out one red herring to attract the
Western dogs of war. While much was ruse and smoke, the State
Department nonetheless realized that it was committed to
Ethiopia's acquisition of at least part of Eritrea, where there were
important American facilities. It was decided, therefore, "as a
matter of policy," to supply *some* arms and ammunition to retain
Haile Sellassie's goodwill.[57] The Pentagon, however, did little to
facilitate purchases and Ras Imru grew frustrated. In January 1948,
he politely requested implementation of his request of July 1947. A
barely respectful answer was delivered on 21 April, advising that the
weapons were not available "from United States Government military stocks as a result of heavy demands created by the necessity of
implementing highly essential military programs," but that the administration had no objection to direct Ethiopian purchases from
manufacturers. Without official involvement, however, Ethiopia
could not qualify for subsidized, low-cost credit, nor installment
payments.[58] Ras Imru persisted, but the Department of Defense
resisted, again recommending commercial sources, an insinuation

54. Farquhar to FO, Addis Ababa, 1 Oct. 1947, and Farquhar to Scott Fox, Addis
Ababa, 23 Sept. 1947, FO 371/63141; Imru to Secretary of State, Washington, 18
July 1947, SD 884.24/7-1847.

55. Department to Minister, Washington, 23 Sept. 1947, ibid./9-2347.

56. British policy in Ethiopia, for discussions in Washington, late Nov. or early
Dec. 1947, FO 371/63158.

57. Beach to Secretary of State, Addis Ababa, 15 Oct. 1947, and Department to
Minister, 26 Dec. 1947, SD 884.24/10-1547 and 12-2647.

58. Imru to Secretary of State, Washington, 28 Jan. 1948, and Secretary of State
to Imru, Washington, 21 April 1948, ibid./1-2848 and 4-2148.

of how unimportant Ethiopia then was to America's geopolitical strategy.

Washington's attitude began to change only in late August, when the legation learned that the Ethiopian State Bank had transferred three million dollars to Czechoslovakia, the first payment toward an eight-million-dollar weapons contract that included construction of a munitions plant in Addis Ababa. With the arms reportedly came a military mission, although "whether the Ethiopians would risk the political repercussions is questionable." The arrangement with Prague stemmed from a "lack of success in obtaining arms in the US and UK on Ethiopian terms."[59] After considering the ramifications of Addis Ababa's action, the State Department informed HMG that Washington viewed "with misgiving the introduction of any considerable number of satellite personnel into Ethiopia and would be interested in any views the British Government might have regarding the practicability of persuading the Ethiopians to terminate the contract."[60]

On 14 December 1948, George Clutton of the Foreign Office told a U.S. Embassy official that, as much as his government disliked the Czech arms sale, it "can think of no way to stop [the] transaction except by either US or UK undertaking to fill Ethiopian arms requirements. At present UK is in no position to do this."[61] At the time, Washington was neither willing to intervene alone nor to offer itself as Ethiopia's arms supplier, and in mid-1949 the first Czech shipment arrived in Jibuti: 15,000 Mausers, 2,750,000 rounds of ammunition, 500 machine guns, and 10 submachine guns.[62] Meanwhile, Washington and Addis Ababa had negotiated a satisfactory lend-lease settlement, and Ethio-American relations turned to civilian matters.[63]

The technical mission of 1944–45 had conditioned the emperor to think about economic development in terms of those infrastructural and capital projects which later characterized his regime. The mission produced a multi-volumed recommendation of projects worth ninety-one million dollars, which Washington re-

59. Legation to Secretary of State, Addis Ababa, 25 Oct. 1948, SD 884.24/10-2548.

60. Lovett to London Embassy, 2 Dec. 1948, SD 884.24.

61. Douglas to Secretary of State, London, 21 Dec. 1948, ibid.

62. Bigelow to Secretary of State, Addis Ababa, 18 April 1949, SD 884.24/4-1849.

63. Agreement on Lend-Lease Settlement by and between Ethiopia and the United States of America, 20 May 1949, SD 884.24.

jected as "out of proportion to Ethiopia's capacity to finance."[64] A revision in 1947 by the Department of Commerce and subsequent redactions nonetheless retained features in common which are central to an understanding of American activities in Ethiopia before and after the coup of 1960.

Many have argued that even the partial implementation of suggested programs supported the growth of the bureaucracy and infrastructure necessary for the working of the U.S.-dominated world economy.[65] Others have implicitly viewed the phenomena associated with American aid efforts as seeking to adjust Africa's traditional economy to monopoly capitalism's changing needs.[66] And a few have considered the introduction of capitalistic structures and techniques into a largely traditional society as temporarily buttressing premodern socio-political structures.[67] Besides agreeing with each of these analyses, I strongly concur with the notion that American aid "freed Haile Sellassie from the limitation of his exports," breaking his dependence on primitive capital accumulation.[68] Interestingly, the emperor did not undertake wholly new programs, but merely enlarged and developed the agenda of change he had sponsored in Ethiopia since achieving power. In other words, the monarch's long-term aspirations and policies coincided with the advent of American financial interest and assistance.

U.S. planners saw three major interrelated economic problems: (1) repairing and maintaining the Italian-built communications network; (2) building modern social, educational, and economic infrastructures; and (3) increasing agricultural production and industrial output. Since the whole effort required foreign capital and expatriate technicians, the revised program emphasized projects which either would add to foreign exchange or diminish external spending: "In this manner, an orderly process of expansion, development and technological modernization can be accomplished." The planners, however, did not intend to restrict Ethiopia's foreign trade but to change its composition: "To the extent that imports of cotton textiles, salt, sugar, and gunny sacks are reduced or elimi-

---

64. James S. Moose memo, 21 March 1949, SD 884.50/3-2149.
65. For example, Addis Hiwet, *From Autocracy to Bourgeois Dictatorship*, p. 41.
66. Samir Amin, "Underdevelopment and Dependence in Black Africa, Origins and Contemporary Forms," *Journal of Modern African Studies* 10 (1972):517–18.
67. Aidan Foster-Carter, "The Modes of Production Debate," *New Left Review* 107 (Jan.-Feb. 1978):51.
68. Cooper et al., "A Case Study," p. 23.

nated, Ethiopia will be enabled to purchase machinery, fuels, and other goods abroad in larger quantities than heretofore."

The new scheme thus retained the technical mission's integrated program, "which cannot be arbitrarily altered without impairing the efficiency and coordinated nature of the development anticipated." For example, the growth of lumber and cement mills had been keyed to the demand for building materials during the peak period of industrial construction. Throughout the program's progression, there would be a regular flow of materials to avoid isolated and useless facilities, bottlenecks, and imperfect coordination. The plan even connected the growth of ground transportation and new roads to the supply of mechanics, garages, tires, and fuel. Also intrinsic to the program was provision of a modern public health system to ensure the well-being of Ethiopia's new working class, and an educational organization that would yield trained and skilled workers and foremen, "to displace foreign engineers and highly skilled technical personnel . . . ."

Most of the new men would exploit the agricultural sector, since Ethiopia, in the opinion of American experts, lacked the resources for heavy industry. The country did enjoy "perhaps the largest expanse of fertile arable land in Africa" and local farming techniques were "well adapted to the natural soil environment." Erosion was not so severe as elsewhere in Africa, and even with the continent's largest per capita cattle population, "overgrazing has not reached such serious proportions as to threaten the grass cover." Improvements in animal husbandry would come through selective breeding and culling; and agricultural development would be facilitated by "the vigor and natural intelligence of the population," the excellent climate, "the existence of a fairly extensive road network in relation to the level of economic development," and Ethiopia's proximity to areas of chronic food shortage.

Certain adverse factors would have to be overcome before the country's natural advantages could be exploited. Educational levels were low, marketing techniques were antiquated, technology was lacking, and the government was inefficient. The fact that the country was landlocked constituted a special problem which tended "to perpetuate the primitive character of Ethiopian economic development." The country's rugged topography also impeded progress by isolating peoples and multiplying the costs of health, education, and transportation. The last was likely to be the major expense in any program of economic development, and the technical mission therefore had emphasized production of high-value commodities which would remain profitable after absorbing the high costs of collection and road and rail transport to the sea. Finally, since capital, technology, and managerial skills were scarce, development was keyed to a relatively few projects, rather than spread over a large number of schemes "at the possible risk of not accomplishing any of them effectively."

Paradoxically, however, the mission viewed the cooperation of the peasants as the "cardinal precondition" for success, since they would have to adapt the most to meet the needs of Ethiopia's new export-oriented economy. The government would have to provide "the economic incentives necessary to induce him [the peasant] to produce for the national market, rather than exclusively for his personal needs." The Americans realized that the subject related to Ethiopia's political economy, an area outside the scope of their report, but they understood that only an adequate supply of consumer goods, particularly textiles, would stimulate the peasant "freely" to enter the money sector.

Cotton goods manufacture was therefore retained as a major component of the revised development scheme of 1947, which recommended a three-year $11,740,000 program to establish three industries: six meat-processing centers, each containing slaughterhouses, canneries, and byproduct plants; six associated tanneries to process hides; and a cotton textile complex capable of producing ten million pounds of cloth annually. Although initial foreign exchange requirements would be high, Ethiopia soon would garner valuable hard currency by exporting hides and packed and canned meats and by supplying half its own textile requirements.

The net growth in foreign exchange would finance complementary industries, including logging and a sawmill, the last with an estimated annual capacity of four and a half million board feet of lumber, "most of which will be required immediately for plant construction"; a cement mill with a thirty-thousand-ton capability; and a machine shop and a tire-recapping plant, to serve Ethiopia's growing fleet of vehicles. Later would come a leather works, a wool handicraft unit, and coffee-grading and processing facilities. Finally, the plan called for a salt-refining complex to increase supplies and "to reduce a large and bulky import"; a potash plant able to produce thirty thousand tons; a chemicals company; a powder and dynamite works; a carbide, acetylene and oxygen unit; a burlap and bagging mill; vegetable oil refineries; a soap factory; a shoe industry capable of producing 180,000 pairs annually; a wood products and veneer plant; and a sugar mill with a capacity of five thousand tons and one million gallons of alcohol. With the remnants of the Italian-built modern sector, the new undertakings would provide enough profit to stimulate further economic development.

Infrastructure and supporting services were to be developed through a three-year, ten-million-dollar program, one-third of which would go to transportation. The planners appreciated that the sum would not maintain existing roads, build the additional routes required for the industrialization scheme, and simultaneously provide Ethiopia with new and desperately needed trucks. The Americans hoped that Ethiopian ingenuity would make the difference: manual labor in place of machines, hand-crushed rock instead of gravel and asphalt, "and, for the next few years, at least, much reliance . . . on animal and wagon transportation."

Education, however, would not even reach the horse-and-buggy stage. The three-million-dollar allocation would do little to bring about the "mass education, training of teachers and training of specialists [which] are the main keys to Ethiopian economic and social progress." Neither the technical mission nor the Department of Commerce planners had any understanding of the type of practical education necessary for a people about to undertake modernization. The low priority afforded education was not so shocking, therefore, as the disregard American experts had for Ethiopia's agriculture and animal husbandry, the country's economic mainstays.

Somehow or other, a little over three million dollars would have to sustain land surveyors, crop and land use specialists, and the extension agents who would implement programs. It was assumed that Ethiopia's farmers would rapidly adopt the schemes which agile foreign experts would specify to solve the country's agricultural problems. Postwar Washington enjoyed a blithe trust in the ability of "modernization" ipso facto to erase tradition and an entrenched political economy. Truly, it was a religious age, a time of faith in the new deities of technology and progress. When it came to dollars and cents, however, pragmatism was evident.

In 1945-46, Ethiopia reported a net foreign exchange surplus of eighteen million dollars, enough to finance development schemes, although the future did not appear so rosy. World agricultural

markets presumably would normalize, once war-ravaged areas returned to production, sharply decreasing Ethiopia's grain sales,
which, since 1943–44, had accounted for twenty-five percent of the
country's export revenues. Second, under the pending International
Monetary Fund Agreement, Ethiopia would be unable to market its
gold at more than the U.S. price of thirty-five dollars per ounce.
Finally, the reappearance of Brazilian coffee in Near Eastern markets was already reducing the price paid for the Ethiopian product.
The 1947 memorandum assumed, therefore, that under the worst
circumstances Ethiopia's foreign exchange surplus would amount
to only two to three million dollars obtained from newly mined
gold.

If, however, the projected development program were implemented, it would yield as much as $13.5 million from sales of meat
and animal by-products, leathers, vegetable oil, potash, and ve-
neers. Moreover, domestic manufacturing, particularly of textiles,
would displace imports costing $11 million. Even so, industri-
alization and supporting schemes would place additional burdens
on the Ethiopian balance of payments. Imports of raw materials,
fuel, supplies and technical services could amount to $8.9 million
annually, assuming that Ethiopia made no progress in cultivating its
own cotton, banana fiber, sugar, salt, etc.; but might cost $4.2
million if raw materials were produced locally and if Ethiopians
displaced foreigners in technical positions. In either case, Addis
Ababa would be able to borrow $22 million at $3\frac{1}{2}$ percent over a
thirty-year period, with annual service charges of about $1.6 mil-
lion. Thus, at worst, the country would net $10.5 million in foreign
exchange, and at the best, $18.7 million. As the 1947 memo ob-
served: "it is worth noting that, even on conservative assumptions,
the program under consideration should substantially improve the
balance of payments position of the Empire, provide assurance of
regular servicing of foreign credits, and yield substantial balance of
payments surpluses in addition."[69]

The additional earnings could be used to increase consumption of
imports "and consequently raise . . . living standards," to expand
industrial development, to accumulate gold or foreign exchange

---

69. There is evidence that these aims were achieved, at least by the sugar and
textile industries, but at the expense of the consumer, who paid considerably more
than the world price for heavily protected and taxed domestic products. See Duri
Mohammed, "Private Foreign Investment in Ethiopia (1950–1968)," *Journal of
Ethiopian Studies* 7 (1969):66.

reserves as a hedge against economic crises, or to effect "the broad program of public works development, including public health, education and social services for the people, which was envisaged in the Technical Mission's report." Of course, such a decision rested with the Imperial Government, which, by the time a choice had to be made, would have benefitted from the experience gained in implementing the original plan. The authors of the revision therefore strongly recommended advancing Addis Ababa credits of not more than twenty-two million dollars and financing "further development . . . through currently accruing surpluses of foreign exchange receipts over expenditures." The Ethiopian government would thereby avoid accumulating onerous foreign obligations and would "be free at all times to change the plans and direction of further development in accordance with the experience gained in the first years of the effort."[70] Addis Ababa, however, was less cautious about its freedom of action, more optimistic about economic development, and as ambitious as the technical mission.

In January 1948, the Imperial Government advised Washington that it would request a loan of $130,088,870 to carry out "projects necessary to the rehabilitation and the economic development of Ethiopia." It was a maximum shopping list reflecting the technical mission's report which, although never officially transmitted, was fully known to Addis Ababa. The first part of the request called for $108,500,000 for the development of infrastructures. Twenty million was to be devoted to the rehabilitation and expansion of road transport "essential to the development of [Ethiopia's] agricultural, mineral, and industrial resources." Next came a $55 million railway project involving the construction of 890 kilometers of new line, "to augment the wholly inadequate present facilities," and of new terminal facilities. Fifteen million dollars was to be invested in the development of airports and related installations. The restoration, extension, and improvement of post, telephone, and telegraph systems was calculated at $5.3 million; and various hydro-electric, irrigation, and water control projects were assigned a cost of $13,300,000.

Industrial requests totalled $21,588,870, differed little from the American revision, and emphasized meat packing and related undertakings; sugar and alcohol production; textiles; logging and

70. Department of Commerce Memo based on the Fellows Report, in Palmer to Glendinning, Washington, D.C., 2 July 1947, SD 884.50A/7-247.

lumber; vegetable oils and soaps; salt; chemicals; leather and tanning; glass, cement and bricks; and batteries manufacture and repair. The Ethiopian design was more ambitious but not so well-documented and detailed as the American scheme. Nonetheless, Addis Ababa considered that its projects were "soundly conceived," the subjects of "careful study" either by the technical mission or various expatriate experts. It argued that the industrial projects would be self-sustaining: "So high are the demands and needs for the products involved that all give assurance of operations with substantial profit margins."

Next, the Ethiopian proposal turned to public works which, while not "directly self-sustaining [were] essential to the development of the agricultural and industrial economy of Ethiopia"; they would justify themselves by stimulating production, internal commerce, and external trade. The enlarged tax base and increased supplies of foreign exchange would easily permit Addis Ababa to retire the U.S. loan, most of which would have been expended on "the acquisition of American supplies, machinery, equipment and personnel." The Ethiopians stressed that the development program fostered U.S. interests: "American industry will . . . be aided through the increased exports to the United States, of hides, goat skins, sheep skins, leopard skins, coffee and other raw materials."[71]

The State Department's Development Bureau studied the scheme critically from two vantages: need and ability to repay. Its analysis was, of course, hindered by a lack of accurate data, but available information indicated outstanding foreign debts of $15,177,133, not a particularly high figure in light of Ethiopia's prosperity from 1943 to 1947. The bureau reckoned that this run of good luck was over because Ethiopia was beginning to lose its Middle Eastern grain markets to Canada, Australia, and the United States, which no longer had to feed a reviving Europe. Moreover, although Ethiopian coffee was good, it could not long continue to compete in the Middle East with Brazil's large exports of cheap beans. Finally, demand for hides had dropped considerably because buyers now could obtain better quality skins elsewhere. Ethiopia's import situation, however, was favorable: the price of textiles, its main need, was dropping in face of world oversupply and some high-demand items—gunnysacks, tobacco, and liquors—were now being pro-

71. Imperial Ethiopian Loan Request, in Yilma Deressa to Loy W. Henderson, Washington, D.C., 29 Jan. 1948, SD 884.51/1-2948.

duced locally. In 1948, therefore, Ethiopian imports amounted to $35,898,947, but exports were valued at $45,209,031.

In 1947, Ethiopia had shipped hides, skins, and coffee valued at $5,583,000 to the United States, from whom she imported $8,085,000 worth of textiles. The $2,502,000 deficit was partially covered by selling grain for dollars in neighboring countries, particularly Saudi Arabia. The same year, Ethiopia ran a deficit of $3,150,000 with Great Britain but easily acquired the necessary sterling in Eritrea, Aden, and British East Africa. Given these figures, it was clear that Ethiopia would experience great difficulty servicing either a large sterling or dollar loan if imports remained at present levels and if Addis Ababa were unwilling to make payments in gold, which fetched a better soft-currency price elsewhere. As a matter of fact, the State Department reckoned that if Ethiopia reduced American imports ten percent, and if exports did not fluctuate sharply, then only $392,320 would be available to service a $5,000,000 loan for fifteen years at three percent, representing an annual repayment of $343,333. Such a program would also require stringent Ethiopian banking, currency, and foreign exchange regulations.

Currently, the Imperial Government was facing the expected fiscal crisis: anticipated revenue for 1948 appeared to be less than fifty million Ethiopian dollars, a decline of fifteen million from 1947, when trade was at a high point. To meet current expenses, Addis Ababa had been borrowing against its accounts and holdings in the State Bank and had sold gold. The State Department noted that the government could save money by reducing peculation and inefficiency but could do little about a bad harvest, a deteriorating road system, and excessively high railway freight costs. It was no wonder that trade, and therefore revenues, had declined, but the department's pundits insisted that Addis Ababa could not afford an extensive public works program, no matter how desirable or necessary, although they anticipated that Washington might be able to provide grants for some technical projects, including road construction.

Turning their criticism to the industrial request, the planners found some merit in specific undertakings. Surprisingly, textiles manufacturing was dropped because "it may be cheaper for Ethiopia to continue to buy textiles on the world market, than to develop an industry which would require imports of cotton, technicians, train a labor force, and secure spare parts and spindles . . . ."[72] Instead, Ethiopia ought to concentrate on small-scale meat-packing and leather industries, since both products would find immediate markets and "provide sufficient foreign exchange to enable Ethiopia to service a loan far in excess of the one [considered] here . . . ." For now, however, Ethiopia would have to be satisfied with a five-million-dollar loan, rigidly supervised by U.S. or International Bank officials.[73]

Addis Ababa had been led by the Report of the Technical Mission to believe that the United States would spend tens of millions of dollars to modernize Ethiopia. That belief had been reinforced when Washington had sponsored Addis Ababa's membership in the United Nations, granted lend-lease, provided diplomatic support against the British, and when President Roosevelt had honored Haile Sellassie by meeting with him in Cairo. No one in the U.S. government had bothered to advise Addis Ababa that in 1947, the assistance package had been scaled down; and, of course, the Ethiopian government overlooked the fact that, in 1948–49, the United States had no genuine political interest in the Horn of Africa that had to be ensured through extensive technological aid and capital transfers. Thus, when it came to Ethiopia, Washington tended toward a utilitarian view of assistance, which even undermined showcase American efforts.

For example, though the Import-Export Bank readily extended the expiration date of a three-million-dollar credit to purchase ground transport items, it refused to permit the funds to be used to buy aircraft for Ethiopian Airlines. The company—managed by TWA—had been successful and had contributed to U.S. prestige and influence. It desperately needed three Martin 202 transports to expand its profitable services, but the State Department argued that: "On balance, the need for additional aircraft is considered secondary to the need for surface transportation in the primitive economy of Ethiopia."[74] Such pragmatic calculation was dominant until the cold war and the Korean crisis cast Ethiopian aid requests in a

72. Duri Mohammed, "Private Foreign Investment," pp. 69–71, and see note 69 above.

73. Carwell memo, "The Fellows Mission Report and Ethiopia's Application to the International Bank for Reconstruction and Development," Washington, 13 July 1949, SD 884.51/7-1349.

74. Melembaum to Thorp, Washington, 5 July 1949, SD 884.51/7-549.

different light. Thus, up to 1950, *no* American-sponsored pattern of dependency in Ethiopia emerges from the data.[75] To the contrary, the Addis Ababa Government worked assiduously to link its economic destiny with the American world system.

The legation reported that "the Government will try to keep body and soul together and to reorient the economy towards export sales for United States dollars." Addis Ababa was selling gold for dollars and liquidating its reserves in sterling, devaluation of which appeared imminent; and was introducing modern capitalistic devices. A securities market was established in the capital; the State Bank's loan criteria were redefined to accord preference to "borrowers whose enterprises . . . offer the most productive potential with respect to the over-all economy"; and business laws were rewritten to provide suitable guarantees for the repatriation of profits and capital, "thus making the interest of the foreign investors coincident with the interests of Ethiopian nationals [?!]."[76] In other words, the emperor and oligarchy, not surprisingly, chose to expand Ethiopia's capitalism, a process spurred in 1949 when drought in Brazil and floods in Guatemala forced coffee prices up. Although Ethiopia's seventeen-thousand-ton crop was small by most standards, it provided valuable dollars and stimulated further production. The prices paid for hides and skins also held up well, considering the non-devaluation of the Ethiopian dollar, which made the country's produce more expensive in terms of sterling. Finally, even the grains market was relatively strong, notwithstanding all pessimistic projections. And working far better than expected was the newly imposed currency control, which captured most of the country's foreign-exchange earnings.[77] In fact, contrary to State Department forecasts, 1949 was a good year for the Ethiopian economy, permitting the Imperial Government to project revenues of E$63,120,000 for September 1949–September 1950, and expenditures of E$62,988,726, for a slight surplus.[78]

The same years had not served the British empire so well. London's power was largely illusory by this time, its responsibilities

---

75. For various definitions of dependency, see Theotonio dos Santos, "The Structure of Dependence," *The American Economic Review* 60 (May 1970); and James Caporaso, "Dependence, Dependency, and Power in the Global System, A structural and Behavioral Analysis," *International Organization* 32 (Winter 1978).

76. Merrell to Secretary of State, Addis Ababa, 16 Aug. 1949, SD 884.51/8-1649.

77. Merrell to Secretary of State, Addis Ababa, 7 Nov. 1949, SD 884.51/11-749.

78. Merrell to Secretary of State, Addis Ababa, 21 Feb. 1948, SD 884.00/2-2148.

unmitigated by resources. HMG's position in the Horn of Africa was irremediably weak, even if it appeared to Addis Ababa in April 1946 that the British had every intention of retaining the Ogaden. Then, Foreign Secretary Ernest Bevin had proposed to the "Big Four" (Britain, France, the United States, and the USSR) that Italian Somaliland be united with the British Protectorate and the Ogaden "to form a single region called Somalia," which should be placed under a British Trusteeship.[79] The proposal, like Britain's empire, had no future: the USSR criticized the idea as imperialist and the United States found it colonial. The French, eager to demonstrate Paris's loyalty to its Latin neighbor against the Anglo-Saxons, wanted to see Italian Somaliland returned to Rome, and Italy, of course, desperately sought to reestablish her old empire, even if cloaked in a U.N. Trusteeship. Addis Ababa, needless to say, viewed the scheme as anathema: the proposal was so daunting that Ethiopian policymakers envisioned their reveries about Eritrea transmogrifying into a landlocked nightmare. Access to the sea was Addis Ababa's overriding concern, and the emperor despairingly proposed to London that the Ogaden be exchanged for the port of Zeila and a connecting corridor.

Ironically, Addis Ababa unveiled its scheme in June 1946,[80] when it was becoming obvious that Bevin's plan, however sensible,[81] would not be implemented. Indeed, the foreign secretary, in the House of Commons on 4 June 1946 had already signalled failure and admitted his own naiveté at having raised the matter. Bevin described the "innocence" of the proposal as stemming from a desire "to give these poor nomads a chance to live, [to] organize the thing decently" by eliminating the "constant bothers on the frontiers." But if the other powers misrepresented and misunderstood the wellspring of British altruism, "we will not be dogmatic . . . we are prepared to see Italian Somaliland put under the United Nations' trusteeship."[82] When the Ethiopian government realized that the Bevin plan was stillborn, and as it became obvious that at least part of Eritrea would be transferred to Addis Ababa, the emperor quickly retreated from his government's own proposal. A

79. *Times* (London), 30 April 1946.
80. See FO 371/53467.
81. John Drysdale, *The Somali Dispute* (New York, 1964), p. 68.
82. As quoted in Saadia Touval, *Somali Nationalism* (Cambridge, Mass., 1963), p. 79.

year later, it was clear that the Ethiopians were not serious about the exchange and were only "spinning the whole thing out" until other issues were settled.[83]

If the attempt to recreate "Somalia" failed, the Bevin proposal was nonetheless a boost for the nationalism of the "Somali Youth Club." Established in May 1943 as a social organization, it had, by 1945, enrolled about five thousand more or less educated government functionaries who shared a trans-Somali perspective. By the end of 1946 the possibility of a united Somali state had attracted twenty-five thousand members, and one year later there were an estimated eighty thousand on the roster, including at least seventy-five percent of the gendarmerie, the majority of the enlisted men in the fifth battalion of the King's African Rifles, and most local members of the British Military Administration.[84] In late 1947, responding to the needs of a vastly increased membership and the international situation, the club transformed itself into a political organization, the Somali Youth League (SYL), which sought: (1) to unite all Somalis; (2) to educate all Somalis; (3) to develop a written Somali language; and (4) "to take an interest in and assist in eliminating by constitutional and legal means any existing or future situations which might be prejudicial to the interests of the Somali people."[85] The SYL became so popular that in January 1948 it would claim the support of ninety percent of all Somalis, including traditional rulers.[86] Even if its assertions of strength were only half true, the facts suggest that the British ruled only through the cooperation of the SYL, as the military itself admitted to the Foreign Office in early 1948.[87] Thus, any active opposition by the SYL would necessarily undermine the premises of British rule in the Ogaden, where the Sinclair Oil Company was surveying possible drilling sites.

Haile Sellassie had told the American minister that granting the concession to an American firm was a political act,[88] and the Ethi-

83. Minute by I. W. Bell, 25 July 1947, FO 371/63136.
84. War Office report on the Somali Youth League, 15 Nov. 1947, FO 371/69424.
85. As quoted in I. M. Lewis, *The Modern History of Somaliland* (New York, 1965), p. 123.
86. "Statement of the Somali Youth League on 20 Jan. 1948," in Four Power Commission of Investigation for the Former Italian Colonies, *Final Report* (London, 1948), Vol. 2, Appendix A, Section II, Chapter IV.
87. Note on British attitude toward the Somali Youth League in Reid to Bell, WO, 31 April 1948, FO 371/69424.
88. Cole to Secretary of State, Addis Ababa, 2 April 1947, SD 884.6363/4-247.

opian Ministry of Interior issued the Americans passes valid for one year's stay in the Ogaden. British military authorities honored the documents, since London was anxious not to provide Addis Ababa any pretext for denouncing the 1944 agreement: "our attitude . . . is that we are prepared as far as possible to allow [Sinclair] the same facilities as they would receive if the Ogaden were administered by Ethiopia."[89] In sharp contrast, the Jijiga branch of the Somali Youth League rejected Addis Ababa's sovereignty and advised Sinclair that its presence in the Ogaden was based on an authority "which we do not recognize and would never recognize as we are not willing to be ruled by the Ethiopian Government." It cited the Atlantic Charter as a basis for Somali sovereignty and asked the Americans "How can you trespass our country on the sole authority of our oppressors?"[90] In SYL eyes, the Sinclair operation was "a political move sponsored by the Emperor of Ethiopia."[91] Neither the SYL nor local Somali authorities, however, took action to alter the status quo until just before the arrival in Mogadishu of a four-power commission to ascertain local opinion about the disposition of the Italian colonies.

On the afternoon of 4 January 1948, Mr. Wells, the general superintendent of the main Sinclair camp near Wardere, was handed a note addressed to "The Sinclair Oil Company (Americans)" and signed by various local notables. It asserted that "you entered our land (Somalia) without any permission from us, and then did many kinds of work not caring for its people"; the note demanded the cessation of all activities until an agreement, particularly in regard to day laborers, had been negotiated.[92] Wells immediately drove to Wardere, to consult with the British civil affairs officer, who, after local inquiries, asked the American to return the next day with his colleagues for a conference with various clan leaders and the president of the SYL branch.

During the meeting on 5 January, Sinclair's men were again told that the company had no right to operate in Somali territory. When Wells and his associates failed to respond satisfactorily and made for a waiting airplane, apparently to travel to Harar, the Somalis

89. FO to Legation, 1 Oct. 1947, FO 371/63160.
90. Somali Youth League to Representatives of Sinclair Petroleum Co. passing through Jijiga, Jijiga, 6 Aug. 1947, ibid.
91. Civil Affairs Officer, reserved area, to HQ, Middle East Land Forces, Jijiga, 12 Aug. 1947, ibid.
92. Copy of memo handed to the Sinclair camp on the afternoon of 4 Jan. 1948, FO 371/69295.

became irate. The Americans were threatened and beaten, and the plane was stoned and seriously damaged. The local gendarmerie did not intervene until the incident was over, and as a ranking British Officer in Mogadishu wrote, "There is no means whereby local protection at Wardere or in [the] Ogaden would in itself meet [a] situation [of civil insurrection]."[93]

The Ethiopians were the first to react to the incident. In Addis Ababa, the British chargé was told that the emperor, his private secretary, and the vice-foreign minister "had been astonished" at what had happened.[94] The three men were being disingenuous, however, since throughout 1947 the Ethiopian Government had organized a Somali cadre which kept Addis Ababa well informed of SYL activities and pretentions in the Ogaden. In fact, the government had countered the nationalists by convening its Somali supporters in Addis Ababa for consultations and for the signature of a petition to the emperor requesting the immediate return of the Ogaden to Ethiopian administration and registering full support for the Imperial Government's arrangements with the Sinclair Oil Co.[95] The signatories were traditional men who understood government and authority in terms of patron-client relationships and not at all within the framework of modern nationalism; they were also, of course, more intrigued by oil royalties than by spartan republicanism.[96]

The American government was not interested in such purely local political considerations, and complained that the Somaliland administration apparently could not offer Sinclair the same protection it routinely provided for British firms. A Foreign Office minute explained, at least to its author's satisfaction, that "If a British Company . . . were working in the Ogaden, the local inhabitants would *not* regard it as the vanguard of the Ethiopian return, and, consequently, would not be hostile to it."[97] But such a flippant apologia was beside the point, as other British officials quickly noted. The nub was military weakness, and a mortified high com-

---

93. Civil Affairs Officer to WO, Mogadishu, 14 Jan. 1948; Weld Forester to FO, Addis Ababa, 6 Jan. 1948, ibid.

94. Weld Forester to FO, Addis Ababa, 22 Jan. 1948, ibid.

95. Merrell to Secretary of State, Addis Ababa, 16 May 1948, SD 884.014/5-1648.

96. Commander in Chief, Middle East Land Forces, to WO, 28 Oct. 1947, FO 371/63160.

97. Douglas to Wright, U.S. Embassy, London, 4 Feb. 1948, and minute J829/G by Lascelles, 8 Feb. 1948, FO 371/6920B.

mand, knowing that there could be no improvement, advised immediate withdrawal from the Ogaden and the reserved areas, thus terminating any responsibilities for Sinclair and Washington. The Foreign Office agreed reluctantly, even if it were obvious "that we are clearing out as a direct result of our failure to protect the Americans in the Ogaden. [But given] the state of our military administration . . . then regardless of prestige it is high time we . . . withdraw."[98]

Before the conclusion evolved into decision and implementation, British strategists assessed the impact of withdrawal on imperial policy and the disposition of Italy's colonies. Everyone agreed that an independent Somaliland would succumb immediately to Moscow's subversion and that a Western trusteeship was therefore necessary. Although there was some anxiety about Italy becoming a communist state, its return to the Horn of Africa would be the best solution, to help keep the country in the "free world" and to compensate Rome for the loss of Libya, which would be placed under British trusteeship to protect the Mediterranean Basin and the lines of imperial communication.[99] The only opposition to Whitehall's evolving Somali policy came from Field Marshall Montgomery. He considered Ethiopia "a hopelessly corrupt feudal state," and believed that the Somalis so hated the Ethiopians that they "would fight rather than be handed back to them." He therefore insisted on an "all-British, united Somalia," which would be an integral part of a proposed East African federation. A Foreign Office analyst simply wrote, "these recommendations are not realizable."[100]

And so, on 17 March 1948, Prime Minister Clement Atlee informed Haile Sellassie that "notwithstanding the risk of unfortunate repercussions in other Somali areas, it has been decided to withdraw the British troops from Jijiga at an early date as a first step towards a larger evacuation of the Ethiopian territories now under British Military Administration." The British leader conceded that a permanent administration might have an easier time dealing with the Sinclair problem and reported the removal of SYL flags flying

98. Scott Fox minute of conversation of meeting at Colonial Office (CO) between CO, WO, and FO officials, 14 Jan. 1948, ibid.

99. Stapleton to Lascelles, Ministry of Defense, 14 Jan. 1948, FO 371/69327; "Future of the Ex-Italian Colonies in Africa," Brief for the Secretary of State, Cabinet Paper CP (48), 11 Feb. 1948, FO 371/69328.

100. Analysis of Field Marshall Montgomery's report for Mr. Bevin, 28 Jan. 1948, ibid.

over Ethiopian territory.[101] Haile Sellassie was "particularly pleased" to learn of the imminent British evacuation and recommended a meeting between competent British and Ethiopian parties to ensure an efficient evacuation, thereby decreasing the "risk of unfortunate repercussions in other Somali areas." He thanked HMG for banning SYL flags, which he called "subversive emblems," and asked if Sinclair could recommence operations immediately.[102]

The military administration refused to consider the matter in its unconscionable and unmannerly haste to leave the Ogaden. London explained that its army could not "guarantee the company against a recurrence of incidents," and therefore that it "could not accept responsibility for the consequences."[103] Meanwhile, Addis Ababa worked tirelessly to construct an administration which would secure the Ogaden for Ethiopia. The Somali cadre prepared to assume local government, and police and army units were trained and moved into place, ready for the orders of handpicked and highly qualified sub-governors.[104] So effective were the government's preparations that when Jijiga and adjacent areas were handed back from 15 April to 14 May, "no disorder of any kind was experienced and the population generally behaved in a most exemplary manner," giving the Ethiopians "great satisfaction."[105] Doubtless, however, the Imperial Government obtained more pleasure on 24 July 1948, when Britain agreed to begin the Ogaden evacuation on 24 August 1948, and to finish one month later.[106]

The Ethiopian Government organized its reoccupation from Jijiga, which Donald Bigelow of the American legation visited on 23 July, in order to ascertain if Sinclair could resume its operations under secure conditions. He was greatly impressed with the French-speaking Major Demeke Retta, the sub-governor-designate of the Ogaden, an experienced soldier, diplomat, and administrator. A forceful, intelligent, diplomatic man, Major Demeke reported the

101. Atlee to Haile Sellassie in FO to Legation, 17 March 1948, FO 371/6920B.

102. Haile Sellassie to Atlee, Addis Ababa, 30 March 1948, in Weld Forester to FO, 30 March 1948, FO 371/69291.

103. Atlee to Haile Sellassie, in FO to Legation, 3 April 1948, ibid.

104. Weld Forester to FO, Addis Ababa, 5 April 1948, ibid.

105. Brig. R. H. Smith, "Report on the Handover of Jiggiga and that Part of the Reserved Areas West of the Grazing Line," n.d., in WO to FO, 7 Aug. 1948, FO 371/69293.

106. Protocol of Withdrawal, Addis Ababa, 24 July 1948, ibid.

preparations complete for Addis Ababa's resumption of government and assured Bigelow that Sinclair could go forward "without encountering difficulty from the Somalis." He suggested unofficially that the company make a cash present to each of the chiefs in the drilling area, thus oiling and giving them "some concrete advantage from the operation," and permit the headmen to distribute surplus water and to recruit locally hired laborers.

The major recounted that he had recently travelled into the Ogaden, to reassure the population and its leaders of the benevolent nature of the forthcoming Ethiopian administration. He told Bigelow, however, that any violent opposition would be countered by two regiments of well-equipped and well-trained troops under his command.[107] When the British evacuated the bulk of the Ogaden by 23 September 1948, these units garrisoned the area,[108] and quickly imposed order because the Somalis knew that the Ethiopians, in sharp contrast to their recent experience with the British-officered Somali troops and gendarmerie, would shoot to kill. In any case, incidents were unlikely because SYL militants had withdrawn from the Ogaden rather than face the renewed police power of Ethiopian colonialism and its Somali agents.

The returning Sinclair workers therefore found the Ogaden "quiet [with] the Ethiopian forces . . . in good control of the situation and in a position to cope with any tribal uprisings," in contradiction to official British reports of instant rebellion. The U.S. legation explained the discrepancy by pointing to colonial officialdom's propensity to give "undue weight to comparatively unimportant incidents because of their personal distaste for the Ethiopians and their lurking fondness for the idea of the creation of Greater Somaliland."[109]

Still, British weakness and Ethiopian strength had resolved the issue of a pan-Somali state, at least for the time being. Relations between Addis Ababa and London improved, even as the British minister bemoaned Whitehall's inability to supply the weaponry "the Ethiopians clamoured for through the British Military Mission to Ethiopia." He consoled himself with the notion that the emperor

107. Bigelow to Minister, 25 July 1948, enclosure in Merrell to Secretary of State, Addis Ababa, 29 July 1948, SD 884.6363/7-2948.

108. Tefera Worq to Sinclair Oil Co., Addis Ababa, 2 Oct. 1948, in Merrell to Secretary of State, Addis Ababa, 5 Oct. 1948, SD 884.6363/10-548.

109. Merrell to Secretary of State, Addis Ababa, 21 Oct. 1949, SD 884.00/10-2149.

was "disappointed . . . with the U.S. Government as a potential Father Christmas,"[110] but returned ruefully to the impoverishment of Britain and, consequently, to decreasing British influence in Addis Ababa. He appreciated that the Ethiopians sought only money and arms: "But in our present state of penury and rapid rearmament [brought on by the Berlin Crisis and the establishment of NATO] we can't supply either. No, the balance . . . seems . . . to be very much against us. The fact that we surround him [Ethiopia], and could in the old days have squeezed him flat with very little difficulty, is of course irrelevant in the age of Lake Something [Success, where the United Nations had its temporary headquarters]."[111] The frustrated diplomat wanted to wind down British activities in Ethiopia, but was not supported by either the Foreign Office or the War Office, both of which viewed the survival of the BMME as essential to keeping the communists out of Ethiopia. Neither of the ministries, however, was especially keen on paying the mission's annual costs, now a niggardly fifty thousand pounds.

The War Office had concluded that the Ethiopian army would never be a valuable ally in time of war, and regarded the force as helping "the Emperor to maintain stability and to prevent the spread of communism." In the ministry's opinion, the value of the BMME, therefore, "lies largely in the political rather than in the military field," and it again sought a Foreign Office subvention.[112] The diplomats ridiculed this argument, basing their refusal on the clear fact that military missions were obviously in the purview of the War Office.[113] That unhappy and financially straitened organization was forced to concede the point, but only because retention of the BMME ensured "against some ill disposed country such as Czechoslovakia stepping into our place, supplying arms, and spreading communism."[114]

While the subsidy issue was resolved, the harsh fact was that the BMME had insufficient funds to operate properly, and constant requests to the Ethiopians for money to purchase necessary equipment and weapons for training went unheeded. Meanwhile, Ras Abebe's War Ministry squandered resources on showy but tactically

110. "Review of Principal Events in Ethiopia in 1948," in Lascelles to FO, Addis Ababa, 9 Feb. 1949, FO 371/73765.
111. Lascelles to Gov. G. E. Reece, Addis Ababa, 9 Feb. 1949, FO 371/73788.
112. Morgan to Wass, WO, 30 Dec. 1948, FO 371/73701.
113. Minutes, J104, ibid.
114. Charteris to Scrivener, WO, 18 March 1949, ibid.

useless heavy artillery, the relatively ineffective territorial army (the ras's political base), and a top-heavy administration.[115] British frustration with this state of affairs reached its apogee in early 1950, when the Ethiopian government announced that it shortly would receive a consignment of twenty tanks from Czechoslovakia, at a cost of US$627,000. The BMME had advised against this acquisition, since the army did not have the technical skills to maintain the armor, and really needed such unassuming items as ammunition, uniforms, and trucks. "The fact that the Ethiopian Government are prepared to waste a large sum of American dollars on buying these tanks reveals the extent of their irresponsibility and of their desire to maintain at all costs their facade of modern technical development in the military as in other spheres."[116]

The despair permeated subsequent memoranda and reports, and in May 1950, one Foreign Office functionary posited: "The Ethiopian army must be a fantastic affair, and it does not seem worthwhile to keep the BMME there to help train it."[117] The emperor also had concluded that the British connection had finally to be broken, and the onset of the Korean War offered rich possibilities. In early August 1950, Haile Sellassie's private secretary had brought an Amharic document, "which in all probability was written by the Emperor himself," to the American ambassador for transmittal to Washington. In it, Ethiopia declared itself a loyal ally of the West, even if Great Britain and the United States had done little to assist her and to strengthen her defenses against the communists. Nevertheless, the Imperial Government offered one thousand troops for service with the United Nations in Korea, provided that the United States equipped and otherwise supplied them and that Ethiopia received a substantial amount of American weaponry.[118] This telegram was never sent; apparently the emperor, on advice of his Foreign Ministry, had second thoughts about the way his offer had been framed. He therefore toned down his complaints and withdrew his second condition. "This does not mean that the Emperor no longer wants arms from America. He has apparently asked that an entirely separate message on the subject be sent to the State

115. Memo on the Imperial Ethiopian Army by Gen. Turnbull, Addis Ababa, 31 May 1949, ibid.

116. Chancery to FO, Addis Ababa, 24 Feb. 1950, FO 371/80262.

117. Minute by Baxter, 25 May 1950, JA 1201/4, ibid.

118. Memo on internal political developments in Ethiopia, by Arthur L. Paddock, Jr., n.d., in Merrell to Department, Addis Ababa, 31 Oct. 1950, SD 775.00/10-3150.

Department. He has clearly seen the wisdom of not linking the two matters."[119]

The British mission in Addis Ababa took the opportunity to recommend that the BMME be withdrawn.[120] The military concurred: "Far from enhancing our position politically . . . [the BMME] has become a political liability. Militarily it has no value and we can use our officers and money to far better purpose elsewhere."[121] On 30 November 1950, the British ambassador advised the Ethiopians that the BMME would be withdrawn in three months. "My Government are now faced, as a result of the international obligations which they have assumed in regard to the organisation of the joint defences of the Western Hemisphere against aggression, with exceedingly high demands on their manpower and financial resources."[122] British hegemony in Ethiopia was over, and its last symbol of authority was giving way to the conquering lion. The period of American ascendency was about to commence, and Ethiopia looked forward to economic and military benefits. The U.S. connection already had proved its political worth by helping Addis Ababa win Eritrea.

119. Bell to Allen, Addis Ababa, 8 Aug. 1950, and Bell to FO, Addis Ababa, 14 Aug. 1950, FO 371/80247.

120. Bell to FO, Addis Ababa, 23 Oct. 1950, FO 371/80262.

121. Robertson to WO, via Asmara, 10 Nov. 1950, ibid.

122. Lascelles to Ethiopian Government, Addis Ababa, 30 Nov. 1950, ibid.

4. American Security and Ethiopia, 1950–1960

Acquisition of Eritrea was a basic element in Ethiopia's postwar foreign policy. Whenever and wherever possible, the emperor and his officials repeated Addis Ababa's line that Eritrea had been an integral part of Ethiopia before being colonized, that retrieval would give Addis Ababa access to the sea, and that reversion to Solomonic sovereignty was compensation for wartime cruelties and losses. In August 1945, the emperor called in the diplomatic corps and proclaimed his dissatisfaction that Ethiopia had not been asked to the forthcoming foreign ministers meeting in London, where an Italian peace treaty would be discussed. Ethiopia, the "principal victim of Italian aggression," had been invited only to submit a position paper, whereas Italy was to be fully represented. He admonished: "The small nations of the world must be accorded a fair opportunity of representation in regard to decisions affecting their soil and future if there is to be . . . a peace founded upon the principles of justice." He therefore demanded the return of Eritrea as "simply the rectification of a wrong which for sixty years had deprived Ethiopia . . . of the oldest part of the Empire and . . . of access to the sea."[1]

Churchill and Roosevelt already had agreed that Ethiopia should be ceded southern Eritrea, including the port of Assab, which had been designed by the Italians to serve northern and central Ethiopia.[2] Haile Sellassie, of course, lobbied for it all, making all the familiar arguments to President Harry Truman, although he added that "unless we can obtain access to the sea, the possibility of

---

1. Government of Ethiopia, Press and Information Department, *Eritrea and Benadir* (Addis Ababa, 1945 [?]), p. 4.
2. "Eritrea, Port of Assab," *Intelligence Report*, Aden, 1 March 1944, U.S. National Archives, Record Group 226, OSS 64047.

developing the oil concession which we have granted to a large American corporation and which holds forth unlimited possibilities for the alleviation of the hard lot of our beloved subjects, must also vanish."[3] To other powers, he emphasized the importance of Massawa: "It is through it alone that the four great and densely populated provinces of Tigre, Gondar [Begemdir], Wollo, and Gojam can be supplied with their needs for imported goods, and it is the only port through which their exports of hides, coffee, and other agricultural products can find an outlet to the sea."[4] These views were seconded and amplified by Haile Sellassie's faithful claque in Great Britain which also emphasized that Eritrea had remained culturally a part of greater Ethiopia during its long occupation. "In no sense is there a separate Eritrean people; and it would be contrary to the trend of the political and social order which is promised after the war, and looks to larger economic and political units, to encourage any movement for political separation."[5]

In Eritrea, much the same position was taken by the "Patriotic Association for the Union of Eritrea and Ethiopia" led by Dej. Beyene Beraki and Ato (later Dej.) Tedla Bairu. Its members called for the unconditional integration of the colony into the "motherland," totally opposing partition or trusteeship. The party was headquartered in Asmara, where Col. Nega Haile Sellassie, Ethiopia's liaison officer to the British Military Administration, also advised and subsidized the unionists out of monies collected in Addis Ababa by the "Society for the Unification of Ethiopia and Eritrea." This organization had been formed in 1944 by the redoubtable Wolde Giorgis, who, as minister of pen, was the head of the Imperial Secretariat and therefore the emperor's de facto *chef de cabinet*. Many officials and other members of the national bourgeoisie participated in the society's efforts to dramatize the government's determination to rule *all* of Eritrea.[6]

3. Haile Sellassie to Truman, Addis Ababa, 4 April 1946, File 85E, Truman Library.

4. Government of Ethiopia, Ministry of Foreign Affairs, *Memoranda Presented by the Imperial Ethiopian Government to the Council of Ministers in London, Sept. 1945,* revised ed. (London, 1946).

5. Norman Bentwich, *Ethiopia, Eritrea and Somaliland* (London, 1945), p. 16; see also E. Sylvia Pankhurst, *British Policy in Eritrea and Northern Ethiopia* (Essex, 1946), and her newspaper, *New Times and Ethiopia News*.

6. Lloyd Ellingson, "The Emergence of Political Parties in Eritrea," *Journal of African History* 18 (1977):267–69.

Addis Ababa's Eritrean adversaries also agreed on the importance of retaining the colony's integrity. Christian and Moslem nationalists alike had established the "Love of Country Society" in 1943, and pledged "to work together to serve the causes of the country without any distinction." Unfortunately, however, religious parochialism proved a more decisive factor than secular nationalism, and by the beginning of 1947, Eritrean nationalists split into factions "on the basis of their confessional affiliations and they fell for [the] manoeuvres of British and Ethiopian colonialism." No matter how hard they argued for immediate independence or a period of trusteeship followed by national sovereignty, the very atavism of their divisions blocked them from achieving their goals. As a longtime nationalist put it, "In the final analysis, the Eritrean people were the losers."[7]

So were those Italians who dreamed of the colony's retrocession to the "new Italy" and who sought to retain the country intact to preserve "the integrity of the [colonial] effort."[8] The Rome Government supported "the Pro-Italy Party" composed of settlers and ex-soldiers who sought the return of the colonial power under the auspices of a U.N. trusteeship.[9] The party had little impact on the four-power commission which visited Eritrea from 12 November 1947 to 3 January 1948, but its testimony helped the visitors to decide that there was general opposition to dismembering the country, even if this consensus was "not indicative of a definite feeling of national consciousness."

Quite to the contrary, the commissioners concluded that people's consciousness did not extend beyond families and clans "in their appreciation of political and social life," and that existing political parties "are insufficiently developed to assume the responsibility of leadership in the country." They also found that Eritrea had a backward agriculture, a crude industrial base, and poor natural

7. Othman Saleh Sabby, *The History of Eritrea* (Beirut, 1975), pp. 208–11.
8. Italo Papini, "L'Eritrea ha ragione di esistere," *Affrica* 2 (15 June 1947):95–96.
9. Ellingson, "Political Parties," pp. 275–76. Of more than passing interest are letters sent to President Truman by various Eritrean notables, arguing for Italy because Rome would feed, house, and clothe the people, whereas Britain would not, and Ethiopia could not. See Truman Library, File 319, Ethiopia. Many others in Eritrea agreed with the judgement, if not with Italy's restoration, and Othman Saleh Sabby recalls the following aphorism: Italian policy was "'fill your stomach and shut up!', the British policy was 'speak and go hungry!', and the Ethiopian policy was 'shut up and go hungry'." Othman, *History,* p. 213.

resources, so that "The national wealth and revenue at the present level cannot assure the country an independent existence or provide for its development." Even if many Eritreans had voiced their desires to live in an independent country, "these wishes are not mature or the result of independent thinking. They are not founded on serious political and economic considerations."[10] Although some form of dependency was the obvious answer, neither the commission nor the Council of Foreign Ministers could decide on a recommendation, and the matter was referred to the United Nations, where the anti-imperialist Arab-Asian bloc came to consider the Eritrean case as somehow or other "symbolical of the anti-colonialist struggle."[11] Such thinking obviously worked to the advantage of Ethiopia, which went on a diplomatic campaign to obtain Eritrea.

On 30 July 1948, Addis Ababa acknowledged its paramount interest in Eritrea.[12] In London, policymakers were willing to give "some degree of satisfaction" to Ethiopia by giving over "Assab and the Danakil as an outlet to the sea," but the Foreign Office wanted northern Eritrea granted to Khartoum.[13] The latter's subsequent unwillingness to administer the area led Whitehall to consider transferring the whole colony to Solomonic sovereignty; such a gesture might mute Addis Ababa's complaints about the return of Italy to Somalia, and it might be manipulated to induce the Imperial Government to permit the construction of a Lake Tana dam, vital to an expansion of irrigated cotton land in Sudan's Gezira region.[14] The only possible obstacle was Washington.

The United States sought to shift only southern Eritrea to Ethiopia, with Britain remaining in control of the north. There, the U.S. Navy had an oil facility at Ras Dogan, but Washington's main concern "undoubtedly" was Radio Marina, an Italian facility on the outskirts of Asmara, taken over by the U.S. Army Signal Corps in

10. Four Power Commission (Deputies), *Final Report on Eritrea* (London, 1948), pp. 116–17.

11. Sir Duncan Cumming, "The U.N. Disposal of Eritrea," *African Affairs* 52 (April 1953):130.

12. "Statement made by Aklilu Habte Wolde to the Council of Foreign Ministers Outlining the Supplementary Views of the Ethiopian Government," London, 31 July 1948, FO 371/69340.

13. "Paper on Italian Colonies," the result of several interministerial meetings, in Lascelles to Sargent, London, 17 Jan. 1948, FO 371/69327.

14. "Ex-Italian Colonies," Minutes of meeting held in Secretary of State's room on 30 July 1948, FO 371/69340.

1942. It had since been considerably expanded; three forty-kilowatt transmitters were in continuous use, and there were plans to expand operations. At seven thousand feet, Asmara was ideally sited in a latitude little affected by daily variations in weather or by seasonal changes, thus reducing the need for numerous frequency shifts. Radio Marina functioned as a relay station, forwarding messages to and from naval vessels, and as part of a global network that gathered and beamed intelligence to the Pentagon.

About 150 American servicemen staffed the facility, but they managed to remain "remarkably inconspicuous" in Asmara, where they lived in a large compound containing barracks, canteens, playing fields, and other amenities. The men rarely socialized with the British and were not often seen in restaurants, bars, movies, "nor even in the streets." Yet, American commanding officers had told their opposite numbers "how important it is for the station to be in territory under British (or presumably American) control."[15] When London made it clear that it soon would decamp, the need to have a friendly and cooperative administering power finally convinced Washington that an Ethiopian Eritrea would be best for America's global security.

The National Security Council advised the White House "to prevent any potentially hostile power from obtaining a hold in the Middle East, the Mediterranean area, or in Africa." This policy precluded independence for Eritrea, inevitably a "weak state . . . exposed to Soviet aggression or infiltration."[16] Russia and world communism were viewed as the collective enemy, a worldwide threat which made Radio Marina an increasingly valuable asset. The State Department therefore recommended against an Italian trusteeship in Eritrea, not only because the Rome Government might fall to Marxists but also because its fascist history would lead the General Assembly "severely" to restrict "the use of the territory for military purposes." Finally, the State Department considered Massawa to be Ethiopia's "only satisfactory outlet," whose cession would also yield control over Asmara, the adjacent highlands, and over the Islamic areas to the northwest: thus, "we cannot see any other solution than to give this area to Ethiopia."[17]

15. Mason to Bevin, Asmara, 23 Oct. 1948, FO 371/69445.
16. U.S. National Archives, National Security Council, The Executive Secretary, "Disposition of the Former Italian Colonies in Africa," A Report to the NSC, n. 19 (1949).
17. Lovett to Souers, Washington, 3 Aug. 1948, n. 19/2, ibid.

The Joint Chiefs of Staff (JCS) also came to favor Ethiopian dominion. Admiral William Leahy, the chairman, emphasized America's determination to keep the oil-rich, Red Sea–Indian Ocean area in friendly hands. He foresaw the need for social and economic aid, "together with such military assistance as may be practicable, to insure collaboration of the indigenous peoples in the common defense of the area." He was generally concerned with establishing U.S. facilities to fulfill "our over-all requirements within the framework of our global strategy," and particularly interested in retaining the signals base and other facilities in Eritrea:

> . . . the Joint Chiefs of Staff would state categorically that the benefits now resulting from operation of our telecommunications center at Asmara—benefits common and of high military importance to both the United States and Great Britain—*can be obtained from no other location in the entire Middle East–Eastern Mediterranean area. Therefore, United States rights in Eritrea should not be compromised.*[18]

Thus, it became hard American policy that "in the light of their particular strategic importance to the United States, every effort must be made to assure the maintenance of essential U.S. military rights, particularly in the Asmara-Massawa area."[19] Not surprisingly, therefore, in November 1948, Secretary of State George Marshall offered to support Addis Ababa's claim to most of Eritrea, in return for retaining "unhampered use of the radio station in Asmara and possibly other military facilities such as airfields and ports in the Asmara-Massawa area." The Ethiopians were immediately willing to provide written assurances, but Washington then preferred a verbal commitment, fearing that a formal action would be misunderstood by London and also embarrass Rome.[20]

18. Leahy to Secretary of Defense, Washington, 5 Aug. 1948, n. 19/3, ibid. Italics mine.

19. State Department to NSC, Washington, 4 Aug. 1949, n. 19/5, ibid.

20. "Briefing Memorandum to be used in Discussion with the Foreign Minister of Ethiopia, Ato Aklilu," Washington, 25 Sept. 1950, in Berry to McGhee, Washington, SD 777.00/9-2550. The verbal agreement might be the "secret mutual defense pact" which Bereket Habte Selassie and other Eritrean liberationists claim was signed before the British evacuated the colony; Bereket Habte Selassie, "From British Rule to Federation and Annexation," in *Behind the War in Eritrea*, ed. Basil Davidson, Lionel Cliffe and Bereket Habte Selassie (Nottingham, 1980), p. 38. While he and the others are obviously wrong, it is easier to agree with their notion that American agreements with Ethiopia about Eritrea were "conditioned by priorities . . . which proved catastrophic to the cause of Eritrean freedom and independence"; Richard Greenfield, "Pre-Colonial and Colonial History," in *Behind the War in Eritrea*, p. 31. On the other hand, one must view with extreme skepticism Dr. Bereket's asser-

It was the Korean War that convinced the United States that all of Eritrea should be integrally federated with Ethiopia. The rationale reflected U.S. global anxieties, and was based upon the geopolitical logic defined earlier by the National Security Council and the Pentagon. Lurking in the background were unstated fears about the security of American facilities in Massawa and Asmara:

> Eritrea is neither socially, politically, administratively, nor economically qualified for independence, nor will it be for some time. An independent regime would be unable to maintain law and order against the internal ravages of border marauders, or to prevent a move for secession and union with Ethiopia—which would not be unlikely—by the people of the Central Plateau. If attacked from outside, it would be unable to maintain its territorial integrity without external aid.[21]

Washington had been gratified by Addis Ababa's offer to contribute troops to Korea and to identify Ethiopia's interests with those of the "free world."[22] The gesture yielded favorable comments in July 1950, at a meeting of American, British, and Italian officials, who agreed that a satisfied Ethiopia might play an important role in the defense of the Middle East.[23] It became obvious to all that an Eritrean-Ethiopian federation offered the perfect compromise: the Solomonic crown would hold sovereignty; the colony would remain intact, assuaging the feeling of Muslims and others who wished to remain separate from Ethiopia; and Rome could argue that Italy's achievement in Africa would retain its integrity and that settlers would remain insulated from Addis Ababa's direct control. Washington applied pressure on the emperor, who acquiesced "because the United States has made the proposal and the Emperor has great faith in United States judgement."[24]

---

tion that the needs of U.S. global policy overwhelmed "the *unqualified* [italics mine] wish of the Eritrean people for independence"; Bereket, "From British Rule," p. 39.

21. U.S. National Archives, State Department, Office of Intelligence Research, Division of Research for the Near East and Africa, "The Capacity of Eritrea for Independence," *Intelligence Report,* n. 5311 (25 July 1950).

22. "Prepared Statement by David Newsom, Assistant Secretary of State for African Affairs," in 91st Congress, Senate, 2nd Session, *United States Security Agreements and Commitments Abroad,* part 8 (Ethiopia) (Washington, 1970), p. 1883. See also "Long-term Analysis by Principal Officer—Ethiopia," Addis Ababa, 11 April 1956, SD 775.00/4-1156.

23. British translation of the text of an informal memo of conversation prepared by the Italian Embassy of the meeting at the Foreign Office on 3 July, in Palmer to Secretary of State, London, 19 July 1950, SD 770.00/7-1950.

24. Memo of conversation between Aklilu Habte Wolde, John Spencer, and Assistant Secretary of State McGhee, et al., Washington, 7 Aug. 1950, SD 770.00/8-750.

Immediately after accepting the federal solution, the Ethiopian Government began to pressure Washington for military assistance. In May 1951, the research component of the Joint Chiefs of Staff concluded that Addis Ababa's request for equipping three divisions was excessive. "It is currently impossible, and will be for some time to fulfill these demands, particularly in view of rapidly expanding United States and western European forces and the requirements of United Nations forces in Korea . . . of which those from Ethiopia are a part." Any spare material would go to areas such as Malaya, where there was "direct or subversive Communist aggression." Since Ethiopia remained unthreatened, there was no compelling need for a military mission or advisory personnel, although the facilities in Eritrea "naturally" intensified America's interest in the area's defense, at least obviously enough, it was hoped, to satisfy the emperor's yearning for security.[25]

The Air Force chief of staff was distressed by the implicit disrespect. He pushed for meeting Haile Sellassie's needs: "for a period of fifty years the Ethiopian Government has slanted its policies towards the western powers with scant material rewards for its cooperation." He raised the specter of Soviet-bloc intervention in the strategic Red Sea–Indian Ocean area, particularly if the Arab states turned against the West. The presence, therefore, of a U.S. military mission in Ethiopia would not only dramatize the country's importance but would also counter Soviet subversion. His arguments were impressive, and the chiefs voted to send a military mission to Ethiopia.[26]

In June 1951, around the anniversary of the Korean War, Lt. Gen. Charles L. Bolte, U.S. Army, visited Addis Ababa, where he was welcomed by Brig. Gen. Abiye Abebe, the new minister of war, who remarked that Ethiopia's contribution to the U.N. police action testified to Addis Ababa's commitment to the West. When he asked for assistance in the establishment of a small mobile army and air force, Bolte responded that Korea was Washington's "preoccupation" but that "Ethiopia's needs would not be lost to sight." Asked directly about a military training mission, the American was generally agreeable, but his recital of U.S. global priorities placed

25. Memo by the Director, the Joint Staff, for Lt. Gen. Charles L. Bolte, JCS, "Visit to Ethiopia by a Representative of the President," JCS 210.482 Ethiopia (5 Sept. 1951), U.S. National Archives, Record Group 218.

26. Memo by Chief of Staff, United States Air Force, 28 May 1951, JCS 2197/2, ibid.

Africa last, although he admitted that Asmara's Radio Marina was an area of mutual interest and testified that Washington would "always take with great concern any danger to Ethiopia."[27] The entire episode masked no conundrum or hypocrisy but revealed the texture of subsequent United States–Ethiopian relations.

Gen. Bolte reported to the Pentagon that, except for internal security, Ethiopia had "little reason" to maintain national armed forces; that a U.S. training mission would not be "useful" militarily and was "inadvisable" politically; and that military assistance would lead to demands for equipment beyond justification for a low-priority country. Still, he believed that Ethiopia's pro-Western activities deserved the concession of a modest training "detachment . . . as opposed to a formal military mission" to demonstrate Washington's goodwill.[28] Although the JCS fought to keep the unit small and temporary,[29] geopolitics dictated that America's military involvement in Ethiopia would become permanent.

Israeli independence, the phenomena of Nasser and a radicalized Egypt, and Soviet pressure in the eastern Mediterranean and the Red Sea heightened Washington's sensitivity to the security of the Suez Canal and the Straits of Bab el Mandeb. Moreover, John Foster Dulles, President Eisenhower's secretary of state, viewed world politics in Manichean terms—the good, free world led by Washington versus the bad, totalitarian world directed by Moscow.[30] Since the forces of evil were active everywhere, Dulles constructed defensive positions around the globe, among them a treaty-wall comprising an alliance between Turkey, Iraq, Iran, and Pakistan, to block Russian access into the Middle East. The secretary also conceived of a secondary tier of Arab states, strongly anchored in British-dominated Egypt, which was to keep the Soviets out of the West's oil reserves. Cairo's revolutionaries, however, would have none of this scheme when they came to power in 1952; instead, they

27. Minutes of meetings of 13 and 15 July 1951, in Childs to Department, Addis Ababa, 21 June 1951, 775.5/7-2151. Bolte told the British minister that his instructions were to take "a politely discouraging line and to point out as tactfully as possible that Ethiopia inevitably stood very low on the list of priorities for the available materiel." The general confessed that he had not felt justified in being so negative, "for Ethiopia was at least entitled to some consideration for her effort of cooperation in Korea." Lascelles to FO, Addis Ababa, 16 June 1951, FO 371/90080.

28. Report by the Joint Strategic Plans Committee, 10 July 1951, JSPC 974/2, in JCS 210.482 Ethiopia (5–Sept.–51), U.S. National Archives, Record Group 218.

29. Chief of Staff, Army, to JCS, 30 July 1951, JCS 2197/3, ibid.

30. Stephen E. Ambrose, *Rise to Globalism*, rev. ed. (New York, 1976).

opened a campaign for the British evacuation of the Suez Canal Zone. Washington, therefore, began to fall back upon Ethiopia as its turnkey in the Red Sea,[31] and sought to negotiate a formal base agreement for Radio Marina and the other U.S. facilities in Ethiopia. The American need offered Haile Sellassie an opportunity he eagerly exploited.

In October 1951, the Ethiopian Government transmitted a note requesting a complete program of military assistance on the basis of loyalty "to the policies, programmes, and measures being pursued by . . . America and other peace-loving countries."[32] The State Department temporized as long as possible but finally conceded Ethiopia's eligibility for "Reimbursable Military Aid."[33] In October 1952, negotiations were opened in Asmara to formalize the status of the communications base, now called Kagnew Station, after the Ethiopian battalion which had returned from Korea in May 1952. The draft treaty which the United States tabled guaranteed almost sovereign privileges at the American facilities in return for a limited program of military aid for Ethiopia.[34] Aklilu Habte Wolde, foreign minister since 1949, commented that the bestowal of such substantial rights would open his country to the verbal attacks of its adversaries and considerable risk in wartime, when the installations would be "desirable targets for our common enemy." To meet the challenges, Ethiopia needed "more military support . . . than the agreement now provided."

The American ambassador, J. Reeves Childs, rejected any notion of military risk, since Kagnew Station was "not [a] military base in the strict sense of the word, but is just a communications center," and remarked that the draft was only a formalization of the Ethiopian commitment of 1948. The Ethiopian explained that the draft went beyond the earlier verbal agreement, since it dealt with more than Radio Marina by including a commitment (Article one) to negotiate for future installations sited in *"all of Ethiopia* [italics

31. Townsend Hoopes, *The Devil and John Foster Dulles* (Boston, 1973), p. 182.

32. Ethiopian Government to American Embassy, Addis Ababa, 25 Oct. 1951, SD 775.5—MAP/10-2551.

33. "Exchange of Notes Concerning Eligibility of Ethiopia for Reimbursable Military Aid," 19 June 1952, SD 775.5—MSP/6-1952.

34. Draft Agreement as delivered to the Ethiopian Government on 11 Oct. 1952, attachment 6 in "Record of U.S. Negotiations with Ethiopia for Base Rights Agreement during the period Dec. 15–Dec. 22, 1952," Washington, 9 Jan. 1952, SD 711.56375/1-953.

mine], and that was certainly not mentioned in 1948." As compensation, Addis Ababa sought a permanent training mission and enough equipment for a small, modern army—in other words, aid "proportionate to the strategic value [of] Ethiopia."[35] A stalemate was reached, and the talks were adjourned until mid-December, when the scene shifted to Washington, where Aklilu met with State Department officials, and New York, where John Spencer, Ethiopia's American-born foreign affairs adviser, talked with representatives of the Departments of Defense and State.

In the interim, realizing that the Ethiopians knew the value of the base agreement, the Pentagon diplomatically had conceded some military assistance and a training mission. In New York, Spencer voiced the emperor's concern that the commitments be long-term, particularly the provision of training.[36] In Washington, when Aklilu was subsequently informed that an exchange of notes would demonstrate U.S. sincerity, he remonstrated that he needed more than sincerity to convince his government to devolve near-sovereign privileges for Kagnew Station. He wanted a specific and broader U.S. commitment to keep Ethiopia "fully informed on all matters directly related to or of interest to the defense of East Africa" and prompt consultation "in respect of any such matters." The Americans regarded Aklilu's declaration as an effort to "obtain a defense commitment" and immediately rejected inclusion of any such statement in the notes to be exchanged.[37] The negotiations thereupon stalled, until Addis Ababa realized that Washington would make no further concessions.

On 22 May 1953, the United States and Ethiopia signed an agreement governing the use of Kagnew Station and other facilities in Eritrea until 1978; and a standard military assistance treaty regulating the delivery of weapons and other equipment and providing for a Military Assistance Advisory Group (MAAG). Washington agreed to train and equip three six-thousand-man divisions at a total cost of about five million dollars, a generosity then and sub-

35. "Minutes of Meetings in Asmara, 9–10 Oct. 1952, Covering Formal Negotiations for Ethiopian Base Agreement for Eritrea," in Childs to Department, Addis Ababa, 17 Oct. 1952, SD 711.5637A/10-1752.

36. "Minutes of U.S. Base Negotiations in New York, on 15-16 Dec. 1952, between John Spencer, and Messrs. Utter and Root of State Department and Lt. Cols. Kurth and Davis of Defense Department," attachment 1 as in note 34 above.

37. Acheson to Embassy, Washington, 23 Dec. 1952, attachment 2 as in note 34 above.

sequently considered a form of rent.[38] Some have characterized the treaties as "an immoral accord" which placed Ethiopia "under the effective control of American imperialism and of the Zionist world."[39] Others have suggested that the Ethiopian case was merely one of a series of U.S. responses to the decline of colonialism and of the power of western Europe. Washington had to assume the "primary responsibility for the defense of the capitalist system," which it accomplished by establishing a worldwide system of bases, by raising huge forces, and by arming client states, which were incorporated into "the imperialist network."[40] Following this logic, Ethiopia was therefore a party to world imperialism and a participant in the world capitalist economy, albeit on the periphery.

Yet, the data reveal that neither the U.S. Government nor American capitalism eagerly poured millions into bastion Ethiopia, either to make it into a militarily significant factor or to transform its economy. From 1950 to 1974, private American investment was minuscule, and, until 1956, Washington's development programs remained largely devoted to technical assistance administered under a Point Four Agreement signed on 15 May 1952. The latter's piece-meal approach revealed the totality of Addis Ababa's needs and of America's original determination to solve problems within Ethiopian terms, a sensitivity later lost. For the first few years, the U.S. assistance mission "was a rather simple structure in which . . . technicians did most of the planning, originating, and keeping in contact with the host government."[41] It was a period of earnest experimentation, during which much good was accomplished. Each side participated equally in terms of outlay, if not in the provision of experts and technology. The Americans worked alongside their counterparts, on projects defined by Ethiopian civil servants and not determined by strategies established in Washington and then nego-

38. Ambassador Don Bliss and his successors understood the *quid pro quo*. In April 1960, just before he left his post, he wrote, "Fundamentally the 1953 agreements constituted a bargain which matched a limited military aid program against extensive base rights"; Bliss to Department, Addis Ababa, 12 April 1960, SD 775.5—MSP/4-1260. See also Robert A. Diamond and David Fouquet, "American Military Aid to Ethiopia and Eritrean Insurgency," *Africa Today* 19 (Winter 1972):38.

39. Petros Desta, "Le Secret de la Politique étrangère de Hailé Sellassié," *Remarques Africaines* 281 (1967):18.

40. Harry Magdoff, "Militarism and Imperialism," *American Economic Review* 60 (1970):239–40.

41. Stanley Andrews, "Ethiopia," typescript, Agency for International Development Reference Center (Washington, probably 1961).

tiated by government. Since high-level bureaucrats and foreign policies rarely impinged, immediate utility was the most compelling criterion for adopting a project.

During 1952–54, a wide variety of schemes were planned and effected. In the area of agricultural education, a high school in Jimma, the college at Alemaya, and a crop improvement center in the Cobbo-Alamata area were established. Other agricultural projects included locust control, a machinery pool in the Ministry of Agriculture, a coffee cooperative venture, animal disease control, a water resources survey, and well-drilling. There were various educational programs, the largest of which was an intensive survey of almost every aspect of Ethiopia's academic needs. Most important, however, was the establishment of the public health college and paramedical training center at Gondar and a nurse and midwife training school in Asmara. Other projects included a water supply and sewerage survey for Addis Ababa, the empress's handicraft school in the capital, rural vocational and industrial arts in provincial centers, a commerce and industry development center, health advisory services, an institute of public administration, and a program providing scholarships abroad.[42]

In 1955, an animal improvement scheme was undertaken in Arsi, followed by a veterinary training project in 1957. That year, the Point Four Program established regional agricultural productivity programs which involved farming and breeding improvement centers and stations, a cotton and oilseed demonstration farm, and five forest nurseries. An ambitious commodities development program, which included improvements to existing facilities and the establishment of another agricultural high school in Ambo, as well as extension services, coffee research, and cooperative marketing was also funded. In 1958–59, projects that concerned production and export of commodities were begun.[43] Throughout, the Ethiopian government was dissatisfied with the limited American effort and pressed for the financing of ports, highways, and airfields.[44]

42. U.S. Operations Mission to Ethiopia, *The Point Four Program in Ethiopia* (Addis Ababa, 1954), passim.

43. Albin D. Molohon, "Report, USOM/E Agricultural Program, 16 July 1956–31 July 1959," typescript, Agency for International Development Reference Center (1959), pp. 21, 33.

44. Memo of conversation between the Secretary of State and Aklilu Habte Wolde, the Ethiopian Foreign Minister, and Yilma Deressa, the Ethiopian Ambassador, 2 July 1954, SD 775.5–MSP/7-254.

The emperor opened the campaign on his first visit to the United States in spring 1954. In an address before a joint session of Congress, he remarked, "We have a profound orientation to the west. . . . We read the same Bible. We speak a common spiritual tongue." Then he sought access to a common pocketbook: "so great are your power and wealth that the budget of a single American city often equals that of an entire nation." More to the point, he declared his intention to remake Ethiopia through "the closest possible association with the United States."[45] Yet, as his foreign minister later learned, it was difficult to move the American Government by appealing to its idealism and sense of justice. Washington's bureaucrats might listen intently to Haile Sellassie's request for a whopping hundred-million-dollar aid package; they might even be sympathetic to the country's aspirations; but, above all, they were Yankee traders who wanted fair returns, and they believed that they already had bought Ethiopia. Aklilu's only tactic, therefore, was to threaten his country's withdrawal from the Western camp: "Ethiopia must ask itself again, just what place does Ethiopia actually hold in the eyes of the U.S.?"[46] In a Washington hypersensitive to the competition between the East and West, even so clumsy a thrust was parried only by a further concession of military assistance.

By 31 March 1954, the Pentagon had shipped $3,800,000 worth of small arms, vehicles, and artillery to Ethiopia, out of the five million dollars originally appropriated.[47] No additional funds had been authorized, however, and the State Department maneuvered to obtain a more or less permanent U.S. military program from a Pentagon curiously reluctant to involve itself in the Horn of Africa. Therefore, instead of proceeding through channels, the State Department's Near Eastern and Africa Bureau (NEA) grasped the opportunity presented by Aklilu's outburst and guilefully committed the U.S. Government to "follow-through in the program underway." The Ethiopian foreign minister was told that much depended on congressional appropriations but more on administrative adjust-

45. Government of Ethiopia, Ministry of Information, "Address to the United States Congress (26 May 1954)," *Selected Speeches of His Imperial Majesty Haile Sellassie First, 1918–1967* (Addis Ababa, 1967), p. 109.

46. Memo of conversation on "Ethiopian Proposals for Further Discussions with the United States Government," Washington, 7 July 1954, SD 775.5—MSP/7-754.

47. Memo by Major Gen. G. C. Stewart, Washington, 16 May 1954, SD 775.5—MSP/5-1654.

ments, since "Here the question is what other programs to reduce, since there is no specific provision in the budget for Ethiopia."[48] So, Addis Ababa had been correct to worry about a long-term American commitment, and the emperor's visit and Aklilu's anger, feigned or otherwise, yielded a change in American attitude, at least among the civilians.

NEA justified its purely political decision in terms that would become familiar to a generation of American diplomats: the Addis Ababa government had supported the United States in Korea; Ethiopia occupied a strategic position in the Middle East; and "military assistance would be one of the few tangible benefits obtained by the Emperor's visit, in contrast to the Emperor's very substantial shopping list." Nevertheless, ranking officers in the State Department had been upset by NEA's action—however much they approved in principle—and the bureau was advised that "it is unwise to commit the United States Government to provide assistance when other interested agencies have not concurred or refused to concur in a proposed assistance program."[49] Still, the secretary of state was moved to write Charles Wilson, his colleague at the Pentagon, that military aid would save the American position in Ethiopia, a country whose friendship was worth more in propaganda value "than the relatively small cost of arms which we feel should be given to them."[50] Another five million dollars of military aid was granted Ethiopia in October 1954.[51]

American administrative machinery operated very slowly, and the Addis Ababa Government noticed very little additional military assistance and no new economic aid coming its way. To spur the process, in early May 1955, the emperor called in Joseph Simonson, the U.S. ambassador, and offered additional American facilities in Ethiopia. A few days later, Aklilu told Simonson of his deep concern "over the lack of collaboration" between his government and Washington; Ethiopia, he said, took the relationship with the United States very seriously, but he was not certain that America reciprocated. The ambassador expressed the sincerity of Wash-

48. Memo handed to Aklilu Habte Wolde by Utter at 3:45 PM, July 8, 1954, at Washington National Airport in St. Cyr to Jernegan, Washington, 25 Aug. 1954, SD 775.5—MSP/8-2554.
49. Frechtling to Nolting about "Additional $5 million MDA Program for Ethiopia," Washington, 3 Sept. 1954, SD 775.5—MSP/9-354.
50. Dulles to Wilson, Washington, 15 Sept. 1954, SD 775.5—MSP/9-1554.
51. Dulles to Embassy, Washington, 27 Oct. 1954, SD 775.5—MSP/10-2754.

ington's commitment to Ethiopia but also reminded the foreign minister that the United States had worldwide interests and involvements but not unlimited resources of manpower and money.[52]

To mollify imperial authorities, the Pentagon agreed to send Gen. Orval R. Cook to Addis Ababa to survey Ethiopian military requirements. Upon arrival in November 1955, Gen. Cook received a Ministry of Defense memo which charged that the delay in American shipments had permitted certain, but unspecified, foreign powers to disseminate "subversive propaganda" suggesting that the relationship with the United States was worthless: instead of strengthening Ethiopia, it made the country vulnerable to attacks it did not have the weapons to counter. The document explained that malcontents in the Ethiopian army argued that the American connection should be severed in favor of an arrangement with an unspecified power which could supply "arms in adequate quantities . . . without delay [prophetic words, indeed!]." To rebut such propaganda, Washington should facilitate the "fuller implementation" of the military assistance program, not only by providing weapons but also by supporting new military schools, housing, and medical facilities. The Imperial Government justified its requests in terms that echoed statements made in Washington: "Ethiopia has unequivocally ranged itself on the side of the Western Powers"; it was the most stable power in the Middle East; it dominated the Horn, a position made even more important by the British evacuation of the Suez Canal Zone; and it permitted the United States its "only military base on the Red Sea."[53]

The embassy's "country team" (composed usually of the mission's top military, political, intelligence, and aid officials) naturally agreed and recommended that more military aid be furnished "to maintain the present friendly government in power and to keep it oriented to the West . . . [and consequently to] insure the continued availability of U.S. bases in Ethiopia—Kagnew Station at the present time and air and naval facilities when and if required." The team also argued that an increased military program would permit Ethiopia, in the event of general war, to contribute "one or two light

52. Simonson to Department, Addis Ababa, 17 May 1955, SD 611.75/5-1755.

53. Memo, "Defense Needs of Ethiopia," presented by Gen. Mulugeta Bulli, Chief of Staff, Imperial Ethiopian Army, to Gen. Orval R. Cook, Deputy CINEUR, Addis Ababa, 18 Nov. 1955, in Simonson to Department, Addis Ababa, 23 Nov. 1955, SD 775.5—MSP/11-2355.

divisions of proven quality" to the Western alliance.[54] Given the new situation in the eastern Mediterranean, the Pentagon finally began to see the value of the State Department's political goals in Ethiopia, and the Joint Chiefs of Staff agreed to "a minimum U.S. aid program of $5,000,000 per year augmented by direct sale of air force and naval equipment."[55] By this time, Ethiopia's economic situation had improved greatly, permitting the government to dispose sufficient funds to support the local costs of MAAG and of the increasing infrastructure required to sustain the military effort.

For the Ethiopian year ending September 1949, Ethiopia's imports amounted to E$90,984,804 (at this time, the Ethiopian dollar was worth forty U.S. cents), of which Italy, India, Japan, the United States, and the United Kingdom accounted for almost two-thirds; exports were E$77,191,200, four-fifths of which went to Aden (for forwarding), Eritrea, America, Italy, and Great Britain. Yielding E$17,004,350, coffee was the most important export commodity, but hides, skins, grains, peas and beans, and oilseeds brought in approximately E$40,000,000.[56] The government's budget was E$60,000,000, of which E$24,000,000 came from customs duties, and the rest mostly from indirect taxes, although there was a personal business and income tax that produced some revenues.[57]

The revival of the economies of western Europe and the increased demand for primary commodities stimulated by the Korean War made 1950 a good year for Ethiopia. Hides, skins, grains, peas and beans, and oilseeds brought in E$30,300,000, but the value of coffee almost doubled to E$32,538,000, even as the quantity shipped only grew from 17,828.8 to 21,151.6 metric tons. Revenues from duties consequently rose from E$24,000,000 to E$31,650,000.[58] For 1951, the value of coffee soared to E$56,500,000, accounting for 50.5% of all Ethiopian exports; hides and skins were now 28% of the total, but cereals and oilseeds had dropped to 21.5%. By 1952, coffee, now 54.9% of all exports, was valued at E$83,000,000; the country's total trade was E$158,000,000, which yielded customs reve-

54. Simonson to Department, Addis Ababa, 2 Dec. 1955, SD 775.5—MSP/12-255.

55. Military Comments on "Defense Needs of Ethiopia," enclosure in original memo; see note 53.

56. "Summary of Current Economic Information," in Embassy to Department, Addis Ababa, 16 June 1950, SD 875.00/6-1650.

57. Embassy to Department, Addis Ababa, 14 Aug. 1950, SD 875.00/8-1450.

58. "Annual Economic Review," in Embassy to Department, Addis Ababa, 5 Feb. 1951, SD 875.00/2-551.

nues amounting to E$42,989,981, against E$36,181,476 for the year before.[59]

1953 was a big year for the Ethiopian economy: the coffee crop had grown to 37,000 tons, which sold at higher world prices for E$122,000,000, nearly 65% of the value of all exports. "This record crop benefitted several groups—land owners, small farmers, farm laborers, traders and exporters, but mostly the government," which had raised export taxes several times, "skimming off most of the extra purchasing power and at the same time increasing its revenue" from export duties threefold.[60] In sharp contrast, 1954 was a disappointment, since Brazilian coffee glutted the market. The Ethiopian crop fetched only E$83,000,000, although astute management ensured a trade surplus of E$20,000,000, the same as the year before. By 1954, the United States was the chief recipient of Ethiopia's coffee and therefore vital to Addis Ababa, whereas trade with Ethiopia was negligible in terms of the huge American economy.[61]

The increasing acceptability of Ethiopian coffee in the world market owed much to new plantings, better care of coffee stands, improved sorting and cleaning of beans, and more thorough harvestings. The spectacular elasticity of production, however, depended on the Italian-built road system, refurbished, maintained, and fully expanded under supervision by a team from the U.S. Bureau of Roads working under a contract with the Imperial Highway Authority, an autonomous agency since 26 January 1951. Through 1957, the American government facilitated loans of twenty million U.S. dollars from the International Bank for Reconstruction and Development to reconstruct and repair roads from Addis Ababa to Assab, Jimma, Lekempti, Gondar (via Dessie and Adigrat), to the Blue Nile Bridge (via Fitche), Shashamane (via Mojjo), and to Assela (via Nazareth), altogether 4,534 kilometers of all-weather, graded gravel roads. Besides promoting Ethiopia's international trade, each highway stimulated interregional commerce and fostered production for the markets of Addis Ababa, where, by

59. "Ethiopia—Economic Review—1952," in Embassy to Department, Addis Ababa, 13 March 1953, SD 875.00/3-1353.
60. "Economic Review—Ethiopia—1953," in Embassy to Department, Addis Ababa, 8 March 1954, SD 875.00/3-854. See also Zbigniew Siemienski, "Impact of the Coffee Boom on Ethiopia," *The Middle East Journal* (1955):65, 68, 69, 73; and P. G. Sylvain, "Note sur le café d'Ethiopie," *Zaïre* 9 (1955):301.
61. "Annual Economic Review," in Embassy to Department, Addis Ababa, 15 March 1955, SD 875.00/3-1555.

1954, there were about 3,600 wholesale and retail establishments.[62] The country's economy grew productive enough to deliver comparatively great wealth to a small group of hierarchs and a relatively high standard of living to a much larger group of urban-based middlemen, bureaucrats, technicians, workers, and security forces, who benefitted from the multiplier effect of the many transactions involved in marketing Ethiopia's commodities.[63]

They also gained from the inception of "large-scale, plantation-farming operations under various forms of ownership and management," the first of which, the Dutch-financed Wonji sugar plantation in the Awash Valley, opened in 1954.[64] By 1956, the Awash Valley Authority was organized, and thereafter it manipulated the development of the entire region, in which foreign capitalists, along with Ethiopia's monied aristocracy and haute bourgeoisie, invested heavily. From its very inception the plantation mode of production destroyed traditional economies and transformed a rural peasantry, however impoverished, into an exploited rural proletariat.[65] It was a harbinger of changes to come throughout the sixties, as planners, economists, and agronomists extended the commercialization of the Awash Valley and also turned their attention to the Omo and Didessa Valleys. These developments, destructive as they were of long-standing patterns of life, strengthened the oligarchy headed by Haile Sellassie and also helped to spawn the social conditions which led to the revolution against the imperial regime.[66] The fulcrum of these developments was Addis Ababa, where the nation's wealth was concentrated.

By 1956, it was evident that the infrastructure of modern life existed in the capital and in a few provincial centers, whereas else-

---

62. H. F. Huffnagel, *Agriculture in Ethiopia* (Rome, 1961), pp. 91–93, 136, 138; Adi Cooper et al., "Class, State and the World Economy: A Case Study of Ethiopia," Conference paper, Sussex University (1975), pp. 23–25; and see note 61.

63. Michael Ståhl, *Ethiopia: Political Contradictions in Agricultural Development* (Stockholm, 1974), p. 11; S. Pausewang, "Peasant Society and Development in Ethiopia," *Sociologia Ruralis* 13 (1973):173, 179.

64. Dale Adams, "Agricultural Development Strategies in Ethiopia, 1950–1970," typescript, Agency for International Development Reference Center (Washington, 18 Sept. 1970), p. 3.

65. John Markakis and Nega Ayele, *Class and Revolution in Ethiopia* (Nottingham, 1978), pp. 56–58; J. W. Harbeson, "Territorial and Development Politics in the Horn of Africa: The Afar of the Awash Valley," *African Affairs* 77 (Oct. 1978):481, 490.

66. Negga Belew, "The Unfolding Class Struggle in Ethiopia," *Pan African Notes* 4–5 (1975):9; Henock Kifle, "Ethiopian Economic Development: An Alternative," *Challenge* 9 (Aug. 1969):14–16; Molohon, "Report," pp. 36–37, 40.

where, modernity was described by the need to acquire money, to pay taxes and to purchase a small range of imported goods. Peasants were increasingly drawn into the market sector, where their surplus was sold off to satisfy national (urban) and world needs.[67] In fact, until its end, the *ancien régime* exploited a largely rustic, nonurban society, upon whose productivity it was dependent. In other words, "the Ethiopian peasant produces not just to support his family but additionally to maintain the State, the Church, and their administrators, who constitute the power-wielding elite of the Ethiopian civilization."[68]

Since Ethiopia's governmental and political elites mostly resided in Addis Ababa, there was a tendency "for . . . finance, internal security, public works, and social services to be concentrated mainly in and around the capital."[69] The disproportionate investment was natural enough but also stemmed from Haile Sellassie's penchant for showmanship and his desire to be associated with every outward aspect of change in Ethiopia. It was government policy to attribute every development to the emperor, sustaining his claim "to be the sole innovator on the Ethiopian scene."[70] Regrettably, his vision was myopic, and his edifices and monuments testified to bad planning and insubstantial formalism, revealing only "the *appearance* of progress." He lavished millions on Paris-style broad boulevards but little on Addis Ababa's broad masses. Even the choice of sites for schools and government buildings placed public relations over human needs.[71] Nevertheless, the semblance of modernity attracted a cross section of the empire's peoples, foreign merchants and capitalists, and an increasing number of European technicians, advisers, educators, and adventurers. Addis Ababa and a few other centers took on the aspects of boom towns, and real estate speculation and development "became a source of enormous income for the . . .

67. S. Pausewang, *Peasants and Local Society in Ethiopia* (Bergen, 1978), pp. 71–72.

68. Frederick C. Gamst, "Peasantries and Elites Without Urbanism in the Civilization of Ethiopia," *Comparative Studies in Society and History* 12 (1970):383–85; for a more passionate view of the exploitation of the countryside, see Hagos Gebre Yesus, "Land Reform; Plus Ça Change. . . ?" *Challenge* 5 (March 1965):3–4.

69. William E. H. Howard, *Public Administration in Ethiopia* (Groningen, 1956), p. 56.

70. Fecadu Gedamu, "Some Thoughts on the Social and Cultural Backgrounds of the Overthrow of the Ethiopian Feudal Regime," Conference paper, Conference on Feudalism, Addis Ababa University, Institute of Ethiopian Studies (1976), p. 8.

71. Donald Levine, "Haile Selassie's Ethiopia—Myth or Reality," *Africa Today* (May 1961):12.

oligarchy."[72] The capital and adjacent provinces exemplified the national characteristic of uneven development, no better represented than in the concentration of schools and other social facilities.[73]

By 1960, most university students were located in the capital, as were nine of the empire's secondary schools. Of the country's 620 government elementary schools, 38 were in Addis Ababa, 126 were in Eritrea, and most of the remaining were in the north, mainly in Amhara regions or in towns populated largely by Amhara.[74] Such inequity was further complicated by the government's prejudice in favor of Amharic language and Christian culture, a policy which obviously benefitted the already favored northerners, and particularly those who lived in Addis Ababa. The Oromo keenly felt this discrimination, which many believed reduced their language "to a mark of illiteracy and shame" and "ruthlessly violated" their traditional faith or their Islamic religion.[75] Beyond such Amhara cultural arrogance, there was the cloying and distressing fact that clinics, hospitals, orphanages, and other social services were relatively overrepresented in the north and in Addis Ababa and probably paid for by southern tax monies. As Gebru Tareke has commented: "A look at the rural-urban dichotomy reveals that the impoverishment of the rural population has been a condition for the growth and relative prosperity of the cities."[76]

To one and all, therefore, it was obviously best to reside in Addis Ababa, but better to be an agriculturalist or urban dweller in the north than to live in a southern town; worst of all was to farm in the south, which meant isolation from modern amenities, indeed, deprivation, and also increasing exploitation as the export-oriented

---

72. By 1974, according to the present revolutionary government, the emperor, nine other members of the royal family, and ten aristocrats owned 95% of Addis Ababa's best 2150 hectares, with the remaining 5% in the hands of ten senior officials and twenty businessmen. See Ethiopian Government Revolution Information Centre, *Ethiopia in Revolution* (Addis Ababa, 1977), p. 10.

73. Gebru Tareke, "Rural Protest in Ethiopia, 1941–1970" (Ph.D. Diss., Syracuse University, 1977), p. 112; Gontran de Juniac, *Le Dernier Roi des Rois: l'Ethiopie de Haïlé Sellassié* (Paris, 1979), pp. 330–33.

74. George Lipsky, *Ethiopia* (New Haven, 1962), pp. 89, 92.

75. Oromo Liberation Front, Foreign Relations, "Oromia Shall be Free," mimeo. (West Berlin, 1978), pp. 2–3; for a dispassionate but highly critical view of Amhara cultural and economic domination of the Oromo, see Paul Taylor, "Internal Security in Ethiopia," Addis Ababa, 20 March 1958, SD 775.00/3-2058.

76. Gebru, "Rural Protest," p. 114; Mesfin Wolde-Mariam, "The Rural-Urban Split in Ethiopia," *Dialogue* 2 (1968):12.

economy burgeoned throughout the 1950s.[77] Thus, in the capital and other urban centers, modernity appeared as a sharp contrast, a contradiction, to the experience of the great Ethiopian mass.[78] Nowhere was this paradox better demonstrated than in the revised constitution of 1955, the emperor's jubilee gift to his people. As two recent writers suggest, "The document, taken as a whole, is a monarchical constitution rather than an attempt to create a constitutional monarchy, and represents an historically appropriate fusion of formal, legalistic elements in an essentially traditional political system attempting to survive through adaptation."[79]

While the constitution did leave the emperor in more or less untrammeled possession of absolute sovereignty and power; and while it is probably true that its proclamation was undertaken with an appraising eye cocked toward western Europe and the United States, it did introduce an elected lower house of parliament, a theoretically independent judiciary committed to the rule of law, the doctrine of the separation of powers, a catalog of human rights, and the idea of bureaucratic responsibility to the people.[80] Haile Sellassie considered the new constitution the symbol of Ethiopia's progress under his stewardship and the guide to "further progress and development." His speech of promulgation recorded not only his sense of achievement but also his limited view of development.

He attributed Ethiopia's population growth to the introduction "of the latest techniques" in medicine and public health and to new facilities "which did not exist here 25 years ago." The forty-eight clinics and hospitals of 1930 had grown to 240 by 1955, resulting, according to the emperor, in longer life for adults and decreased mortality rates for infants. Some of the latter would matriculate in a school system which had grown thirty-five hundred percent since 1930. And some students and adults would have the opportunity to fly "the outstandingly successful Ethiopian airlines," to motor along the country's new roads, or to use the telephone and telegraph systems which tied the country together. The new communications had spurred commerce, which had risen one thousand percent dur-

77. Jean Comhaire, "Urban Growth in Relation to Ethiopian Development," *Cultures et développement* 1 (1968):27, 36.

78. Lanfranco Ricci, "Organisation de l'Etat et structures sociales en Ethiopie," *Civilisations* 14 (1964):22.

79. Heinrich Scholler and Paul Brietzke, *Ethiopia: Revolution, Law, and Politics* (Munich, 1976), p. 39.

80. Ibid.; cf. John Markakis and Asmelesh Beyene, "Representative Institutions in Ethiopia," *Journal of Modern African Studies* 5 (1967):204, 206.

ing the last twenty-five years, permitting the national budget to grow from five million Ethiopian dollars to over one hundred million in 1955. The greater revenues had increased the efficiency of the judiciary and the administration, whose fourteen ministries were "valiantly seeking to cope with the ever-widening perspective of national development." The central bureaucracy had been instrumental in uniting all of Ethiopia's regions "along parallel lines of progress and integrating all into a common national endeavour." Under Addis Ababa's firm direction, "all vestiges of feudalistic and other classes have been wiped out, so that all our beloved subjects may live together as equals and brothers in the same family." Yet, the country, "under Our guidance," must do more; "she must advance yet further, . . . Our sole goal in life." The impressive growth in commerce, industry, and finance deserved to be matched by political evolution, in recognition of which the emperor offered a revised constitution permitting his subjects greater participation in government and policymaking.[81]

It is difficult to assess the emperor's grasp of Ethiopia's reality in 1955. He saw 240 medical facilities, whereas previously there had been forty-eight. Moreover, tens of thousands of Ethiopia's school-age children were actually in school, compared to the meager few thousands of 1931. Haile Sellassie could take pride that these accomplishments had occurred during his reign. One wonders, however, if he really considered the absolute growth in the relative terms which Ethiopia's reality required. The country was poor; most people lived on the fringes of survival; and Ethiopia was backward, even in African terms. Possibly the emperor was such a traditional figure that he really did not comprehend the depth of Ethiopia's problems as he witnessed and presided over changes that would have been unimaginable, for example, to Menilek II, during whose reign (1889–1913) Haile Sellassie was born, reared, and educated.

Menilek had limited his program of modernization mostly to communications and security, both of which strengthened the monarchy.[82] Haile Sellassie sought to accomplish the same goal by constructing a relatively modern central government, and his projects—whether road or school building—were directed towards establishing effective administration and internal security. Thus, the

81. "Promulgating the Revised Constitution" (Speech of 3 Nov. 1955), *Selected Speeches,* pp. 396–406.
82. Serge Groussard, "Entretien avec Haile Séllassié Ier," *Le Figaro,* 25 March 1959.

crown existed as "the most progressive of the rest of [Ethiopia's] traditional power elites in so far as it has to a limited degree shown the will to incorporate modern ideas into the rigid traditional system."[83] Perhaps reality for the emperor was tied to his perception of how programs puffed up and strengthened the sovereign's position. In other words, politics, not programs, was his forte,[84] and the Jubilee celebration amply demonstrated that fact.

The American ambassador, Joseph Simonson, reported that "virtually every event of the celebration [3–13 November 1955] served to dramatize the Monarchy and the Monarch before the country. . . . to impress upon the country the grandeur of the Emperor . . . and the respect in which he was held by the outside world." Consequently, the Jubilee was "a show put on *for* the people and for the outside world by the Emperor rather than a national or folk festival for Ethiopians." Indeed, the entire occasion was staged to conform to Haile Sellassie's notions of progress, and Addis Ababa was given a modern facade "in the greatest outburst of government building activity which this country has probably ever seen." While visiting foreigners and newsmen may have been impressed, there was one profoundly disturbing imperfection for the emperor: he had not as yet received enough American rifles to arm soldiers participating in a military review. Instead, they paraded with obsolete Czech weapons, a sign, so Haile Sellassie believed, of "Ethiopia's weakness."[85]

On the new year, therefore, the Imperial Government dispatched a memorandum to the American Embassy expressing "deep concern over the inadequacy of United States military assistance to date" and requesting a combination of grants and long-term military credits to support the country's defense needs. The State Department long had favored further military assistance, and the deputy undersecretary advised the Pentagon that continuation of good relations with Ethiopia depended on compliance "at least in part" with Addis Ababa's request. The department sought a long-range plan

83. Assefa Bequele, "The Ethiopian Elite and Intelligentsia," *Dialogue* 1 (Oct. 1967):3.

84. Christopher Clapham, *Haile Selassié's Government* (London, 1969), p. 51.

85. Simonson to Department, Addis Ababa, 30 Nov. 1955, SD 775.11/11-3055. For his coronation in November 1930, the emperor took similar measures and directed comparable tableaux; see H. G. Marcus, "Ts'hai Negus (Sun King)," *L'Ethiopie moderne/ Modern Ethiopia*, ed. J. Tubiana (Rotterdam, 1980).

"designed to assure a full measure of internal security,"[86] and the embassy wanted a cohesive program, since it believed that the piecemeal nature of American military aid was *the* problem.[87]

Washington, as usual, took its time, but a response became urgent when the United States Government agreed to provide forty million dollars in aid to Nasser's Egypt. Haile Sellassie voiced irritation by asking how the Americans could grant large sums to the anti-Western, revolutionary Cairo regime when pro-Western, conservative Ethiopia was starved of development capital.[88] Ambassador Simonson made no reply, but he cabled the department that the U.S. position in Ethiopia was more valuable than ever, given "all the swirling currents in the so-called Arab World," and, in light of the competition between the USA and the USSR to influence the Afro-Asian world, he warned of increasing Soviet interest and involvement. It was, he argued, important for America to "help promote the sound and stable economic, social, and political development of [Ethiopia] internally, and . . . to guide it in its external relationships so that it contributes to the peace and stability of the area generally."

Simonson was fully aware of Ethiopia's faults: political repression in Eritrea, xenophobia in government, the "virtually feudal" ruling class that exploited "an inert peasant mass," the emperor's inability to comprehend modern problems, and especially the cultural and political arrogance and exclusivity of the dominant Amharas. Nonetheless, with all its shortcomings, Ethiopia offered the United States the "best possibility" for a trustworthy regional ally "with a potentiality as a base country."[89] So certain was Simonson that Washington would agree to greater amounts of economic and military aid that he permitted the Chief of MAAG to negotiate an agreement with Gen. Mulugeta to reorganize the Ethiopian army

86. Memo, "Additional Military Assistance to Ethiopia," by Allen, Near East and African Bureau, to Deputy Undersecretary via the Secretary of State, Washington, 21 Feb. 1956, SD 775.5—MSP/2-2156; Murphy to Grey, Washington, 27 Feb. 1956, SD 775.5—MSP/2-2756.

87. Simonson to Secretary of State, Addis Ababa, 8 March 1956, SD 775.5—MSP/3-856.

88. Memo of conversation between Simonson and Haile Sellassie, 9 Feb. 1956, in Simonson to Department, Addis Ababa, 11 Feb. 1956, SD 611.75/1-1156.

89. Memo by Simonson, "Long-term Analysis by Principal Officer—Ethiopia," Addis Ababa, 11 April 1956, SD 775.00/4-1156.

into three commands, each of one light division consisting of three brigades, with headquarters in Addis Ababa, Harar, and Asmara.[90]

His action was premature, since the Pentagon questioned the new scheme and did not agree that Ethiopia warranted more military assistance. The Joint Chiefs of Staff were studying a document entitled "FY [Fiscal Year] 1958 Programming Guidance," which made the following points:

> Ethiopia is not vulnerable to internal subversion and is not exposed to local aggression. Her forces are, and will continue to be, too small to be of any consequence in either local or general war. These forces are a heavy drain on her scanty resources.[91] No encouragement should be given to expand or modernize the Ethiopian forces. MDAP support should be tailored to the task of maintaining internal order, and designed to prevent the deterioration of equipment and to improve the military capabilities of personnel.[92]

The embassy in Addis Ababa was furious: it repeated the arguments about the United States's vital strategic interests in the Middle East and raised the specter of an Ethiopian estrangement so complete that the Soviets would be invited to supply Addis Ababa's military and economic needs.[93] The emperor would have no other alternative, even if he feared the communists.[94] Moreover, Moscow's Ethiopian allies—a "left wing" youth group led by Ras Imru, "at least an intellectual pink"—would quickly grasp the opportunity to undermine the United States.[95] In agreement with such casuistry, the State Department appealed to the authority of the White House, which instructed the National Security Council (NSC) to undertake a policy review.

The Imperial Government and the American Mission immediately began campaigning for an outcome favorable to their interests. From Addis Ababa came reports that Haile Sellassie was bitter "that the amount of U.S. dollar aid is much more substantial to many countries less friendly to the U.S. than Ethiopia."[96] The country

90. Simonson to Department, Addis Ababa, 6 Jan. 1956, SD 775.5—MSP/1-656.
91. In the tentative Ethiopian national budget for the year beginning 11 Sept. 1956, the military was allotted US$14 million, or 27% of the total. See Taylor to Department, Addis Ababa, 26 July 1956, SD 775.5—MSP/7-2656.
92. As reported in Taylor to Department, 23 May 1956, SD 775.5—MSP/5-2356.
93. Ibid.
94. Same as note 88.
95. Same as note 89.
96. Taylor to Department, Addis Ababa, 26 May 1956, SD 775.5—MSP/5-2656.

team found, not surprisingly, that the royal rancor ramified throughout the Ethiopian government, and heard "disturbing" criticism of the United States and its contributions to the country's progress.[97] From the embassy's military attaché came the worrying intelligence that Gen. Mulugeta had declared that without more American aid, the "IEG will have to look elsewhere."[98] The Chief of MAAG testified to the "increasing bitterness" and "growing" awareness of Ethiopian officers that the United States was not fulfilling its promised assistance. The colonel was full of regrets in face of a deteriorating Middle East situation that "will almost certainly require American use of Ethiopian airfields and the Red Sea ports of Massawa and Assab."[99] By this time, Egypt had made its arms deal with the Soviet Union, and Nasser was openly critical of the United States's northern-tier strategy, alienating John Foster Dulles, who was already upset by Cairo's recognition of the People's Republic of China.[100] The State Department consequently used the wraith of an unfriendly, belligerent Egypt in the eastern Mediterranean and the wailing from Addis Ababa to win over the National Security Council and to force the acquiescence of the still stubborn Pentagon.

The diplomats' rationale ran as follows: it was imperative to counter "hostile forces" in the Near East and North Africa. Ethiopia's propinquity to the volatile regions made friendship and cooperation with its stable, pro-Western government especially important. Obviously, therefore, it would benefit the United States to help reorganize and modernize Ethiopia's forces, to bolster its economy, and to support Addis Ababa's foreign policy goals in the United Nations and elsewhere.[101] Modest programs of military, economic, and technical aid would guarantee that Ethiopia would serve "as a balance to the rest of the Middle East," as a base for any necessary U.S. expansion in the Red Sea area, and as an anchor "at one end of a crescent of friendly countries to the south and west of

97. Taylor to Department, Addis Ababa, 2 June 1956, SD 775.5—MSP/6-256.

98. Taylor to Department, Addis Ababa, 12 June 1956, SD 775.5—MSP/6-1256.

99. Quarterly Activity Report of MAAG—Ethiopia, 1 Sept. 1956, in Simonson to Department, Addis Ababa, 6 Sept. 1956, SD 775.5—MSP/9-656.

100. Robert Stephen, *Nasser, A Political Biography* (London, 1971), pp. 142, 160, 172, 193.

101. "Strengthening of United States Policy Toward Ethiopia," in Murphy to Allen, Washington, 5 July 1956, and enclosed "Draft Position Paper on Ethiopia," as revised 2 July 1956, SD 775.5—MSP/7-256.

Egypt."[102] The logic was compelling, and the Pentagon finally yielded a "limited military assistance program . . . justified mainly because of overriding political considerations."[103] This compromise permitted the National Security Council to issue its report on "U.S. Policy toward Ethiopia" (23 October 1956), which remained in force until superceded in 1959.

The NSC recommended that technical assistance be maintained; that Washington help Addis Ababa to obtain international funding for economically sound projects; that economic aid be introduced, especially to supplement "Ethiopia's capacity to support the planned reorganization of its armed forces"; and that the Pentagon undertake a narrow military program "suitable for maintaining internal security and offering resistance to local aggression (without establishing a U.S. requirement for the support of a particular mission for the Ethiopian armed forces)." The estimated cost of the proposed programs is shown in the accompanying table.

The military assistance was calculated to provide training support for the previously negotiated three commands (two motorized, one mountain) of three brigades each, with a total manpower of twenty-eight thousand men, including four thousand support troops. The three would be equipped with small arms, mortars, and artillery below 105mm, but not with tanks, jet fighter-bombers, antiaircraft weapons, and the like, which Addis Ababa might purchase if it wished. The army reorganization and other military programs would be completed by FY 1962, when Ethiopia's forces would have reached the following ceilings: army, twenty-eight thousand; Imperial Bodyguard, five thousand; navy, four hundred; air force, six hundred; for a total of thirty-four thousand, which would cost the Addis Ababa Government $19.2 million annually, doubling 1954 defense outlays. Aside from some support monies granted by the Pentagon, and U.S.-supplied Military Assistance Program equipment and the salaries and travel costs of MAAG personnel, Ethiopia was expected to fund its own defense budget entirely.[104]

Ambassador Don Bliss, Simonson's successor, cynically understood that the support funds and the newly instituted economic aid

102. "United States Position on Aid to Ethiopia," in Rountree to Dulles, Washington, 30 Aug. 1956, SD 775.5—MSP/8-3056.

103. Joint Strategic Plans Committee, in collaboration with Joint Logistics Plans Committee, "Survey of Ethiopian Military Air Requirements," a memo presented to the JCS, 11 Jan. 1957, Dept. of Defense 092, Ethiopia (9-26-56), Sec. 2.

104. National Security Council, "US Policy toward Ethiopia," NSC 5614 (23 Oct. 1956), approved 29 May 1957 as NSC 5615/1 with no important changes.

	actual		estimated			
	1955	1956	1957	1958	1959	1960	(1957–1960)
Military aid	$1.0	4.1	4.1	4.8	5.5	6.3	$20.7
Economic aid	–	–	2.0	4.0	5.0	5.0	16.0
Technical aid	2.7	3.0	3.5	3.8	4.0	4.0	15.3
Information services	.1	.1	.2	.3	.5	.5	1.5
TOTALS	$3.8	7.2	9.8	12.9	15.0	15.8	$53.5

(Millions of US $)

would shore up the government's thoroughly inadequate investment program; that Ethiopia's military effort absorbed men and capital which might better have been used elsewhere; and that there was "a danger that the aspirations of the people will in future years outrun the ability of the economy to meet their needs." In 1957, the Ethiopian government devoted twenty-five to thirty percent of its budget to defense and security, and Bliss reflected that American funds kept the proportion from increasing.[105] If the ambassador's view were correct, then one must agree with Addis Hiwet's insightful notion that U.S. economic aid paid for "the enormous cost of maintaining a sprawling and ever expansive bureaucracy (civil and military)."[106]

Moreover, the increased assistance came when the Ethiopian economy had slowed its growth. The international coffee market was replete with the increased production of various South American countries, and Ethiopia's exports of pulses, cereals, oilseeds, haricot and horse beans suffered from the closure of the Suez Canal in 1956 and from competition elsewhere in Africa.[107] By 1958, the Addis Ababa Government was forced to draw heavily on its reserves to pay its bills, and there was labor unrest, particularly in Eritrea, where a general strike began in Asmara on 10 March 1958, completely paralyzing the city.[108] By 1959, the poor economic situation

105. Bliss to Department, Addis Ababa, 2 Aug. 1957, SD 775.5—MSP/7-257.
106. Addis Hiwet, *From Autocracy to Bourgeois Dictatorship* (London, 1976), p. 50.
107. "Economic Review for the First Half of 1956," in Embassy to Department, Addis Ababa, 24 July 1956, SD 875.00/7-2456; "Effects on the Ethiopian Economy of the Stoppage of Suez Traffic," in Simonson to Department, Addis Ababa, 11 Jan. 1957, SD 875.00/1-1157.
108. "Economic Survey, Ethiopia—Jan.–March 1958," in Embassy to Department, Addis Ababa, 25 April 1958, SD 875.00/4-2558.

had led to "diminishing employment opportunities for the growing number of Ethiopians with college degrees." Industry and agriculture languished, trade was depressed, and only the government hired, but on a "make-work" basis; salaries were low, "less than many had been led to expect they would receive . . . a bitter blow to egos inflated by education and by subsidized living abroad."[109] Last but not least, in 1959, a drought and famine struck Eritrea, Wello, Harraghe and Tigre. In fact, the conditions prefacing the abortive coup of 1960 appear remarkably similar to those before the successful coup of 1974, except that in 1959, the government admitted the famine and asked Washington and others for food relief.[110] Nevertheless, the disaster made clear that agriculture was starved of investment diverted to military aggrandizement, a tendency which the United States fed by conceding Ethiopia carte blanche over economic aid funds allocated to support the military assistance program.

Their allocation in 1957–58 required Addis Ababa's agreement to provide matching funds for jointly agreed projects, a standard American technique to retain control over the monies and to test the sincerity of a recipient country. In its straitened circumstances, the Imperial Government refused to exchange notes which referred to matching grants and insisted that the six million dollars in question be regarded as a "gift without strings and under IEG administrative control."[111] When the State Department demurred, Ethiopian authorities became more intransigent, now demanding that Washington simply provide the money, although it could have the right of audit.[112] The matter was a petty annoyance to Washington, which decided that the spirit of the law would be served if Ethiopia would agree to contribute manpower, facilities, and raw materials to jointly planned programs.[113] Addis Ababa only yielded when the State Department conceded Ethiopian primacy in decisions about

109. "Economic Survey, Ethiopia—Jan.–March 1959," in Embassy to Department, Addis Ababa, 14 April 1959, SD 875.00/4-1459.

110. "Economic Survey, Ethiopia—April–June 1959," in Embassy to Department, Addis Ababa, 21 July 1959, SD 875.00/7-2159.

111. Simonson to Department, Addis Ababa, 2 March 1957, SD 775.5—MSP/3-257.

112. Memo of conversation between Aklilu Habte Wolde, the Foreign Minister; Endalkatchew Makonnan, Assistant Minister of Foreign Affairs; John Spencer, Senior Adviser; and Joseph Simonson, U.S. Ambassador, Addis Ababa, 20 March 1957, SD 775.5—MSP/3-2057.

113. Dulles to Simonson, Washington, 28 March 1957, SD 775.5—MSP/3-2857.

the allocation of defense and economic support funds. On 26 April, finally, the notes were exchanged, and Ethiopia had won the day; it was in a legal position unilaterally to allocate United States-supplied funds for internal purposes.[114] Moreover, in April 1957 came Special Ambassador James P. Richards, Member of Congress, to obtain Addis Ababa's adherence to the "Eisenhower Doctrine," devised after the Suez crisis to strengthen America's allies in the Middle East and thereby to block Soviet expansionism in the region. The emperor was gratified to consent and then to receive a few million dollars more in aid, some of which he used to strengthen Ethiopia's internal security apparatus.[115]

After his streak of good fortune, Haile Sellassie ran into temporary difficulty in obtaining American assistance for his air force. In mid-1957, the Commander of U.S. Forces in Europe rejected a United States Air Force survey team's suggestion that the Pentagon should support a program to establish a jet fighter-bomber wing in the Ethiopian Air Force. He did not believe that the Solomonic Empire's internal security depended on advanced aircraft, and he saw "no military requirement for an Ethiopian Air Force to support current U.S. or NATO war plans."[116] In concurrence, the Joint Chiefs of Staff advised against an air force assistance program for Ethiopia,[117] and John Foster Dulles acquiesced.[118] The embassy was horrified, and once more it mounted an attack on the Pentagon.

Bliss reminded Dulles that the USAF team, had, in fact, recommended a jet fighter-bomber wing and emphasized that the Chief of MAAG considered such a force "fully justified [on the] military grounds [of] essential internal security." The ambassador warned that Haile Sellassie was so committed to developing air power that a rejection would "seriously" deplete "our political capital."[119] The State Department did not need much prodding, and soon there was a flow of memoranda going back and forth internally and to the

114. Taylor to Department, Addis Ababa, 26 April 1957, SD 775.5—MSP/4-2657.

115. Bliss to Secretary of State, Addis Ababa, 26 July 1957, SD 775.5—MSP/7-2657.

116. Commander-in-chief, European Command, to Chief of Staff, U.S. Army, Executive Agent for the Secretary of Defense, 18 June 1957, Department of Defense 092, Ethiopia (9-26-56), Sec. 2.

117. Twining to Secretary of Defense, Washington, 27 Aug. 1957, ibid.

118. Dulles to Embassy, Washington, 16 Nov. 1957, SD 775.5—MSP/11-1657.

119. Bliss to Secretary of State, Addis Ababa, 20 Nov. 1957, SD 775.5—MSP/11-2057.

Department of Defense, where Neil McElroy, now the secretary, received a long letter from Dulles outlining the usual political reasons for providing Ethiopia with military assistance. The cold warrior added a new twist, however: he reported that the air force question had assumed "psychological importance" with the emperor. Equally interesting was the following justification:

> [Haile Sellassie] is convinced that an effective Air Force is of such significance that he is prepared to make the economic sacrifices needed to acquire aircraft from other sources, by purchase, if United States aid is not provided. *Such a course would severely impede Ethiopia's economic development efforts and create serious obstacles to the achievements of our political and economic objectives in the country* [italics mine].[120]

Such hollow idealism only led the military to yield once again to the "overriding political considerations" of geopolitics.[121] The diplomats brushed aside the military's view that Ethiopia was of no strategic importance and could contribute nothing to collective security, by stressing that the soldiers did not appreciate Kagnew Station and the possibility of additional base rights. In Bliss's opinion, the Defense Department ignored "the military as well as the political advantages of developing in the Horn of Africa a military power adequate to deter external aggression and maintain internal security as an obstacle to U.A.R. subversion." Even economic development was seen in the broad terms of the East-West struggle, since it sustained "the increasing burden of an expanded defense establishment." Indeed, military aid was the more important American activity, since "We can get more immediate results in the comparatively limited military field than in broad programs designed to lift a whole people up from appallingly low levels of education, public health and primitive methods of production."[122]

American aid officials quickly noticed that their activities had assumed a political function unrelated to economic development programs; they became involved in "an inordinate amount of errand-running for the embassy . . . and concerned with the Amer-

120. Dulles to McElroy, Washington, 15 Jan. 1958, and enclosed memo, SD 775.5—MSP/1-1558.

121. Twining to McElroy, Washington, 10 April 1958, Department of Defense 092, Ethiopia (9-26-56), Sec. 2.

122. Bliss to Department, Addis Ababa, 30 July 1958, SD 775.5—MSP/7-3058.

ican POSITION in Ethiopia, as regards political developments in Africa and possible future military and naval bases."[123] The military and the geopolitical *were* the priorities. As Ambassador Bliss wrote: "Badly needed basic reforms, such as the redistribution of land, a modern fiscal system, a properly organized and administered government, cannot be considered for U.S. action in the predictable future. Interference on our part would encounter political and social obstacles so formidable as to be counter-productive."[124]

Washington's focus on geopolitics and military security was reinforced by the imminence of Somalia's independence, which moved the National Security Council to issue a revised statement, this time entitled "United States Policy toward the Horn of Africa." The president's strategists found northeast Africa to be politically fragmented, ethnically divided, and economically backward. "The conflicting aims and aspirations of Ethiopia and the Somalis are a major source of tension jeopardizing prospects for peaceful and orderly progress in the area." Somali demands for political unification "threatened Ethiopia's territorial integrity and . . . aroused Ethiopian antagonism." In the NSC's opinion, "Greater Somalia" would be a weak, embryonic state easily manipulated by the USSR and Egypt, both of which sought "to exploit existing antagonisms and weaknesses in order to undermine the Western position in the Horn of Africa." Since Somalia was already suspicious of Washington's close ties with Addis Ababa, the State Department was directed to encourage Italy to continue its "major role in the maintenance of Somalia's stability and Free World orientation." On its side, the United States would work with Ethiopia, "making every effort to avoid a military build-up [and] increased tensions in the area." The estimated cost of keeping Ethiopia in the Western camp during 1959-62 was $33 million in military aid, $11.5 million in economic support programs, $20.4 million in technical assistance, and $1.4 million in informational and educational activities, for a total of $66 million. Comparing these costs to the original NSC policy statement of 1956, it is apparent that the amounts for military assistance had grown proportionally, whereas the allocations

123. Andrews, "Ethiopia" (Agency for International Development), pp. 2, 3, 9, 10.

124. Bliss memo, "United States-Ethiopian Relations," Addis Ababa, 11 May 1959, SD 611.75/5-1159.

for economic and technical assistance declined relatively, even if the overall figure remained the same.[125]

Inevitably, Addis Ababa could not handle the additional internal costs of American aid. In 1959, the Ethiopian economy remained in a bad way: low world coffee prices had caused a negative trade balance of twelve million U.S. dollars, net foreign exchange holdings were low, government expenses mounted, the Ministry of Finance ran a deficit in its current accounts, and drought and famine continued in Tigre and Wello, taxing an already overburdened infrastructure.[126] The United States, although providing emergency food relief, was blamed for not being responsive to Addis Ababa's real needs. The government complained that continuing American requirements for counterpart funding of economic and technical assistance projects did not accord with domestic priorities,[127] and Aklilu Habte Wolde grumbled that Washington had not provided "really useful help to Ethiopia," but only a "few drops" of water from "the ocean" of its enormous resources.

Desperate for assistance and as if to force the United States to give more, the emperor announced a trip to the Soviet Union and various socialist countries. Aklilu stated that the move had "no political significance in the sense of portending any Ethiopian orientation toward Communism." When asked directly if the country was aligning itself with the neutralist bloc, Aklilu and the emperor responded negatively, merely alluding to the country's need for assistance.[128] The trip to eastern Europe during the summer of 1959 yielded over one hundred million dollars in credits from the Soviet Union and its allies.

The extent of the proffered assistance stunned Bliss, who warned that the West would now have to take strong measures to nullify the opening to the socialist bloc. He clung to the view that the current U.S. program "was well conceived and . . . adapted to the Ethiopian situation," although there was, he conceded, a need to amplify and advance programs already underway.[129] Washington ought quickly to support Addis Ababa on the Somali problem,

125. National Security Council, "U.S. Policy Toward the Horn of Africa," NSC 5903 (4 Feb. 1959), approved 2 March 1959 with no changes.
126. "Economic Summary, Ethiopia—July–Sept. 1959," in Embassy to Department, Addis Ababa, 20 Oct. 1959, SD 875.00/10-2059.
127. Bliss to Department, Addis Ababa, 22 April 1959, SD 775.00/4-2259.
128. See note 124.
129. Bliss to Department, Addis Ababa, 19 Sept. 1959, SD 775.5—MSP/9-1959.

strengthen naval and air programs, help to develop educational institutions, and facilitate Ethiopian acquisition of loans and grants from Western-influenced banking consortia, international organizations, and multinational corporations. Bliss judged that Haile Sellassie really did not want to use the Soviet aid, since it appeared mostly to be tied to a land-reform program that would have changed the political economy of Ethiopia.[130] He also correctly anticipated that the emperor would use the Soviet credits to "blackmail us constantly with threats to go 'elsewhere'."[131] Meanwhile, of course, the United States began to pay the extortion.

The Development Loan Fund made available two million dollars to the Development Bank of Ethiopia for relending to small, private enterprises throughout the country,[132] and the embassy strongly supported Addis Ababa's application to the same organization for a loan of $80.4 million to sustain a ten-year highway program.[133] The country team recommended increased economic assistance, since it would limit Soviet-bloc credits to "non-sensitive areas," and respond "to the change in Ethiopian expectations and . . . aspirations." The embassy's top officials also advocated a sharp shift from individual projects to ministry-based programs evolved through "national economic planning." Most important, the team counselled "adoption of measures to relieve, in so far as possible, the IEG budget of financial pressures deriving, in the investment stage, from U.S. assistance."[134]

Bliss made the same argument for military assistance, advising Washington to absorb the costs of "high priority" items such as jet fighter-bombers and naval craft, thus indirectly contributing "to social and economic development, as well as serving our own political purposes."[135] He also urged that Addis Ababa's contribution to

130. Memo on "Emperor's Speech on Increasing Agricultural Production," in Embassy to Department, Addis Ababa, 2 Oct. 1959, SD 775.11/10-259. This surmise had substance, since Addis Ababa delayed using the credits and, years later, expended them on relatively non-political projects.

131. "On Russian Competition in Ethiopia," in Bliss to Department, Addis Ababa, 17 No. 1959, SD 611.75/11-1759.

132. Satterthwaite to Acting Secretary, Washington, 17 Dec. 1959, SD 775.5—MSP/12-1759.

133. Bliss to Department, Addis Ababa, 5 Jan. 1960, SD 775.5—MSP/1-560.

134. "Country Team Message on Non-Military Assistance to Ethiopia," in Fisher to Department, Addis Ababa, 9 June 1960, SD 775.5—MSP/6-960.

135. "Country Team Analysis of FY 1961 MAP," in Bliss to Department, Addis Ababa, 8 Oct. 1959, SD 775.5—MSP/10-859.

MAAG support be cut sharply, since he saw no valid reason why Americans should be supported "on standards excessively high in Ethiopian terms."[136] Washington accepted the embassy's views and also agreed to raise the general level of assistance to Ethiopia, in effect accepting an increase in rent for Kagnew Station and the other American facilities in Eritrea.[137]

When Arthur L. Richards, the new ambassador, arrived in August 1960, he was therefore able to offer Haile Sellassie new military, educational, and economic aid, plus the promise of further assistance.[138] Back in Washington, Michael Imru, the Ethiopian plenipotentiary, learned of the U.S. concessions when the State Department officially requested the alienation of another fifteen hundred acres of land for Kagnew Station, which the Ethiopian government accorded, after negotiating an upward revision of assistance for a forty-thousand man army.[139] Thus, on the eve of the attempted coup of December 1960, Ethiopia and the United States had renewed their equation in terms of each nation's vital interests. American devotion to Ethiopia stemmed not from a perceived military need but from practical geopolitics, whereas Ethiopia courted the United States as a hedge against invasion, insurrection, and insolvency. By forcing Washington continuously to increase its commitments, Addis Ababa made the United States an actor in Ethiopia's internal politics, a fact that shortly would become obvious.

136. Bliss to Department, Addis Ababa, 20 Oct. 1959, SD 775.5—MSP/10-2059.
137. "State-JCS Meetings: Proposed Topic of March 25: Future Requirements for Facilities in Ethiopia," in Satterthwaite to Merchant, Washington, 23 March 1960, SD 775.5—MSP/3-2360.
138. Embassy to Department, Addis Ababa, 13 Aug. 1960, SD 775.5—MSP/8-1360.
139. Memo of conversation between Mikail Imru, J. S. Satterthwaite, William Witman II, and J. K. Beard, Washington, 31 Aug. 1960, SD 775.5—MSP/8-3160; USTRICOM to JCS and Secretaries of Defense and State, 29 May 1964, no decimal classification.

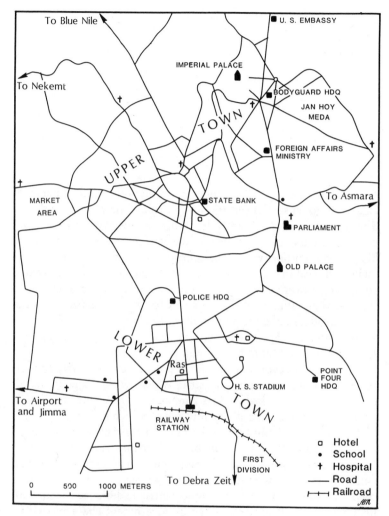

To Blue Nile

U. S. EMBASSY

To Nekemt

IMPERIAL PALACE

BODYGUARD HDQ

JAN HOY
MEDA

UPPER TOWN

FOREIGN AFFAIRS
MINISTRY

MARKET
AREA

STATE BANK

To Asmara

PARLIAMENT

OLD PALACE

POLICE HDQ

LOWER

Ras

TOWN

POINT
FOUR
HDQ

H. S. STADIUM

To Airport
and Jimma

RAILWAY
STATION

Hotel

School

Hospital

Road

Railroad

FIRST
DIVISION

0   500   1000 METERS

To Debra Zeit

Map 2. Addis Ababa, ca. 1960.

5. The Events of 14-16 December 1960

After 1955, Haile Sellassie inaugurated a quinquennium of personal rule as Ethiopia's balancer of power, a role hitherto left to others.[1] The emperor used the recently developed organs of the Addis Ababa government and a spate of newly educated returnees to consolidate his personal authority over the central administration to the detriment of the cabinet and ministers. He characteristically established competing power factions, whose only recourse for decisions was to the monarch. Situated at the apex of various intelligence networks and controlling access to information, the emperor moved and responded to a barrage of competition, here choosing one side, there the other, creating and dissolving a shifting series of coalitions.[2]

The imperial devotion to personal politics led inevitably to indirection and intragovernmental strife which worked against development and modernization.[3] As Ambassador Bliss put it, "HIM is a master of the type of political intrigue by which he has maintained himself in power," but he "has literally no conception of economic or social matters."[4] He was unable to "organize a consistent long-range program for Ethiopian development in a modern world which confronts Ethiopia with unprecedented problems." Haile Sellassie's preoccupation with "internal political intrigue designed to maintain his power unchallenged" resulted in government characterized by "mediocrity [and] incompetence [but] sycophantic loyalty." The cabinet was consequently composed of "individuals less concerned with the efficient operation of their Ministries or of developing

1. Christopher Clapham, *Haile Selassié's Government* (London, 1969), p. 57.
2. John H. Spencer, "Haile Selassie: Triumph and Tragedy," *Orbis* 18 (Winter, 1975):1142.
3. Christopher Clapham, "Imperial Leadership in Ethiopia," *African Affairs* 68 (April 1969):115-19.
4. Bliss to Department, Addis Ababa, 26 March 1959, SD 775.00/3-2659.

programs for the benefit of the country than . . . in competing with each other to gain Imperial favor." The bureaucracy, already underpaid and understaffed, was therefore ineffective and without influence, "and to the extent that it incorporates intelligent young men educated abroad, they are almost to a man restless, unhappy, and critical of the system."[5]

They were watched by a horde of informants who reported to a team of fifteen officials headed by Lt. Col. Workneh Gebeyehu, the autonomous director of security in the Ministry of the Interior. He was alert to the "wide gulf which exists between the young foreign-educated group and older largely ignorant leaders."[6] The rising generation saw their comparatively unlettered superiors as "ignorant of the art of government, with little conception of public service and . . . responsibility." The newly educated could not understand "why the emperor tolerated officials so manifestly inefficient and corrupt." They resented the fact that personal loyalty, even family connections, were more rewarded than was competency, and they were frustrated by their inability to introduce reforms and modern programs. They had a "surprisingly clear conception" of the forces at work in government, "defining . . . [them] as a struggle between the semifeudal forces of reaction and privilege and those of change and progress."[7] The retrogressive nature of the emperor's regime contrasted sharply with governments led by well-educated and progressive young Africans who shortly would lead their countries to independence. Worst of all, though these new states were emerging from a supposedly repressive colonialism, their economies were more modern and certainly less exploitative than that of historically free Ethiopia, a contrast which greatly upset Germame Neway, the intellectual leader of the abortive coup of December 1960.

In almost all ways—except for disloyalty to Haile Sellassie's concept of Ethiopia—Germame represented the effectiveness of the emperor's policy of creating an educated elite to administer the increasingly centralized Addis Ababa government. His immediate family had descended directly from one of Menilek's middle-level functionaries, and he had been reared in comfortable and relatively

5. Bliss to Department, Addis Ababa, 22 April 1959, SD 775.00/4-2259.
6. Memo on internal security in Ethiopia by Paul Taylor, Counsellor of Embassy, Addis Ababa, 20 March 1958, SD 775.00/3-2058.
7. Edward C. Jandy, "Ethiopia Today: A Review of its Changes and Problems," *The Annals of the American Academy of Political and Social Science* 306 (July 1956):107-8, 113; cf. note 6.

modern circumstances in Shoa and Addis Ababa. He was a graduate of Haile Sellassie I Secondary School, a highly selective school noted for the excellence of its teachers and programs. Under the sponsorship of Crown Prince Asfa Wossen, Germame continued his education in the United States, taking his first degree at the University of Wisconsin and then an M.A. in political science at Columbia University. Concern for his native land led to activism in the Ethiopian Students' Association, whose second president he became. His considerable interest in Africa resulted in a thesis on "The Impact of the White Settlement Policy in Kenya" (Columbia University, 1954), which, while badly researched and relatively incoherent, concerned the plight of Africans exploited and oppressed by a powerful elite. It must therefore have been a great shock for Germame to have been posted, upon return to Ethiopia in 1954, to the Ministry of the Interior under Dej. Mesfin Selleshi, the archetypal exploiter.

The minister had been governor of Kaffa from 1945 to 1955, during the years of coffee boom. He had managed to buy thousands of hectares of prime coffee land, often illegally and almost always against the rules of traditional tenure. He augmented his own harvest with peasant-grown beans, which his roving agents bought at low prices; for those immune to his blandishments, he offered a high-cost trucking service which monopolized transport to Addis Ababa. In the capital, Mesfin marketed most of Kaffa's coffee at great profit through the National Coffee Board, whose appointees he controlled. With his wealth, he contributed to the emperor's coffers, a standard practice of Ethiopia's oligarchs; he purchased stock in the country's fledgling industries; and bought land in Addis Ababa, a wine estate in Shoa, and large farm tracts to the south of the capital.

Such profiteering at the nation's expense was one of the primary topics of conversation among Addis Ababa's young educated elite. Although differentiated socially and educationally, they comprehended the world in terms of Western abstractions, whether learned in Paris, Oxford, New York, or even Addis Ababa. They stood against corruption and for modernization, and the many graduates of the Haile Sellassie I Secondary School attempted to establish an alumni association as an important unofficial organization lobbying for progress. When the government, and even the emperor to whom they appealed, refused authorization, some recalcitrants held a few meetings, during which Germame was elected president.

A quiet alarm went off in the heads of four men, each of whom was to die during the 1960 coup: Ras Abebe Aregai, the minister of defense, who considered Germame a dangerous radical; Gen. Mulugeta Bulli, the commander of the Imperial Bodyguard; Lt. Col. Workneh Gebeyehu, the chief of security; and Makonnan Habte Wolde, then minister of two government departments and Haile Sellassie's trusted *homme de confiance.* Together they decided that a post in the provinces would be the easiest way to avoid the threat, and Germame was duly appointed awraja (subprovincial) governor in relatively remote Wallamo, where he was finally able to practice what he preached about development.

He believed that Ethiopia's economic stagnation could be broken only by the full participation of a population freed from exploitation and permitted, under wise leadership, to direct its energies to self-help. Ironically, Germame did not hestitate to accept gifts and bribes from the local elites, but he used them to finance the construction of roads, bridges, and schools. He also organized peasant-manned "surveillance committees" to monitor and to reduce the violence and brutality of the nonlocal police forces. Finally, he distributed government holdings to the landless, thereby sharply reducing the supply of labor available to the large owners, whose loud complaints caused Germame's recall to Addis Ababa. When Haile Sellassie asked why he had given away government property, Germame replied simply that it had been his responsibility to end the suffering of the starving landless. To keep the young idealist from again interfering with property rights, the emperor sent Germame to administer the pastoral Somalis of Jijiga.

Continuing his activities as a zealous reformer, the new governor dug wells and improved existing waterholes, established clinics and improved hygiene, built schools, and planned development schemes. His actions uncovered inertia, corruption, and maladministration, greatly embarrassing the provincial establishment. His incessant demands for equipment, his trips to Addis Ababa to circumvent local authorities, and the startling effectiveness of some of his programs merely determined the bureaucracy to be rid of the young upstart. Officials became totally obstructionist, once and for all convincing Germame that no progress could be made until the existing political system was changed.

The two years before the coup remain an obscure period, with clear glimpses only of a series of increasingly serious discussions among a small group of civilians and military at the Addis Ababa home of Brig. Gen. Mengistu Neway, Germame's brother and since October 1956, commander of the bodyguard. As such, the general's quarters provided excellent cover, since if Germame was considered a dangerous radical, his sibling seemed the antithesis. He was the caricature of the serious and uncomplicated soldier, susceptible only to superiors and sovereign, and on the surface a bon vivant given more to playing than to plotting. Yet, his appearance belied the general's experience as a devoted patriot and as a soldier who had lived modernity in politics and in warfare from the 1935–36 Italo-Ethiopian war to the American-led action in Korea.

He was therefore aware of the material and ideological changes sweeping the world, and he recognized the need for the development of an Ethiopian infrastructure capable of sustaining dramatic growth. He was attracted to his brother's view of the necessity for revolution, since he had also experienced the obstructionism and negativism of the emperor's self-serving system. He agreed with Germame that power should be transferred to the educated, and he also believed that any movememt which sought to destroy the reactionary ruling clique would immediately attract the assent of most lettered Ethiopians of goodwill. Since a wide organization was therefore unnecessary, a cabal could constitute itself as a Council of the Revolution, keep secrecy, and then strike, neutralizing the emperor's partisans and opening the floodgates of support for the new government.[8]

That Germame, Mengistu, and their small group of associates were planning an elitist coup cannot be overemphasized. While they would justify their efforts in terms of the plight of the people, they in fact sought power for themselves and the bureaucratic-military bourgeoisie as the inevitable national saviors. In striking contrast to the popular eruption of 1974, their challenge to the *ancien régime* did not include, nor did it attract, mass support. Nevertheless,

> Although the coup attempt fell short of involving the toiling masses, it . . . opened a new era in the history of the struggle of the oppressed masses of Ethiopia in that it awakened them to the necessity that a fundamental and substantive change was possible only through the violent overthrow of the feudal system and the people's full and active participation in taking their destiny in their own hands.[9]

8. Gontran de Juniac, *Le Dernier Roi des Rois; l'Ethiopie de Haïlé Séllassié* (Paris, 1979), pp. 253–55; Richard Greenfield, *Ethiopia, A New Political History* (London, 1965), chapters 17 and 18.

9. Government of Ethiopia, Revolution Information Centre, *Ethiopia in Revolution* (Addis Ababa, 1977), p. 14.

In this sense, the attempted coup of December 1960 is ontologically related to the 1974 crisis, and must be seen as an event that foreshadowed the future.[10]

By mid-November 1960, Addis Ababa was filled with rumors concerning dissension in the bodyguard and the arrest of several individuals accused of conspiring against the regime. According to a "controlled American source" (rendered CAS in American officialese), on the evening of 17 November, bodyguard officers had met to discuss the injustice of the higher pay given to graduates of the Harar military academy. "At this meeting certain officers reportedly threatened to revolt against HIM but were calmed by others." Interestingly, Workneh Gebeyehu, later one of the coup's three major figures, admitted the existence of "considerable unrest in the bodyguard and [the] consequent concern of [the] Emperor." While the colonel was inclined to blame "[the] situation on the salary differential,"[11] Arthur Richards, the newly arrived American ambassador, advised "that bodyguard grievances [are] much deeper and really based upon dissatisfaction with the regime. Moreover, [these] grievances [are] not limited to the bodyguard." Richards stressed that "Elements of possible trouble [are] inherent in present situation as feelings [of] hostility toward [the] regime (particularly against arch conservative elements surrounding HIM) [are] undoubtedly increasing." The ambassador pointed out that while Crown Prince Asfa Wossen was "no great leader, he is more and more looked upon by many Ethiopians as one who would accept progressive modifications in [the] Ethiopian structure of government including, it is thought, greater political freedom."[12] Of course, what a foreign mission knew was considerably less than Haile Sellassie had learned, and prior to leaving on an extended trip to South America and West Africa, the emperor maneuvered to shore up his position in ways designed to neutralize the bodyguard; characteristically, he did not move directly against the sinners.

On 19 November, the monarch reorganized the army command, replacing the generals of the first, second, and third divisions, and key officers in the Ministry of Defense. The American Embassy's

10. D. C. Watt, "The 'Decembrists': Russia 1825, Ethiopia 1960," *International Relations* 2 (April 1963); cf. Addis Hiwet, *Ethiopia, From Autocracy to Revolution* (London, 1975), p. 88.

11. It is not clear whether thoughts attributed to Workneh really did in fact come from him or were amended by the reporting agent.

12. Richards to Secretary of State, Addis Ababa, 25 Nov. 1960, SD 775.00/11-2560.

army attaché, Lt. Col. W. H. Crosson, reported that mostly "conservative" officers had been placed in all key posts, to watch the activities of "progressive" colleagues. One of the more critical transfers involved Brig. Gen. Aman Andom, [13] who was transferred from the army's logistics office to command of the third division in Harar (where one of his very junior officers might have been Mengistu Haile Mariam). Just by this shift, Haile Sellassie may have engineered the failure of the coup: Aman was so critical of the regime, that, had he remained in Addis Ababa, Mengistu Neway might have found an essential ally in the army. Ironically, though, the emperor made no direct move against the seat of the unrest, the bodyguard. [14] Confident that the army would counter any insurrection on the part of the elite unit, he began his travels on 30 November.

A fortnight after his departure, on 14 December 1960, the U.S. Embassy cabled Washington that before dawn the bodyguard had taken control of Addis Ababa's airport, banning all flights; had blocked all roads leading to the palace; had occupied the telephone exchange; and had seized most of the imperial family and important officials. [15] During the night, a group of officers led by Mengistu entered the grounds of an imperial villa, not far from the American Embassy. There, Empress Menen, the crown prince, Princess Tegnagne Work, Abba Hanna Jimma (the palace chaplain), and Ras Andargatchew (the minister of the interior) had dined together and were watching a film. Mengistu requested and first talked to the trusted Abba Hanna, who was told of an impending coup by the army; Ras Andargatchew was called in, and then the crown prince. The heir suggested that other ranking officials be mobilized, playing into the hands of the plotters, who sought to detain all top officials and thereby paralyze the government. Asfa Wossen telephoned Ras Abebe Aregai, the minister of defense, and Makonnan Habte Wolde, minister of justice, asking both men to come to the villa. [16]

13. Later chairman of the Provisional Military Government, the *dirgue* (Amharic for committee), which overthrew Haile Sellassie; subsequently killed in November 1974 by soldiers loyal to Lt. Col. Mengistu Haile Mariam, the present leader of the Provisional Military Government of Socialist Ethiopia.

14. Wagner to Secretary of State, Addis Ababa, 7 Dec. 1960, SD 775.02/12-760.

15. Richards to Department, Addis Ababa, 14 Dec. 1960, 8:00 AM, critical, SD 775.00/12-1460.

16. Written Deposition of Dej. Kebede Tessema, 20/4/53 E.C., given to the Commission of Inquiry headed by Col. Tamrat Yigezu; Greenfield Collection, Oxford, England.

Thereafter, the night's entertainment gave way to the nightmare of rebellion: the women were placed under house arrest at various locations, and the men were moved down the road to bodyguard headquarters.

When Ras Abebe and Ato Makonnen dutifully arrived at the imperial residence, they were arrested and taken to join the other male detainees. Meanwhile other personages were called in, among them, Ras Imru, the emperor's first cousin and longtime associate. When the latter arrived at headquarters, Mengistu announced to the various captives, among them the crown prince, that the armed forces had taken over the government. When the ras pressed for information, the general talked vaguely about the Committee of the Revolution, which Imru asked to interview. When Mengistu refused permission, the ras railed, "'The Congo became a laughing stock. Are you going to make our country a laughing stock?' But then it dawned on me that we were under arrest, and I sat down and remained quiet." Whereas Mengistu and Germame were able ultimately to convince Gen. Tsigue Dibou and Col. Workneh to join their obviously righteous cause, they were never able to enlist Imru to do more than cooperate to save lives and finally facilitate the emperor's return, even if they called him prime minister.[17]

Meanwhile, word of the coup was circulating in the capital, and two cliques of loyalists had formed spontaneously. One group comprised civilian officials and notables who had not been seduced into arrest. Led by Dej. Asrate Kassa, they hoped to mobilize forces in favor of the emperor and to put down the coup. The other partisans comprised general and field-grade officers led by Major Gen. Merid Mengesha, who was organizing an armed opposition at the first division cantonment in the lower town. Shortly before dawn on 14 December, the two groups learned of each other's existence, united, and formed a civilian authority and a chain of command in the name of the emperor. They also went to the British Embassy, which agreed to transmit the following cable to the emperor, then in Brazil:

> Yesterday Tahsas four (December 13) at 10 PM, the Imperial Bodyguard under command of General Mengistu arrested His Imperial Highness the Crown Prince and leading cabinet ministers. They are now under

17. Written Deposition of Leul Ras Imru, n.d., given to Commission of Inquiry headed by Col. Tamrat Yigezu; Greenfield Collection, Oxford, England.

guard. . . . Princess Tenagne Work and Duchess of Harar are under house arrest at Entoto Villa and the Duke of Harar's children in the main palace. The crown princess and her children are so far safe in their house.

It is believed that the police are cooperating with the bodyguard. The army is thought not to have joined the bodyguard and all available army troops in Addis Ababa are concentrated in First Divisional Headquarters under the command of Generals Merid, Kebede, Izzas [Issayas], Wakgira and Wolde Sellassie. They are awaiting the arrival of troops from the provinces.

Telephones in Addis Ababa cut and wireless controls occupied. . . . Main positions in Addis Ababa are occupied by Bodyguard tanks. The public so far have not been fully informed and security [sic] is quiet.[18]

While this message was being transmitted and delivered to the emperor, Lt. Cols. Willis Gary and W. H. Crosson, the former the embassy's air attaché, were interviewing Workneh and Mengistu at bodyguard headquarters. The two men were affable, even talkative, but revealed little. Behind their Chesire smiles, the two Americans apprehended the fangs and teeth of two Abyssinians contemplating a meal of leonine proportions. Convinced that Workneh and Mengistu were "prime movers" in an attempted coup,[19] the attachés continued their reconnaissance, and, in the lower town, en route to a meeting with Gen. Merid, they encountered jeep patrols around Ras Circle, and soldiers on picket duty from the railroad station and along the line to the first division cantonment. Waiting to be admitted into the camp, the two Americans observed great activity, and, as they were being escorted to Gen. Merid Mengesha, they saw a well-equipped infantry battalion being formed up alongside a heavy weapons company. The general willingly discussed the situation and declared that although he did not know what the bodyguard was doing, they "were up to something."[20]

Merid was understandably confused; his only direct source of information was Dej. Kebede Tessema, who had been directed by Asrate Kassa and his group to mobilize the territorial army in Debre Berhan. Before travelling north, Dej. Kebede had decided to in-

18. British Embassy transmission in Richards to Department, Addis Ababa, 14 Dec. 1960, 11:00 AM, SD 775.00/12-1460.
19. Crosson Report of "Events of 13–17 December 1960," in Richards to Secretary of State, Addis Ababa, 13 Jan. 1960, SD 775.00/1360 (hereafter cited as Crosson Report); interestingly, Crosson marked the report as not releasable to foreign nationals, except for British officials.
20. Ibid.

vestigate the situation, and he had made an unauthorized and daring visit to bodyguard headquarters. Mengistu had received the nobleman cordially and had explained that "having heard that the army, junior and senior officers, had plotted to overthrow the Emperor's regime and to destroy the dignitaries, all because of dissatisfaction over salaries, they (he and his followers) had called the dignitaries in to protect them." The Americans were to blame, but since the bodyguard had refused MAAG training officers, his organization remained loyal to the crown. He also asserted that he had "tried to get in touch with [Gens. Merid and Kebede] but . . . could not reach them," and asked his interlocutor to help him establish communication so that "there would be no bloodshed." Mengistu wanted a conference at bodyguard headquarters, an offer which Merid later refused, although he claimed willingness to "meet on neutral ground," even if he skeptically told Kebede: "I do not believe he has told the full facts and I do not believe that our meeting would straighten matters out." Gen. Issayas, however, thought that every effort should be made to "prevent bloodshed"; he volunteered to parlay with Mengistu, and, with Kebede Tessema, left hastily for bodyguard headquarters.[21]

Meanwhile, Merid was not sitting on his hands; he told Crosson that, "failing a clarification, he intended to use force to restore the situation." He currently had one full battalion under arms, was building two others from various available troops, and would call up provincial units as necessary. Merid was clearly in command, although the attaché learned he was answerable to an ad hoc council composed of the senior officials headed by Asrate Kassa. When a frustrated Issayas returned at noon to report fruitless discussions with Mengistu, the military and civilian leadership concluded that the bodyguard was attempting a coup against Haile Sellassie. Merid immediately began to prepare "for the worst" and handed Crosson a cable for transmission to the emperor, pledging loyalty and requesting his quick return via Asmara or Dire Dawa.[22]

Richards advised delivery, warning, however, that "in no case should it be allowed to become known that [the] Embassy and [the] Department [were] used as a channel for this communication."[23] His caution derived from Crosson's informal briefing to selected personnel about the situation's lack of clarity and the loyalists'

21. Kebede Tessema deposition.   22. Crosson Report.
23. Richards to Secretary of State, Addis Ababa, 14 Dec. 1960, 1:00 PM, critical, SD 775.00/12-1460.

weakness. The ambassador therefore initiated a wait-and-see policy, making it clear to his staff that Americans were "neutrals," a fact immediately supported by Gen. Chester de Gavre, the head of MAAG, who ordered his men away from their assigned units.[24] Shortly after this temporization, the crown prince went on Radio Addis Ababa with a taped speech that promised great changes in the spirit and the administration of government and reflected confidence that the coup would succeed. This possibility also may have accounted for the ambassador's anxiety about the cable to Haile Sellassie.

The question of the crown prince's involvement in the coup has been a source of considerable controversy. When the news of the events in Addis Ababa first seeped out, the West assumed that Asfa Wossen was implicated and deeply committed. On 15 December, the *New York Times* headlined "Coup in Ethiopia ousts Selassie; Son claims rule,"even though it was pointed out that the crown prince, "a retiring, shy man," may have been "the respectable front for other political forces." By 16 December, however, the Western press had begun reporting that the crown prince had "yielded to an ultimatum to save the throne," and that the State Department "had reason to believe that . . . Asfa-Wossen was acting under duress as the leader of Ethiopia's revolution."[25]

The term "under duress" became very popular, and in a leading article for the *Times* of London, Sir Harry Luke wrote that the crown prince delivered his radio message "apparently under duress."[26] *Time* came to agree but had Asfa Wossen delivering his speech, of course, "at the point of a gun," thus conforming to official Ethiopian apologiae on the subject.[27] In a written deposition to an official commission of inquiry, Ras Imru confirmed that the crown prince had not been his own man, that he had acted on Mengistu's instructions, but that he had been consulted, even if perfunctorily, on important matters.[28] Whatever the truth, it was certainly to Asfa Wossen's advantage to cooperate with Mengistu and Germame—he could always claim, if the coup failed, that he

24. Crosson Report.

25. *New York Times,* 16 Dec. 1960.

26. Sir Harry Luke, "Witness of Ethiopian Palace Revolt," *Times* (London), 30 Dec. 1960.

27. "Ethiopia, Time for Apologies," *Time* (2 Jan. 1961); this article argues that Ras Imru, appointed prime minister by the rebels, had acted "under duress."

28. Ras Imru deposition.

had acted under mortal threat—and more than one informant commented to the author that the crown prince rendered his speech in
a rather ordinary fashion, without emotion and with no detectable
sign of duress.[29]

The speech was in any case memorable; for the first time an
Ethiopian leader broadcast the nation's chronic social and economic problems in radical terms. Asfa Wossen charged that life for
the average Ethiopian had not changed for three millennia. He
accused "the favored few . . . of ancestry and heredity," and some
in government, of having manipulated laws and regulations "to
deprive the common people of their rights and privileges in order to
build up riches." The masses now had lost patience and sought
"concrete action aimed at improving their standard of living." He
compared Ethiopia's lack of progress with "the long strides being
made by the newly independent African states"; the country was
being left behind, shattering "the hope that the people have held so
long."

In reaction, during the previous two years, elements of all of
Ethiopia's classes had come together into a movement for progress;
suppression had failed, and "the people who are like bees in a
disturbed hive can no longer tolerate oppression." The movement
had created "an authority that will work for the progress of the
country and the people," whom he also would serve "sincerely in
accordance with the new constitution and on a specific salary like
any other Ethiopian." He stressed that the new government had his
support as well as the backing of the entire nation. "The . . . people
must be united now because they can be sure that history will
restore them to their proper place in the eyes of the world."[30]

Crosson found the speech such "a remarkable performance" that
he set off "to determine its impact on the Army and its leaders." He
arrived at headquarters shortly after 1:00 PM, and found Gen. Merid
in conference with his staff and civilian officials, "obviously as a
result of the . . . speech." After a brief discussion with Gen. Ke-

29. Information from confidential source.
30. Statement of His Imperial Highness, Crown Prince Asfa Wossen, broadcast
over Radio Addis Ababa, 14 Dec. 1960, encl. one in "Report on Attempted Coup
d'Etat," Richards to Secretary of State, Addis Ababa, 29 Dec. 1960, SD
775.00/12-2960 (hereafter cited as Richards Report). There are many versions of this
speech; cf. Greenfield, *Ethiopia*, pp. 398–99 and [University College of Addis Ababa]
News and Views 4 (16 Dec. 1960):11. The latter is the issue that was suppressed, but
a surviving copy can be found in the periodicals section of the library of the Institute
of Ethiopian Studies, Addis Ababa University.

bede, who remarked in passing that "he was sure the crown prince and other detained officials were acting under duress." Crosson conversed with several staff officers. One likened the bodyguard's action to the Ethiopian proverb of the "son taking the bread from the father's mouth," and warned that any fighting would only immerse Ethiopia in a "useless" civil war. Another officer claimed that "no matter how good the cause," it was inexcusable for the Imperial Bodyguard to have broken its oath of allegiance "and that the Army troops were and would remain loyal to the Emperor." Another colloquy yielded the view that the soldiers would fight for Haile Sellassie as "the rightful and legal ruler . . . who had done the best in the face of many difficulties for his country." Crosson judged that there was "a remarkable lack of sympathy for the method chosen by the IBG [but] detected a very faint note of sympathy for some of the objectives stated by the Crown Prince in his speech."

When Merid finally broke away for a short conversation with the attaché, he reported that Eritrea and the army there remained true to the emperor; that he had received messages of loyalty from Begemdir and Gojjam, where irregulars were gathering; but claimed that he had not yet mobilized territorial and regular troops in the provinces, since, above all, he sought to avoid casualties. It was obvious to Crosson "that there was a real reluctance on the part of the army . . . to shed blood, although they would do so if necessary to achieve the aim of maintaining the emperor's position."[31] Interestingly, Merid did not reveal that Gen. Assefa Ayene, the deputy commander of the Imperial Air Force, had given the army access to the air force's communications system; yet, this cooperation must have been comforting, since it demonstrated the general's and, by extension, the air force's preliminary support for the loyalist position. More importantly, Addis Ababa could now communicate directly with the emperor via American facilities at Asmara.

In authority there was Gen. Abiye Abebe, once Haile Sellassie's son-in-law and now his personal representative in Eritrea. His thoughts on the emperor ran as follows: "Ethiopia could become another Congo tomorrow if His Imperial Majesty died . . . If he can live for another ten years, then it will be all right."[32] Despite the general's constancy, after the embassy radioed the consulate about

31. Crosson Report.
32. Memo of conversation between Brig. Gen. Abiye Abebe and Consul M. Looram, Asmara, 10 Dec. 1960, in Looram to Department, Asmara, 13 Dec. 1960, SD 775.00/12-1360.

the crisis in Addis Ababa, all classified files were discreetly shipped to Kagnew Station for safekeeping, and American personnel were ordered to remain off the streets at night until further notice. It was not, however, until 2:00 PM that Abiye called Consul Mathew Looram's home to report the coup attempt and to recommend that the consul, then at Dallol, return at once. Later that afternoon, the general sought permission to use base facilities to broadcast to the capital, and from Dallol, Looram directed his staff to explain that the radio station was powerful enough only for Asmara. When, however, Abiye asked to use the U.S. communications network to call the Ethiopian ambassador in Washington, the request was granted, but the general could only get through to the first secretary.[33]

Abiye found out that Haile Sellassie was in Brazil and directed the astounded first secretary to send "an urgent cable" reporting the coup: "it should read that some malefactors used the name of the Crown Prince and [that] His Majesty's urgent return to Asmara, and not to Addis Ababa, is very necessary." After repeating the message several times, Abiye directed the embassy to deny all reports of the coup as "false and untrue . . . the malefactors claimed that they have the Crown Prince with them, . . . but it is very doubtful that he is involved in it."[34]

Meanwhile, the population of Asmara had learned of the events in Addis Ababa and had remained quiet. The acting commander of the second division, Col. Worku Metafaria, had informed his MAAG adviser that he would not obey orders from the bodyguard in Addis Ababa but would follow Gen. Abiye. The latter reportedly had refused to allow the Asmara-based air force squadron to depart for the Debre Zeit military airport as ordered by the Swedish commander of the Imperial Air Force.[35]

While Abiye was taking steps to secure Eritrea and Haile Sellassie's return, the coup leaders were attempting to consolidate their position as Ethiopia's new rulers. During the afternoon, probably between 2:30 and 3:00 PM, the embassy received a message signed by Blatta Dawit Ogbagzy, the acting foreign minister,

33. Looram Report on "Developments in Asmara during the Abortive Ethiopian Coup d'Etat, Dec. 14–17, 1960," Asmara, 22 Dec. 1960, SD 775.00/12-2260 (hereafter cited as Looram Report).

34. Translation of Conversation in Looram to Secretary of State, Asmara, 14 Dec. 1960, SD 775.00/12-1460; the dialogue took place around 7:00 PM.

35. Looram to Secretary of State, Asmara, 14 Dec. 1960, SD 775.00/12-1460.

officially reporting "a peaceful change in the Government . . . under the direction and leadership of the Crown Prince . . . supported by the general population and the Armed Forces." The substitution, it was claimed, had been undertaken "to eliminate the corruption that has been rampant in the administration and to introduce progressive institutions to foster and advance the general welfare of the people."[36] The note stimulated Richards to drive to the Foreign Office to ask Blatta Dawit to extend official protection to U.S. citizens. The ambassador was received by the chief of protocol who announced that the blatta had, in fact, been removed and was under arrest; he apparently had signed the note "under duress."

Richards was then ushered into the presence of Goytom Petros, a senior ministry official, who declared that he had been instructed by the crown prince to take charge of the Foreign Office pending appointment of a new minister on the morrow. He had been directed to assure missions "that the change in government was in response [to] demands of [the] populace and that [the] Armed Forces [were] merely implementing officials." He sought recognition for the new government since the "transition [was] now completed calmly and without blood-shed"; he declared that the new government would assume and recognize all international obligations, and assured Richards that the authorities "wished [to] cooperate on [a] most friendly basis with us."[37] Upon return to his embassy, Richards learned that the new government also had requested British and Russian recognition.[38] Meanwhile, Crosson had arrived from bodyguard headquarters, where he had gone ostensibly to obtain guarantees of security for American citizens, but in reality to have another conversation with Mengistu and Workneh.

During the interview, the latter voiced the hope that Washington would accord quick recognition, and he assured Crosson that "under the new government, the relationships with the U.S. would be a thousand percent better than in the past." Beyond that, neither Mengistu nor Workneh would discuss the situation except to offer the hope that there would be no "trouble and that they intended there be none." Although with the Ethiopians only briefly, Crosson perceived that both men "seemed sincerely, and, in a sense, deeply moved by the situation although I cannot say that either of them

36. Richards to Secretary of State, Addis Ababa, 14 Dec. 1960, *critical,* ibid.
37. Richards to Secretary of State, Addis Ababa, 14 Dec. 1960, 7:00 PM, *critical,* ibid.
38. Richards Report.

seemed upset or nervous about events." They clearly wanted no bloodshed and hoped the country would support them. "In view of what I knew about the situation on the 'other side of the tracks' I must confess that I thought them most sanguine, particularly since I was reasonably sure that they had made no tactical disposition of the troops available to them to forestall any army attacks." They were so unprepared, in fact, that Crosson concluded that the two leaders did not appreciate the implications of their actions.[39] So overwhelming was this perception that, then and there, the American officer came to believe that the coup would fail.

This impression must have been strengthened when he heard from his air force colleague that Gen. Assefa had permitted Merid to use air force communications to call up four provincial battalions; and had offered to airlift the Neghelli and Jimma units to Debre Zeit, while the Dire Dawa battalion would proceed via the railway and the Debre Berhan component by truck. Crosson also learned later that an armored car company was hurrying from Debre Berhan, and that a tank company from Nazareth was scheduled for arrival during the night and morning of 14–15 December.[40]

Before retiring for the night, Crosson made a sweep around the city, notwithstanding the curfew. He found a few bodyguard patrols, "and not much else." He remained "astonished" that the Imperial Bodyguard still had not made the logical tactical dispositions but had limited themselves to the upper city.

> My strongest impression was one of utter unreality. I could not help but feel that this was a curious coup indeed; one, perhaps, where the instigators were sure of the sympathy or inertia of their possible opponents—the Army and the Air Force. Or else, and this seemed improbable, the conspirators simply didn't know what they were doing.[41]

He consequently told Richards that if Merid's airlift of provincial troops were successful and if the army and bodyguard could not reach agreement, then fighting would begin soon, with air force fighter-bombers doubtless in support of the loyalists. He clung to the notion that both sides sought to avoid bloodshed "but [the] IBG

---

39. Crosson Report.

40. En route, the armor had been stopped by a small roadblock at Akaki, where the guardsmen-defenders explained to an astonished audience that they were preventing an army coup. "The mutual confusion resulting from this verbal exchange enabled the tankers to make a peaceful passage." Ibid.

41. Ibid.

cannot give way entirely since reprisals upon any return of the Emperor [are] sure to be drastic." Since the army was obviously not about to join the coup, "an impossible dilemma . . . will have to be resolved one way or another in the next 24 or 48 hours."[42]

The day's finale was Radio Addis Ababa's proclamation of the guiding principles of "The Peoples Government of Ethiopia." The first point stressed Ethiopia's embarrassment in face of the "constructive progress" of the newly independent African states, and committed the new government "to restore Ethiopia to her appropriate place in the world." The second declared that Addis Ababa would adhere to all international obligations and would "continue its existing relations with friendly nations." The third item guaranteed that foreign investments would not be disturbed so long as they contributed to the well-being and progress of Ethiopia. Fourth was a promise to establish new factories and industries "to help the people improve their standard of living." Only the fifth point dealt with agriculture, in the form of a cursory declaration that "every assistance will be given to the farmers to raise agricultural production." Another perfunctory statement, point six, concerned commerce, whose "due role in improving the country's economy" would be facilitated. Point seven was directed to young Ethiopians who unsuccessfully sought schooling or jobs: "the new government has the aim of educating these young persons and finding employment for those who are not employed." In this regard, item eight confirmed Ethiopia's "lack of technical knowhow," and revealed the government's intention to establish technical schools. Finally the ninth point announced that the bodyguard and the ground forces would be integrated into "The Ethiopian Army."[43] All in all, it was hardly a radical agenda, let alone a revolutionary blueprint.

Yet, it was enough of a departure from Haile Sellassie's platitudes for the embassy's first secretary to argue that sinister forces were at work manipulating the dissatisfactions of young bodyguard officers to destroy the imperial regime. He pointed an accusatory finger at Germame and his cousin Germame Wondefresh, an awraja governor and a member of the Council of the Revolution, both, in McGhee's opinion, dangerous leftist intellectuals. Crosson further

---

42. Richards to Secretary of State, Addis Ababa, 14 Dec. 1960, 9:00 PM, *critical,* SD 775.00/12-1460.

43. Encl. 2 in Richards Report.

surmised that after Haile Sellassie's removal, both Germames hoped "eventually to carry through to a logical conclusion—a people's democracy."[44] Yet, the declaration of "The Peoples Government of Ethiopia" did not alarm Crosson, because he, more than others, realized that bodyguard ineptitude and unpreparedness would lead to the coup's failure. There would be no people's democracy, at least not then. The next morning merely confirmed Crosson's conclusions, and inspired him to pursue a line of analysis which led to direct U.S. involvement on the loyalist side.

At 6:30 AM on 15 December, Crosson began a reconnaissance of the capital. Travelling from east to west, he saw few guardsmen, except those on patrol; in the Jan Hoy Meda area, he found no more than two battalions on bivouac, and he simply could not locate any other large bodies of troops, although he was certain that another two battalions were in the vicinity. In the lower town, he encountered soldiers only near Ras Circle, the first division cantonment, and on the southeastern edge of the airfield. Crosson "was again struck by the unreality of the situation . . . closely resembling the 'phony war' of 1939–40"; he presumed that considerable clandestine activity was occurring, and he was exasperated by his inability to integrate this side of the picture into his analysis.[45]

At 8:00 AM, Crosson and Gary again called at the first division, "where it was immediately apparent that many more troops were under arms," at least two battalions. At headquarters, the Americans met with an exhausted group: Gen. Merid, Dej. Asrate Kassa, Major Assefa Lemma, Lij Worku, Col. Haile Baikedagne, and others, all of whom had worked through the night. Merid remarked that reinforcements were coming in continuously by air, railway, and road; elements of the Debre Berhan battalion already had arrived, as had the tank company from Nazareth. Besides the battalion which Crosson had seen the previous day, Merid reported the successful formation of two others composed of "odd units at hand" and of "individuals culled from all sources, among them several hundred 'old soldiers.'" The general was unable to provide a detailed briefing about his intended troop dispositions and plans, although Col. Haile, the operations officer, said the army proposed

44. Crosson Report.
45. Ibid. Crosson may have been mistaken about the secret negotiations; see below, pp. 143–44, for information about a meeting at the U.S. Embassy which seems to suggest that both sides had not had much contact before fighting broke out.

to seize the radio station but not until it "was thoroughly ready to handle any situation which might arise as a result of this action," the same condition which applied to any move against the airport. Crosson was impressed by "a new and refreshing air of decisiveness in the whole atmosphere"; though fatigued, the officers "were more authoritative and cheerful than . . . the day before." The reinforcements, the messages of support from the provinces, "and the strange quiescence of the IBG" had raised loyalist morale and confidence. The attaché reckoned that army forces were now equal to the bodyguard; moreover, the loyalists disposed fifteen modern tanks, eighteen 105mm howitzers, and the air force. Both Crosson and Gary concluded that "the outcome could not long remain in doubt." The two returned to the embassy to report their judgment to the ambassador. En route, they stopped at Imperial Bodyguard headquarters, but were told that Mengistu was not present.

At 9:00 AM the country team, including the chief of MAAG, met to review major events and to evaluate the state of the crisis. Although Crosson reveals little of his role during the proceedings and the Richards Report does not even mention the meeting, there is little doubt that the army attaché's ideas and judgments were influential. His words certainly must have moved Gen. de Gavre to consider aloud that "the time had come for MAAG to meet its obligations under the MDAP [Mutual Defense Assistance Pact], to give 'advice' to the government forces." The general proposed no material assistance but to follow the terms of an intergovernmental agreement which stipulated that "advice should be given under the prevailing circumstances."

Crosson's report includes the following surprising comment: "The Ambassador *acquiesced* [italics mine] in this course of action," a clear indication that the chief of mission had yielded his authority to the military men, particularly to his army attaché. Crosson knew that de Gavre's decision and Richards' confirmation were sensible in terms of the growing military strength of the loyalists, who were in "a position of such superiority as to leave little doubt as to the final outcome." Yet the colonel worried, perhaps for the record:

> The fact remains that this course of action definitely committed the U.S. to the loyal forces and to the government of HIM. Up to that point it could be said that we were neutral, but afterwards there could be no question but that we were committed. Had our estimates been wrong

and had the rebels won, the U.S. and the Embassy would have been in a decidedly awkward position.

At no time was Washington consulted about what course to take, and Foggy Bottom probably did not learn most of the facts until well after the coup was over and Haile Sellassie was again in power. U.S. policy, as has been shown, was made in the embassy in Addis Ababa, not by its political leadership but by the military establishment, which implemented the decision to intervene.

At 10:30 AM de Gavre and Crosson went to army headquarters, where the American general expounded such military virtues as patience, planning, canniness, and coordination. But, above all, he recommended a peaceful settlement. Merid agreed that de Gavre's sentiments "conformed in most respects with his own views" but warned that "the situation could not remain unadjusted" and that once his forces attained sufficient strength, he would settle the matter "in one smashing concentrated effort." It was obvious to Crosson, however, that staff disorder hampered planning for the offensive. "From the exhaustion evidenced by the general and his staff it was certain that the loyalists had not been able to organize their staff work in any logical way so as to allow for rest." De Gavre's offer of an experienced operations officer was therefore quickly and gratefully accepted, and his arrival at headquarters, along with the return of key MAAG advisers to army units, represented American intervention in Ethiopia's internal affairs.[46]

The U.S. shift from neutrality to partisanship was also occurring in Asmara. On Thursday afternoon, Looram, who finally had returned from Dallol, met with Abiye. "His office resembled a military command post—telephone and radio calls going in and out and people coming and going, giving reports and receiving instructions." The consul discovered that the general was very much in control of Eritrea, and also in continuous contact with all the military and civilian authorities, not only in northern Ethiopia but also in Harar, "who were looking to him for guidance and leadership." As Abiye was also in constant radio communication with Gen. Merid, he was able to provide Looram with an "optimistic and reassuring" report about the situation throughout the country.

He complained, however, that he was unable to counter rebel broadcasts, which "were having a very bad effect and he feared that

46. Crosson Report.

if the rebellion should continue for long and the people were unaware of the real situation, the country might start falling apart." Abiye felt that Haile Sellassie's return would have an "enormous" psychological effect, "but how could he make it known?" Since Looram believed "that the loyal elements had the upper hand and would win out," he now asked the embassy to permit Abiye, and later the emperor, to use Kagnew radio facilities. Before Richards replied, the general was able to arrange a transmitter through the air force, and he broadcast to the country, assuring his compatriots that only a few were in revolt; that otherwise the military remained faithful; and that Haile Sellassie's return was imminent.[47]

In fact, the State Department had informed the embassy that Haile Sellassie's American-crewed DC-6B had left Recife at 10:11; that Dakar air control center estimated the emperor's arrival in Liberia at 17:40; and that the plane should reach Asmara at about 6:40, 16 December.[48] In Addis Ababa, events were approaching anticlimax: the crown prince had gone on the air to announce the formation of a government under Ras Imru and the appointment of Major Gen. Mulugeta Bulli—currently out of the emperor's favor— as chief of staff of the armed forces.[49] Asfa Wossen had declared Gens. Merid and Kebede "enemies of the people," and announced that military salaries would be greatly increased, effective immediately.[50] The most significant event of the morning, and certainly the most instructive and prophetic, however, was the demonstration by college students in the capital.

On the afternoon of 14 December, student leaders were called to bodyguard headquarters to meet with Mengistu, who impressed the young people greatly. One recalled:

> I felt . . . strongly that he was really risking his life. He was extremely nice, too nice for the role he was playing. I felt he had to do something desperate. It was a relief for us to hear him say that most of the 17 ministers he held captive were lice, sucking the [blood of] Ethiopian society and [were] a burden to the country.

As the general spoke about Ethiopia's deteriorating social and economic conditions and its gross social injustices, the students came to

47. Ibid.
48. Secretary of State to Embassy, Washington, 15 Dec. 1960, SD 775.11/12-1560.
49. See above p. 155.
50. Richards to Secretary of State, Addis Ababa, 15 Dec. 1960, SD 775.00/12-1560.

see him as the country's champion. This conviction strengthened when he stressed that he and his colleagues had not acted for "self-enhancement, but in the 'wider interests of all.'" At his urging, the students agreed to hold campus-wide meetings to discuss the coup.[51]

That evening at University College of Addis Ababa many students were at first bewildered;[52] they neither knew what a coup d'etat was nor understood what a demonstration implied. The many political views that were aired added to the confusion—"It was all so fantastic, so dreamlike." The students were hypnotized by authoritative figures speaking aloud what many of them had only dared to whisper. "It was Jesus healing the cripple. We had the same feelings of joy the cripple must have had. The incredible, a miracle had happened." Most came to believe that the coup would succeed, demonstrating a "confidence . . . beyond any real assessment of the situation." The students enthusiastically voted to demonstrate in favor of the coup and worked during the night composing slogans and songs, making banners out of bedsheets, and writing a manifesto.[53]

While self-centered, pretentious, patronizing, and naive, the manifesto augured the politically conscious and activist student movement of later years. The unsophisticated ideas and analyses of 1960 were to develop into the articulated and defined ideology which undermined the emperor's position continuously thereafter. The manifesto opened with an explanation of Ethiopia's backwardness as resulting from a "lack of opportunity and denial of *our* due rights." The students evinced an "ever present ambition to develop *our* dear country, to civilize *our* country and to lead *our* dear country towards a prosperous future," the last a condition not achieved "due to the deprivation of *our* legitimate rights." Though their education was supported by the sweat of the poor, the latter were "surrounded by fear and oppression, [and] *we* have been unable to give any help by which the poor man could improve his life."

51. Randi Rønning Balsvik, "Haile Selassie's Students—Rise of Social and Political Consciousness" (Ph.D. Diss. University of Tromsø, 1979), p. 188.

52. Later divided into the faculty of arts, education, and science; in December 1961, integrated with other institutions into Haile Sellassie I University (now Addis Ababa University).

53. Balsvik, "Students," pp. 189–90. Oddly, Teshome Habte Gabriel offered the new regime his support "provided it is not a military coup d'etat." See *News and Views* 4 (16 Dec. 1960).

The new government would offer students their chance to assist. "Every good thing takes time; the day which *we* have been long awaiting came today, bringing for Ethiopia a new progressive life and prosperity for its people." The young people vowed, "*we* are ready to render *our* advice and service to the new regime." Their "*extensive* study of history and *extensive* research into the world of today" revealed that the former government was the main obstacle to progress. An aristocratic minority controlled most of the land, "while the poor are slaves of the well-to-do, farming for the rich, paying heavy taxes for the rich, while they themselves suffer in poverty." City dwellers also had endured " . . . low pay, delays, and did not even control their own property." In the students' opinion, "this peaceful change of government is aimed at opening a new door to a progressive and prosperous future for Ethiopia and its people."[54]

There has been considerable speculation about the voluntary nature of participation in the demonstration. Greenfield does not refer to the matter, Patrick Gilkes neither confronts the question nor says much about students, and Addis Hiwet only mentions "that the university students came out in full strength," which is factual. [55] Yet, participants, several my friends and many my informants, disclosed being pressured by peers and indirectly threatened by guardsmen to march. Furthermore, a foreigner who accompanied the demonstrators for quite a while recounted that "a substantial minority were not happy; they felt pressured; [the marchers were] not jubilant and triumphant [but] kind of fearful."[56] Official American observations are unanimous in viewing the student action as coerced and contrived,[57] although this conclusion seems extreme. The students may have felt anxious and uncertain, perhaps even coerced psychologically, but the actions of at least a great many of them were spontaneous and heartfelt.[58]

Whatever their reasons, the young people placed themselves and their successors at the epicenter of Ethiopian politics. Singing, waving placards, and yelling slogans, the students marched from the

54. Manifesto in Wagner to Secretary of State, Addis Ababa, 22 Dec. 1960, SD 775.00/12-2260.
55. Greenfield, *Ethiopia,* pp. 414-15; Patrick Gilkes, *The Dying Lion* (London, 1975), pp. 236-42; Addis Hiwet, *From Autocracy to Revolution,* p. 75.
56. Confidential source.
57. Crosson Report.
58. Balsvik, "Students," p. 190.

upper town towards army headquarters, hoping to garner the support of the people. They chanted:

> Wake up, my compatriot, do not forget yourself for you have a history behind you. Erase your slavery and review your freedom today. Wake up. Wake up. Do not forget yourself. Your dignity will be safeguarded and you will be rewarded with eternal happiness. Wake up, wake up. Do not forget yourself.

The banners proclaimed: *for everyone—a bloodless revolution; you who have suffered injustice—wake up; Let us stand peacefully with the new Government of the people; our goal is Equality, Brotherhood and Freedom.* To all of this, the people responded "with confused curiosity," but with little enthusiasm and participation, foreshadowing the failure of the students with the military.[59]

Shortly after noon, the idealism of youth encountered the reality of a platoon of soldiers who refused to permit the students to advance beyond the railway station, and appeared quite ready to confirm their refusal by shooting. A massacre was averted by the quick and assured intervention of several Ethiopian academics who read the contours of the situation as one might interpret a map.[60] The student collapse in face of army determination merely signalled the miscarriage of the coup, now in its penultimate stage.

Meanwhile, another drama was being played out at the Genet Leul Palace, where increasing frustration would lead to the use of weapons against the loyalists and the hostages. With Mengistu's approval, Ras Imru had attempted to obtain the church's intercession to arrange a meeting between Mengistu and Merid. The effort failed, and the patriarch instead issued a leaflet contrasting the treason of the bodyguard with the army's "abiding faith" in the emperor and urging the people to serve the crown and not "listen to the traitors."[61] Worst of all, word also reached the palace that "General Merid and the other senior officers had no wish to come and have any meeting at all." To these developments, a deeply resentful Mengistu "retorted that since the army officers refused to come, he was going to give [the] order to attack. . . ."[62] At about 2:50 PM, approximately when the American Embassy received a

59. Ibid.
60. Confidential source.
61. The Patriarch's Leaflet, Greenfield Collection.
62. Ras Imru deposition.

government note requesting recognition,[63] rifle fire commenced, spreading rapidly from east to west, soon punctuated by mortars.[64]

Crosson "assumed the IBG was at last beginning to deploy its forces in defensive positions" and at 3:30 PM drove to bodyguard headquarters to make inquiries. On arrival, he found the senior officer present, Col. Asfaw Andarge, seated on the front steps surrounded by a group of fully armed junior officers. Crosson could elicit little from Asfaw except that "all is going well enough." The American found the tableau "quite astonishing and amusing. I had never seen a battle run so casually." Since there was no haste, no messengers, no obvious military activities, the American correctly assumed that the command post was elsewhere. "Needless to say, I never found it."[65]

After reporting to the embassy at 4:30 PM, Crosson attempted two different routes to army headquarters but was turned back each time by firing, particularly near the airport. "I later found out that [the] action near the airport was, in fact, the loyal troops taking over from the rebels, during the course of which some of the latter became the former by a mere switch of hats."[66] The rebel collapse here might well have been stimulated by two late afternoon air force overflights, one of which dropped the patriarch's leaflets denouncing the rebels and supporting the emperor, while the other cracked the sound barrier, causing a terrifying sonic boom.[67] It was widely believed, then and later, that U.S. pilots were involved "in action against the Ethiopian rebel government." Upon inquiry, Richards learned that American personnel had flown a reconnaissance mission and had made the flight which cracked the sound barrier "in [an] effort to frighten rebels holding [the] palace."[68] However irresponsible, the activities of United States Air Force officers were of one piece with general embassy policy and reflected the increasingly obvious conclusion that, for exclusively Ethiopian reasons, the coup would fail.

63. Richards to Secretary of State, Addis Ababa, 15 Dec. 1960, SD 775.00/12-1560; the note was written on new official paper with the heading, "Government of Ethiopia," not "Imperial Ethiopian Government."

64. Ibid.

65. Crosson Report.

66. Ibid.

67. Richards to Secretary of State, Addis Ababa, 15 Dec. 1960, SD 775.00/12-1560.

68. Richards to Secretary of State, Addis Ababa, 20 Dec. 1960, SD 775.00/12-2060. The ambassador told his French colleague that there had been no American participation in air missions. See de Juniac, *Roi des Rois*, p. 263.

Indeed, that same afternoon, Haile Sellassie's rumored return had sparked a spontaneous and happy demonstration near the palace. The "traditional cries of joy" magnified the failures of the day for Mengistu, who "showed increasing anxiety."[69] His fitful sleep that night would have become insomnia had he known that Haile Sellassie was now directly involved in the mutiny's suppression, thanks to the technical help of the United States Air Force and its international communications network. During an early-evening stopover in Liberia, the emperor used USAF radio facilities at Robertsfield to communicate with Gen. Abiye, who advised a quick return to Ethiopia via Asmara.[70]

Thereafter, Haile Sellassie had a brief meeting with Liberia's President Tubman and issued a statement published the next day:

> The confused situation in Addis Ababa is something that will pass soon. Such confusion is caused always by irresponsible people. . . . Since this confusion is confined only within Addis Ababa we are confident that peace and security reign in the rest of the country.
>
> The loyalty and fidelity of the army and our bodyguard have been shown during the first stage of the Congo crisis when we decided to send contingents to this trouble spot area.
>
> We are the one who initiated a constitutional measure for the keeping and maintenance of rights and privileges of our people.[71]

After delivering this hopeful message, the emperor and his entourage left at 19:30 local time for Khartoum via Fort Lamy.[72]

While the imperial plane made its way across Africa, Col. Crosson, after a restless night, was attempting to contact the army command. En route at 6:15 AM with Col. Gary, he heard the loyalists open fire on bodyguard headquarters with 105mm howitzers. At 6:40 AM, just as the two attachés found the field command post east of the Bishoftu (Debre Zeit) road, jet fighters swept over the town, machine-gunned the IBG headquarters, and dropped some bombs.[73] After learning that the loyalists had taken the airport the evening before, the two Americans were told that the army had just

69. Ras Imru deposition.
70. Ambassador to Secretary of State, Monrovia, 15 Dec. 1960, 10:00 PM, SD 775.11/12-1560; Looram Report.
71. *Liberian Age,* 16 Dec. 1960.
72. Cable as in note 70.
73. Richards to Secretary of State, Addis Ababa, 16 Dec. 1960, 9:00 AM, SD 775.00/12-1660.

pushed off to attack the bodyguard, now occupying various defensive positions along the upper town. Crosson reflected that the troopers would have difficulty finding the IBG, let alone fighting them, since at 6:00 AM, when he had made his way to the lower city, "IBG troops were not in much evidence." Observing that all the army officers "seemed quite optimistic as to the eventual outcome," Crosson decided to report to the embassy; Col. Gary, however, made for the airport, to assist American employees of Ethiopian Airlines in establishing radio contact between Addis Ababa and the emperor,[74] whose plane had been delayed in Fort Lamy by propeller trouble but was again airborne.[75]

During Crosson's short stay at the embassy, firing became general and heavy, but at 8:00 AM, the attaché set off once more for the army field command. Skilfully circumventing the fighting, he arrived there to learn that loyalist forces had successfully undertaken a two-pronged attack on the flanks of the upper town. Crosson observed that "General Merid was running what might be termed a one man show . . . now issuing orders to an officer, now communicating with others via police radio cars," although he also reported that "a rump Crown Council [was] in session and passing on actions taken by the Army." Before the attaché left, MAAG advisers told him that, notwithstanding all the activity, "things were still in confusion and the situation not at all clear."[76] They were wrong; the outcome of the crisis was becoming almost transparent.

At 8:00 AM, Capt. Kebede, an emissary from Col. Workneh, arrived at the embassy and invited American mediation.[77] Mr. William McGhee, the first secretary, was dispatched to the palace, and subsequently Germame Neway sent for Ras Imru, who was told, "the Americans are dropping bombs from the jets. Will you not therefore talk to them?" The incredulous ras saw "no point" in discussions, but Germame pleaded, "In order to bring peace and stop the fighting, please talk to [McGhee], who has just come here." Imru relented, and according to his testimony, he asked for a conference with the ambassador and delivery of a message to Haile Sel-

74. Crosson Report.

75. Looram Report; for the heroic version, see Greenfield, *Ethiopia*, p. 408; and de Juniac, *Roi des Rois*, p. 264.

76. Crosson Report.

77. Richards to Secretary of State, Addis Ababa, 16 Dec. 1960, 1:00 PM, SD 775.00/12-1660.

78. Ras Imru deposition.

lassie.[78] McGhee's account stressed, however, that Imru was concerned about saving lives and sought the embassy's intervention "to arrange a meeting with General Merid or one of his officers to discuss a cease fire."[79]

The diplomat immediately reported to the embassy, and Richards quickly relayed word to Merid via Asmara. In forwarding the message, Gen. Abiye commented that the offer merely reflected the reality of the weakening rebel military situation, and recommended that Merid immediately demand unconditional surrender, since traitors could not be trusted to fulfil conditions.[80] Although Abiye strongly opposed U.S. mediation, Richards concluded "that for humanitarian reasons we could not have decided otherwise."[81] Crosson, who had just returned, was briefed and sent to Merid to explain the ambassador's position and to request that he meet with Imru at the embassy. The loyalist leader "flatly" refused direct contact with the ras but agreed to send a delegate and to suspend air attacks as a sign of goodwill. He designated Major Assefa Lemma, vice-minister of the interior, as his agent, and he and Crosson arrived at the embassy at 10:00 AM.[82]

Since Richards had not yet returned, Crosson dropped off Major Assefa and drove down the road to the palace. There he joined a conference between the two Americans Richards and McGhee, and Gen. Mengistu, Col. Workneh, Germame Neway, Germame Wondefresh, and Gen. Tsigue Dibou of the police. The ambassador relayed the substance of Crosson's whispered report, and, after some discussion, the coup leaders decided on Germame Neway as their delegate. As he watched, Crosson

> was struck by the calmness of manner of all those present. None of them seemed nervous or upset and their greetings . . . were almost normal in manner. I must confess I was impressed, for I felt their cause was lost and I am sure they had made the same assessment else they would not be asking for a parley.[83]

Shortly thereafter, Germame and Assefa—old acquaintances, now antagonists—met at the embassy in the presence of Richards,

79. Richards to Secretary of State, Addis Ababa, 16 Dec. 1960, 1:00 PM, SD 775.00/12-1660.
80. Looram to Secretary of State, Asmara, 16 Dec. 1960, ibid.
81. Richards Report.
82. Crosson Report.
83. Ibid.

Crosson, and others. Thanks to the attaché, we have a full account of this important session. Germame opened the deliberations with a rehearsal of the reasons for the attempted coup: the regime was corrupt and dishonest, the common man never really had a chance, the country's development had been retarded, and the present government was incapable of reform. Major Assefa retorted that:

> the rate of progress was determined not by wishes but by the economics of the situation; that the Emperor had done all he could to insure progress; that it was the Emperor who had seen to the education of the young men—Germame and himself included—so that they could assist Ethiopia, that it was wrong to attempt to right whatever might be felt to be wrong by a civil war.

After these preliminaries, there could be no compromise.

Assefa only conceded that he would try to arrange a meeting between Imru and Merid.[84] Germame emerged "ashen grey" from Richards' office and remarked to an American friend that "even if we are totally defeated, if nothing of this succeeds, at least we would have spoken a true word."[85] Thus, the main ideologue of the coup understood that the game was up, even if the uncomprehending American mediators continued to be "optimistic" that Imru and Merid would meet; that there would be a cease-fire; and that further bloodshed would be avoided.[86] Crosson learned the truth when he accompanied Major Assefa back to the army command post.

There Merid and the rump crown council discussed the possibilities of a cease-fire and of a meeting between Merid and Imru. They decided that neither the general nor anyone else would meet with the rebels and "that the army was in a position to force the issue quickly and decisively." Crosson intervened by asking Merid to sketch out the loyalist position in a communication to Ras Imru. The general agreed, a letter was prepared and handed over to Crosson, who thereupon left for the embassy, reaching it at 12:30 PM.[87]

Merid's words were unrelenting, "stating in essence that the Army would continue operations unless the rebel forces immediately laid down their arms."[88] Nonetheless, the ambassador,

84. Ibid.
85. Confidential communication.
86. Richards to Secretary of State, Addis Ababa, 16 Dec. 1960, 1:00 PM, SD 775.00/12-1660.
87. Crosson Report.
88. Richards Report.

McGhee, and Crosson were quickly on their way to the palace, perhaps spurred by the visit that morning of Ato Mulu, the crown prince's secretary. He had emphasized to Mr. Joseph Wagner, the embassy's counsellor, that the crown prince had acted "under duress," and that Asfa Wossen was afraid that the bodyguard "out of last minute vengeance might try to murder CP, Crown Princess and perhaps even Empress." The counsellor had assured Mulu that the embassy would use its good offices to ensure the safety of the royal family.[89] Thus, Richards and his colleagues went to the palace, at least in part, to save lives; in the event, they not only failed, but were almost killed themselves.

When they arrived at the palace's main gate at 12:40 PM, Crosson heard heavy firing coming from about a mile down the road. Thinking little about the shooting, the Americans drove to the main building, where, in a small office to the left of the portico, they found Mengistu, Germame, Workneh, and Germame Wondefresh. Gen. Tsigue Dibou appeared and then shortly after him Ras Imru, who received and silently read Merid's letter with obviously increasing dismay.[90] In the interim, Crosson leaned over and quietly asked Mengistu if bodyguard forces still held the old Gibbi hill, which, of course, controlled the main line of retreat from the Genet Leul Palace. The general replied affirmatively, but "At this point Colonel Workineh said in an aside to Mr. McGhee, 'You had better get His Excellency (The Ambassador) out of here. There is going to be trouble'." Then Imru read the note aloud, which was followed by a "very short" discussion, whereupon the ras said to Richards in English, "I wish to see the emperor in Asmara. Is there any possibility that this could be arranged?" The ambassador responded ambiguously but suggested that Imru reply in writing to Merid, since time was passing and the fighting continued. Just as the ras had finished one sentence, "a burst of submachine gun fire was let off by one of the guards at the front entrance." All remained calm, if shaken, even when some bullets hit the outside wall of the room.

It was now 1:00 PM, and advanced units of the army obviously had brought the palace under fire prior to assault. Mengistu, however, claimed, "it is nothing. There is a patrol and a tank at the entrance of the Palace grounds (about 300 yards away). We can

89. Richards to Secretary of State, Addis Ababa, 16 Dec. 1960, 1:00 PM, SD 775.00/12-1660.
90. De Juniac, *Roi des Rois*, p. 265.

hold them and there is nothing to worry about." If Mengistu was confident, "Ras Imru was the coolest of the lot." He actually walked to the window and threw back the drapes to look out, to Crosson's considerable consternation: "Frankly, I shuddered (I was standing directly behind him) but nothing happened." If, perhaps, Imru's gesture invited death, Crosson thought only of living:

> At this point it was obvious to me that we should make ourselves scarce. Three dead Americans—one of them an Ambassador—in rebel head-quarters would certainly make lurid headlines as well as having the disadvantage of [our] being dead in a quarrel not our own.[91]

Richards obviously agreed "for he calmly arose" and announced his departure. Although the ambassador later reported that he "left forthwith,"[92] the getaway was a bit more complicated than that.

Crosson and McGhee followed their leader into the hall and to the entrance, only to discover that the embassy car was not there, having been moved north of the palace for protection. Back inside again, Crosson asked Mengistu if there was a rear entrance; "he was extremely non-committal about this point, while around us the guard of young officers (about 15) were busily loading rifles and submachine guns." The colonel found their technique "appallingly awkward," and he was afraid that there would be accidental firing, "so [I] kept ducking under the muzzles of their guns." Meanwhile, the ambassador had made an unsuccessful reconnaissance toward the rear, by mistake entering the Green Salon off the throne room where the hostages were being detained. By this time, Col. Workneh had persuaded the Americans to return to the small office, there to vault through the window to safety. Although firing erupted just before Workneh and another bodyguard officer made the first leaps, the three Americans jumped during a lull. Crosson comments approvingly on Richards' sangfroid, but it was not until they reached the back of the palace that the ambassador "reduced his pace to a dignified walk." Following Workneh and two other officers, the Americans proceeded to the palace garage where the Ethiopians started up a DKW and Richards a Pontiac station wagon. Both rebels and neutrals left through the rear gate, but the Americans took the high road to the embassy, while the fugitives took to the hills.[93]

91. Crosson Report.
92. Richards Report.
93. Crosson Report.

Thereafter the group in the office scattered, the military to join the fight and Ras Imru to seek sanctuary with the crown prince upstairs. Imru recollected that "the fighting continued with great fierceness. . . . The smoke of the battle was everywhere, both inside and outside the Palace, to such an extent that I thought the building was on fire, but it was not." At about 5:00 PM, one of the crown prince's hysterical servants reported, "There is not a single person remaining—all have left, even those who were guarding us." Then Dej. Bezabe Selleshi made a spectral appearance, only to be welcomed by Asfa Wossen with a laconic, "So you have survived,"[94] as if the prince had known that the officials detained early in the crisis were to be executed if the coup failed.

The loyalist attack on the palace doubtlessly had triggered uncontrollable emotions of despair and frustration that led to the killing of most of the captives. At 4:00 PM commenced the action undertaken, as Mengistu reportedly said, so that, "Ethiopia should never be the same again."[95] The brothers Neway and Germame Wondefresh shot and killed fifteen of the hostages, wounded three, and left two others unhurt but feigning death.[96] After the *Götterdämmerung,* the three remaining rebel leaders—Workneh had fled and Tsigue Dibou had been killed in the fighting—along with a platoon of troops, held out until dark, when they left the now hostile city for the alleged security of the countryside. By this time, however, Haile Sellassie was back in Ethiopia; the country was his and therefore antagonistic to those who had attempted to put him aside.

A relief Ethiopian Airlines plane had flown to Khartoum to await the emperor, who arrived there at 12:30 PM, and was met with full honors by President Aboud and members of his government. An hour later, Haile Sellassie left for Asmara,[97] which he reached at 4:20 PM. All businesses had been closed, and the government had spread the word for everyone to demonstrate their loyalty. The airport and the access road to the city were jammed with people. The emperor emerged from the plane "looking somewhat tired, understandably so [but] relaxed and self-assured." He was visibly moved by the "wildly enthusiastic ovation of the crowds." While reviewing troops and greeting officials and the consular corps, "the

94. Ras Imru deposition.
95. Greenfield, *Ethiopia,* p. 430.
96. Crosson Report; see above pp. 155–57 for a complete listing.
97. Dorsey to Secretary of State, Khartoum, 16 Dec. 1960, SD 775.11/12-1660.

hysteria of the mobs had almost gotten out of hand and the Emperor was soon surrounded by innumerable screaming people. Had anyone wished to assassinate him, it would have been very easy."

When Haile Sellassie finally made his way to an awaiting car, Gen. Abiye pushed the chauffeur aside and drove the sovereign into Asmara. After a brief rest at the palace, Caesar rendered thanks to God at Asmara's two leading Orthodox churches. That evening, the emperor made an apparently "incoherent, indecisive, and unimpressive speech over the radio,"[98] but specifically absolved the crown prince and Ras Imru of any guilt in the rebellion. By the time the emperor was asleep in Asmara, fighting had ended in Addis Ababa, at least for the night, although soldiers were firing their weapons in celebration, and crowds of cheering civilians roamed the thoroughfares.[99]

The next morning, it remained unclear whether Addis Ababa was a safe haven for both emperor and entourage. Yet, Haile Sellassie could not long delay his victorious return, since the coup had been suppressed in his name. Moreover, the monarch worried about the safety and health of the empress and the welfare of other members of the imperial family, even though Looram had delivered a message from Merid which declared the capital secure and the entire royal family safe.[100] The emperor nevertheless sought an independent assessment of the situation and sent a teletype message to Ambassador Richards from Kagnew Station "in [an] unusual move seeking advice as to whether he should return to Addis Ababa." In response, Richards emphasized "the psychological advantage" which an early return would yield, "provided General Merid assured military calm and personal safety."[101] Later that morning, Merid and Haile Sellassie conversed through Kagnew facilities, and "on the basis of that conversation and following a subsequent conference with General Abiye, the Emperor abruptly decided to return to Addis." The departure "was marked by secrecy and haste," with hardly anyone present to see the monarch off.[102]

98. Looram Report.

99. Richards to Secretary of State, Addis Ababa, 16 Dec. 1960, SD 775.00/12-1660.

100. Merid to Haile Sellassie, Addis Ababa, 16 Dec. 1960, in Richards to Secretary of State, Addis Ababa, 16 Dec. 1960, 8:00 PM, ibid.

101. Richards to Secretary of State, Addis Ababa, 17 Dec. 1960, 7:00 PM, SD 775.11/12-1760.

102. Looram Report.

He arrived in Addis Ababa at 4:15 PM, welcomed by the crown prince, Gens. Merid and Kebede, other loyalist leaders, the patriarch and clergy, and high-ranking officials and aristocrats. Also present, invited by Merid, were Crosson, Gary, and Richards, the last the only ranking member of the diplomatic corps admitted to the field. After greeting his compatriots, the emperor called Richards forward "and with some emotion expressed sincere gratitude [for the] assistance given those who put down the revolt. He asked [that] his gratitude be conveyed to the President."[103] Observing him closely, Crosson found Haile Sellassie "alert and energetic and [he] gave the impression of being calm and collected, his usual air." The monarch must have been buoyed, however, by the cheering multitudes who lined the route into the city in an emotional and apparently spontaneous demonstration.[104] His arrival had not been announced, and many believed that the people sensed its imminence. In fact, however, the population realized that the emperor was coming when they saw hundreds of security men lining up along the airport road. Haile Sellassie went to Jubilee Palace, to begin the process of learning the truth about the events of the previous few days.

103. Richards to Secretary of State, Addis Ababa, 17 Dec. 1960, 7:00 PM, SD 775.11/12-1760.
104. Crosson Report.

6. Pathology, 1960

Crosson was not a man given to speculation, yet even he fell prey to considering what might have happened *if:*

> . . . the tactical planning and execution [had] been good and the attack been put in Wednesday morning at daybreak. I believe the IBG would have been successful, under the circumstances, in establishing local control. They could then either have persuaded the Air Force at Debra Zeit to come over to them or they could have seized Debra Zeit and neutralized, if not destroyed, that portion of the IEAF. (Even if the IEAF had flown planes out, the fuel stocks would have fallen to the rebels.) Possibly at this point the 3rd Division would have declared for the rebels. It is even conceivable that uncommitted troops outside of Eritrea would have come over. But even so the provinces which declared for the Emperor would have mobilized and marched. The end result could only have been a guerrilla war of long duration during which the country would have been rent from end to end for many months.[1]

Thus, it is clear that the coup leadership early missed the possibility of success. As the *Times* of London reported on 22 December, "enough can be pieced together now to suggest that the immediate reason for the failure of the palace *coup* was hesitation on the part of the rebel leaders soon after they had proclaimed their authority."[2] An American academic witness stressed the naiveté of the rebels who, "apparently with *no* plan beyond the initial takeover, firmly believed that if they held the capital—in fact, not even the entire capital, but just the palace and the downtown area—they held the nation."[3]

1. Crosson Report, SD 775.00/1-1360.
2. "Ethiopian Rebels Beaten by Hesitation," *Times* (London), 22 Dec. 1960.
3. Francis A. J. Ianni, "Ethiopia: A Special Case," in *The Transformation of East Africa*, ed. Stanley Diamond and Fred G. Burke (New York, 1966), p. 423.

Crosson pointed to haphazard planning and lack of contingency arrangements: "the conspirators, once committed, seemed to have left action and counteraction to occur without any attempt to take the initiative and sat on their hands, seemingly to await developments." This inertia was matched by the sloppy way in which the rebels carried out their arrests: "As a result some of the most important men—e.g. Generals Merid and Kebede—escaped arrest and immediately got to work to counter the coup d'etat. This was a major blunder." If this error were not enough, Crosson could not understand why Mengistu and the rest had avoided contacting elements or individuals within the air force and army, "whose sympathy or active assistance were absolutely essential to the success of the plot." The only explanation comprised the unstated assumptions upon which the coup was based: "the appeal of their program, the appeal of the Crown Prince's name, and the degree of dissatisfaction existing in the Army and Air Force." Without support from the last two, "the plot was doomed to failure and anyone but a fool or a wishful thinker would have recognized the weakness immediately the plot was proposed."

The attaché also believed that the leadership had exaggerated "the degree of support which could be expected from the population and even from the intelligentsia" and had erred by considering that "Addis Ababa is Ethiopia and that he who holds Addis controls Ethiopia." This misapprehension had led to the consequent failure to enlist any of the provincial authorities, leaving the emperor a great reservoir of strength in the countryside: "in some areas horsemen were mobilized and were enroute before the Army could finish off the IBG." The baseless presumption of peer support and the arrogant devaluation of the provinces' importance led the rebels "into another fatal error, that of doing nothing during the 14th, thus allowing their enemies to build up military strength undisturbed. . . . Had their planning and preparations been adequate . . . the next logical step, force, would have been taken immediately the emotional and political appeal failed."

Even if a more forceful approach had been attempted, Crosson believed that inability to agree upon a single leader would have thwarted success. Instead all decisions were made by committee, with "procrastination and delay . . . not to mention errors in military judgement." He cited Workneh's seminal realization that the air force base at Debra Zeit should be neutralized, a proposition which "failed to gain the support of other leaders." Yet, as the attaché was quick to stress, "even accepting the committee decision, the military situation was not completely lost had the IBG troops been deployed early Wednesday morning between the city and the Army troops." As it was, the decision made in the late afternoon of 15 December was too delayed for any kind of reasonable defense, and "The implementation of the attack order was frightfully inept." Deployment was made only by company; the commanders were unable to make an adequate reconnaissance, "hence did not really know where they were going"; there was no reserve; there was no real main effort nor adequate tactical direction; and the artillery and mortars were used ineffectually and not in support of infantry.

"It was a most distressing performance. Too little, too late [because of the] weakness . . . of allowing humanitarian impulses to govern military decisions." From the first, both sides had declared their desire not to shed blood, "and were scrupulous about this." Neither the army nor the IBG therefore used their weapons with any efficiency, and their forbearance saved civilian life and property; "even the strafing and bombing by the Air Force was done in what one might term a restrained fashion."[4]

If the Imperial Bodyguard's indecision led to defeat, Gen. Abiye Abebe's certain hand played a vital role in holding the northern provinces for the crown. American officialdom "had always feared that should Addis Ababa ever be torn by internal dissension, the latent dissatisfaction in Eritrea might erupt." Instead, the major towns were calm, and "there were no signs of a coalescence of hostile Muslim elements," thanks largely to Abiye's immediate declaration of loyalty to Haile Sellassie. Also, in the absence of Eritrea's chief executive, the general called in members of the state government and instructed them to mobilize support for the emperor; he assumed command of the Second Division; and openly toured Asmara, showing his confidence in the favorable resolution of the crisis. "His decisive stand and general conduct were of enormous psychological importance at that juncture." Abiye also enjoyed the support of Col. Tedla, the commissioner of Eritrean police, whose men were quickly in evidence in Asmara and elsewhere. "The people were thus given to see at the outset that Abiye was determined to maintain order and to back the Emperor's cause."

4. Crosson Report.

While Looram believed that most Eritreans considered the events in Addis Ababa an internal Amhara affair, he had learned that some young Eritreans were sympathetic to the rebel government's program. "Nevertheless in this police-controlled territory, most were very discreet about their feelings." Still, the consulate had sufficient evidence to conclude that if the emperor had not returned quickly, or had the outcome in Addis Ababa been delayed, "serious problems would have broken out here." In fact, "a so-called 'Independence Party' was allegedly organizing a revolt." Abiye thus had saved the day, but there was no guarantee for the future; "having learned their lesson once, dissatisfied Eritrean elements might . . . be quicker the next time to take advantage of dissension in Addis should such happen again." Looram ended on a further negative note, even while lauding Abiye: "with a less decisive, loyal and well respected individual at the helm here, the outcome, at least in the northern part of Ethiopia, might have been quite different—and might be quite different on another occasion."[5]

The same type of augury, albeit differently couched, was made by Ambassador Richards. He stressed "the complete failure of the rebels to win any important degree of popular support," although "in general young educated Ethiopians greeted the coup with enthusiasm." The masses, however, accepted "the news with sullen apathy and apprehension," the difference being that "the rebel program . . . was obviously over the head of the masses and struck no responsive chord in them." The coup's leadership had "failed to measure the temper or the degree of understanding yet existing amongst the vast bulk of the Ethiopian people."[6] Richards hoped that the crisis had forced the emperor to appreciate "the urgent need for social and political reform in Ethiopia and the appointment of new blood to positions of real responsibility." This anticipation was, however, adumbrated by the emperor's press interview of 20 December, during which Haile Sellassie emphasized that there would not be "the slightest deviation from the [previous] path of progress worked out for Ethiopia" and that "there will be no change in the system of Government or in the Government's programs." Richards soberly ended his report with the following perception: "If the Emperor does nothing . . . it is not unlikely that a

5. Looram Report, SD 775.00/12-2260.
6. Donald Levine was told that Ras Imru made a similar remark: "Germame did not understand the temper of the Ethiopian people."

similar recourse to violence will reoccur at some future date, possibly with greater success."[7]

Throughout the night of 17–18 December, however, only sporadic and apparently indiscriminate violence continued in a darkened Addis Ababa, where just the palace, a few embassies, and several other lighted places enjoyed electricity generated by portable units. Shooting could be heard during the 18th, but at a much diminished rate, almost in direct relation to the growing effectiveness of the restored government. When Radio Addis Ababa finally went on the air, it warned that "Blood will again be shed by anyone who should in future attempt to defy the Emperor's authority." A statement by the Ministry of the Interior advised that the hunt was continuing for the leaders of the coup and other participants. With the increasing security, refugees returned to the capital, and foreigners left the safety of embassy compounds to see to their affairs. Little was known about the provincial situation, and nothing could be learned since censorship was tight. Meanwhile, a few shops and bars opened, and air force planes flew overhead, skywriting the emperor's name. Finally, the monarch broadcast to the nation.[8]

He attributed the attempted coup to a "small handful of willful men who sought, for their own ends, to retard and impede the progress which Ethiopia is achieving in the modern world." He condemned the bloodshed and the "irreparable harm and injury to Ethiopia as a whole." Alluding to his significant political strength in the provinces, the emperor queried, "Why should Addis Ababa be troubled, when the entire Empire is peaceful?" Changing the subject somewhat, Haile Sellassie was quick to exonerate the crown prince and others who apparently had cooperated with the rebels: "We have understood what impelled the traitors to implicate Our beloved son . . . and Our dignitaries, in whom We repose high confidence, that their plot might become more plausible." He then insinuated that the plotters were cowards who refused to attack him directly but only when he was abroad on "a voyage which We were confident would contribute, through the contacts We were making with other world leaders, to the continued advancement of Our nation."

7. Richards Report, SD 775.00/12-2960. See also "Selassie Pledges Unchanged Rule," *New York Times*, 21 Dec. 1960.

8. Richards to Secretary of State, Addis Ababa, 18 Dec. 1960, SD 775.00/12-1860; *Times* (London), 19 Dec. 1960.

Progress for Ethiopia had been the hallmark of his life, and he had pioneered a modern educational system, "but trees that are planted do not always bear the desired fruit." He had sent students abroad for higher studies, "expecting that they would return and devote their learning to the service of their nation." He had not played favorites: "We have loved all equally. We gave authority to persons whom We judged on their face value." The newly educated had served the people according to the constitution which "We conferred upon Our people," and had implemented "some of the many plans We have formulated for the advancement of Our nation." And although "Our trust has been betrayed . . . Our hopes . . . shattered [and] they have repaid Us with treachery and banditry, let there be an end to bloodshed." At this point, the emperor offered a form of amnesty to rebels still at large who did not "create further obstructions . . . We desire peace . . . peace is justice, justice peace; the two are complementary."[9] Finally, the emperor thanked loyalists in the armed forces, his other supporters, and "Almighty God who elected Us to lead Our people."[10]

The next day, 19 December, the government propaganda effort opened with a press conference held by Major Assefa Lemma, now the acting minister of information. He handed out a special issue of the *Ethiopian Herald,* the first to appear since 14 December, and announced the following very low casualty figures: for the army, 29 killed and 43 wounded; bodyguard, 174 dead and 300 hurt; and 121 civilian dead and 442 injured. In response to questions, Major Assefa insisted that there had been "absolutely no trouble" outside of the capital and that all provinces had remained loyal to the emperor; that Gen. Mulugeta Bulli had died ignorant of his appointment as chief of staff of the armed forces; that Ras Imru had never agreed to serve as prime minister; and that the emperor had received him shortly after arrival. The major announced that a 7 PM to 6 AM curfew remained in effect, that domestic and international telegraph and telephone services had been restored, that urban utilities were again functioning, and that Ethiopian Airlines had resumed its normal services. He reported that survivors of the palace killings were Brig. Gen. Makonnan Deneke, vice minister of the imperial court; Haji Farer, vice minister of the interior; and Ademu

9. "Amnesty Offered to Ethiopian Rebels," *New York Times,* 19 Dec. 1960.
10. "His Imperial Majesty Pays Tribute to Heroic Ground and Air Forces, Police and People," *The Ethiopian Herald,* 19 Dec. 1960.

Tessema, assistant minister of public works and communications, each badly wounded but expected to recover. Ras Andargatchew Masai, minister of the interior, and Senator Dej. Bezabe Silleshi had escaped unharmed by feigning death.[11]

In a separate press release, the government defined the assassinations as "a desperate act of wanton cruelty," and characterized the dead "as brave men, true to the last to their Emperor and their nation, in fulfillment of the solemn oath which they had sworn before God to render undying loyalty to His Imperial Majesty and the Empire of Ethiopia." First among the victims was the septuagenarian Ras Seyoum, governor of Tigre, "a man of great dignity, holding a high position among Ethiopian nobility. Does youth survive and prosper only through the death of their fathers?" Driving the point home, the government asked: "Is the flower of Ethiopia's progress to bloom only if watered by the blood of those who have devoted a long lifetime to the development of their country?" Next cited was Ras Abebe Aregai, minister of national defense, "the greatest of the patriot leaders . . . a man known for his qualities of leadership . . . for his sagacity and wisdom . . . A great figure is lost to the Ethiopian scene, and the Empire of Ethiopia is poorer for this passing." Then came Makonnan Habte Wolde, a person who had devoted his life to "tireless and devoted service of his Emperor and his country [during the exile] he laboured ceaselessly for the restoration of his Emperor and his nation. In his death, Ethiopia bids farewell to one of the greatest of its civil servants."

Senator Blatta Ayale Gebre, at his demise already mortally ill, "had served faithfully and well as a member of His Imperial Majesty's Government [and had] devoted himself to the cause of the Ethiopian people." This laconic citation was followed by a longer obituary for Major Gen. Mulugeta Bulli, minister of national community development and former chief of staff of the armed forces. Saying little about his career, the piece stressed that the officer had neither known about nor accepted the rebel appointment as chief of staff. "To what lengths did the traitors carry out their deceit!" They announced his "defection . . . to persuade Ethiopians that there was substance to their plot and that it had the support of a man admired and respected by the Ethiopian people." As for Likemakwas Tadesse Negash, minister of state in the Ministry of Justice,

11. Wagner to Secretary of State, Addis Ababa, 20 Dec. 1960, despatch 184, SD 775.00/12-2060.

his traditional role was to impersonate the emperor in battle, to divert "the blows of the enemy directed against His Imperial Majesty. He received such a blow and has died of it." Eulogizing Afanegus Ishete Geda, vice minister of the interior, the press release characterized him as "an able administrator and a tireless civil servant [who] had demonstrated qualities of energy, determination and intelligence." Blatta Dawit Ogbagzy, minister of state in the Ministry of Foreign Affairs, was defined as "an honest, able man, who served selflessly in the post entrusted . . . to his care [he] was liked and respected by all, no less for his great personal charm than for his manifest dedication to the advancement of Ethiopia."

Both Amde Mikael Dessalegne, vice minister of information, and Gabrewold Ingedaworq, minister of state in the Ministry of the Pen, were depicted as "competent and able" men who "had worked to further not their own interests or ends but the cause of the people of Ethiopia . . . each leaves a gap which will be difficult to fill." The rebels also murdered Abba Hanna Jimma, who had no political position but was "a priest and church man, a man of God [who] had devoted himself unstintingly to the spiritual advancement of the Ethiopian people and to the moral well-being of the leaders for whom he laid down his life." Then came Senator Dejatch Lelibelou Gebre, a man who had gained fame "as a great patriot fighter . . . in the glorious days of the liberation . . . a man who time and again demonstrated his willingness to shed his blood on behalf of the freedom and independence of the Ethiopian people." Finally Lemma Wolde Gabriel, vice minister of finance; and Kebrete Astakkie, assistant minister of the interior, were mentioned "as industrious and efficient civil servants."[12]

In the face of such losses, Ambassador Richards was busily recommending a package of support for Haile Sellassie's Ethiopia. He urged that United States assistance activities be speeded up wherever possible, "in particular DLF [Development Loan Fund] actions planned for [the] December board meeting. In addition [to] EAL and airport loans, [I] urge early approval [of the] INDEVCO [International Development Corporation] loan for sawmill equipment." He reasoned that formal announcement of the various loans and programs "would evidence faith in [the] future of Ethiopia at [a] time when such evidence [is] needed and [will be] appreciated by

12. Government Press Release of 19 Dec. 1960, in ibid.

[the] IEG and thereby pay exceptional psychological dividends."[13]
The obvious support led to strong Egyptian criticism of "US action
in blocking social revolution,"[14] a policy which the State Department confirmed by instructing Richards to dispel "any possible
doubts [about] our attitude which may enter HIM'S head."[15] One
can only wonder what strange anxieties afflicted Washington, since
the emperor and everybody else knew where the White House stood
in relation to the Imperial Palace.[16] Indeed, Washington's stance
strengthened Haile Sellassie's resolve to maintain the status quo.

On 20 December, the emperor held a news conference, and announced that he would continue implementing pre-crisis policies.[17]
He stressed that the revolt was the work of a "very small group [of]
bodyguard officers and minor civil servants" and that the "principal
conspirators [were] all closely associated, either by family ties or by
background. They constitute [a] small isolated group." The monarch asserted that many had participated because they were early
duped into believing that they were fighting for the crown; they
continued in error even after learning the truth because they believed that they were mortally implicated in treason. Haile Sellassie
announced a thorough investigation to separate the innocent from
the guilty, the "real plotters from those who became stupidly involved," and advertised mercy for those "who, caught in a web of
circumstances beyond their control or comprehension, acted fool-
ishly or stupidly, but not out of ill-will or convictions." The true
culprits, however, "would be tried and punished according to [the]
constitution and [the] law."

Assuming no outside subversion, the "force which motivated [the
conspirators] was clearly personal ambition and lust for power. [It
is] easy to cover one's real intentions with high sounding phrases,
but their actions betrayed them." As for the rebels' eleven-point
agenda, the sovereign argued that it was "only a copy of existing
programs" and therefore proclaimed that recent events

13. Richards to Secretary of State, Addis Ababa, 20 Dec. 1960, cable 571, SD
775.00/12-2060.
14. Richards to Secretary of State, Addis Ababa, 20 Dec. 1960, cable 572, SD
775.00/12-2060.
15. Herter to Richards, Washington, 20 Dec. 1960, SD 775.11/12-2060.
16. John Franklin Campbell, "Background to the Eritrean Conflict," *African
Report* 16 (1971):22.
17. Jay Walz, "The 'Conquering Lion' Still Reigns," *New York Times [Sunday]
Magazine* (15 Jan. 1961):9.

would not cause the slightest deviation from [the] path of progress he [had] initiated for his country. [He was] convinced [that the] programs he [had] initiated [were] those best calculated [to] secure achievement and progress . . . and [he was] determined [to] pursue them with all [the] vigor and energy at his disposal. There [would] be no change in [the] system of government or [the] government's programs.[18]

The *Times* correspondent warned, however, that reforms must come soon, "if another *coup* is not to follow, and next time perhaps to succeed." Land reform headed his list: "there is no security of tenure anywhere in the country and most of the land is concentrated in the hands of large, often absentee, landlords." Administrative change was next in precedence and required "a reduction of the Emperor's personal responsibility and the encouragement of Ministerial authority." In each ministry, especially justice, finance, and interior, "specific reforms are needed in abundance to drag Ethiopia into the twentieth century." The reporter foresaw a danger, however, in weakening the monarch's hold over the central government: national identity had historically been imposed through loyalty to the person of a single ruler, and diminution of the role of the sovereign "may encourage the Eritreans and Somalis to revolt." Still, the "country must make the transition to the nation-state in which loyalty to kings becomes at best a symbol of loyalty to country." Finally, the correspondent suggested that the abortive coup had signalled "that a new concept of nationhood has arrived physically upon the Ethiopian scene and will not be forgotten. . . . If the old regime cannot accept it and adjust to it, a new regime will force its way in."[19]

Meanwhile, however, the government was pursuing the business of reaction, hunting down the attempted coup's minor and major figures. By 23 December, the Addis Ababa area had become much quieter, and firing had diminished considerably as guardsmen surrendered in the city's suburbs and exurbs. Many had been killed, and others, among them Col. Workneh, chose suicide rather than to experience the emperor's justice; his body, however, suffered the indignity of being strung up on a hastily erected gibbet. Loyalist forces relentlessly hunted down the brothers Neway, whose stars were eclipsed by an earthly king on Christmas Eve. The two men

18. Official Resume of the Emperor's Press Conference in Richards to Secretary of State, Addis Ababa, 21 Dec. 1960, SD 775.00/12-2160.
19. "Transition Period Ahead for Ethiopia," *Times* (London), 22 Dec. 1960.

were surrounded in their refuge near Nazareth, some seventy kilometers southeast of Addis Ababa. After a shoot-out, Germame was dead, and Mengistu wounded in the face but alive to face his calvary. On 26 December, Ambassador Richards could report that Addis Ababa was "calm" and that "all principal rebels [had been] killed or captured."[20]

Richards hoped that the emperor now would get on with the business of improving government and ameliorating social wrongs. By the new year, however, he was becoming uneasy about Haile Sellassie's inertia and apparent inability to act.[21] The delay in naming a new government was resulting in growing uncertainty, the paralysis of normal government functions, and a spate of unusually disturbing gossip, leading to growing anxieties among the people. One story had the army threatening to "take action" unless personnel were granted the pay raise promised by the rebels; another rumor absurdly placed Gen. Merid in danger of arrest on charges that he was involved in the coup, and the same was said of Brig. Gen. Aman Andom. Finally, it was current that senior civil servants had refused to serve in the new government unless Haile Sellassie declared a constitutional monarchy. Richards believed that the emperor must assert himself and quickly undertake constructive programs having popular appeal, or discontent would transmogrify into violence. At the least, Haile Sellassie had to shake himself free of melancholia, self-pity, and self-doubt.[22]

By 6 January, when Richards was received in audience, it appeared that the emperor's spirits had revived, and he now "seemed composed, in good health and more vigorous." In response to the ambassador's expressed hope that Ethiopia would "move forward promptly with [a] new . . . vigorous [and] forward-looking government," Haile Sellassie described himself as still shocked by the

20. Richards to Secretary of State, Addis Ababa, 23 and 26 Dec. 1960, SD 775.00/12-2360 and 2660. In the coup's final irony, Germame, before committing suicide, allegedly shot Mengistu in the head, but the bullet passed through the face and jaw without causing a mortal wound. Personal communication, Richard Greenfield, Oxford, 15 June 1978.

21. At another crucial moment in his life, immediately after the Ethiopian defeat at Maichew in April 1936, Haile Sellassie suffered a breakdown; he withdrew from reality and entered the mystical world of religion and faith. See Col. Th. Konovaloff, "Notes on the Battle of Mai Chio, March 31 1936," n.p., n.d., in Report by Major Taylor to charge, Addis Ababa, 22 June 1936, F.O. 371/20167. Except for the deletion of all references to poison gas, the same material appeared in Col. Th. Konovaloff, *Con le Armate del Negus, Un Bianco Fra i Neri* (Bologna, 1938).

22. Richards to Secretary of State, Addis Ababa, 4 Jan. 1961, SD 775.00/1-461.

murder of "so many of his friends and officials [upon] whom he had long relied." Nonetheless, he had already survived many trying times, "specifically mentioning previous attempted revolts and [the] Italian occupation. He had overcome these and was determined [to] overcome [the] present crisis." But to prevail would take time "because of [the] paucity [of] qualified men." The emperor also asserted that he must continue lengthy security interrogations "to be sure of [the] men he wished to appoint to high position." However, he realized "[the] urgency [of the situation] and was proceeding accordingly."

Haile Sellassie declared himself pleased by Washington's decision to facilitate various programs "as evidence [of] business-as-usual and had given instructions [to] move forward [as] fast as feasible on various projects." In this context, the ruler said "it was his wish" to use local currency proceeds of a $1.5 million grant to begin work on the new Hilton hotel. Richards advised Washington to "place no roadblocks in [the] way [of] this project. To do so would nullify any favorable psychological and political impact [of] this grant and thus vitiate its purpose." Then Haile Sellassie expressed his pleasure over receipt of the George Washington Carver Memorial Award, stating that such recognition "and [the] resulting favorable publicity (which he clearly encouraged), came at [a] most happy time [as] far as he was concerned." Finally, the emperor commented at some length on news stories about the attempted coup. "On [the] whole he thought [that the] world press had handled [the] matter well. He never objected to honest factual criticism and was the first to recognize [the] need for reform." He did, however, regret *Time*'s and *Newsweek*'s sensationalism and inaccuracy," devices he characterized "as [a] cheap appeal to increase sales . . . regrettable [since] it handicapped those trying [to] do good and [the two magazines] misled [an] uninformed public."[23] Richards' recapitulation of the interview and his facile recommendations to Washington reveal the diplomat's lack of vision, a failing matched by the monarch a few days later, when he tried to entice the apparently disaffected young educated elite into active support.

On 9 January, the *Voice of Ethiopia* featured Haile Sellassie's Christmas address as "A clarion call to the youth of the land to

23. Richards to Secretary of State, Addis Ababa, 6 Jan. 1961, SD 775.00/1-661. For an analysis of the emperor's early appreciation of propaganda and the manipulation of media, see my "Ts'hai Negus," in *L'Ethiopie moderne/ Modern Ethiopia*.

dedicate themselves to the colossal task of advancing Ethiopia along the road to education and technical development, and to leave aside impatience and immaturity. . . ." In fact, the speech was a clear but shrill reiteration of past achievements and already established priorities and goals, uttered as though the attempted coup had not occurred. Haile Sellassie opened by avowing "that ever since We became leader of Our nation until the present time, We have never ceased to labour with all Our efforts for the welfare and prosperity of Our beloved and loyal people and for the growth of Our country." History, he claimed, would testify that Ethiopia, "guided by her own civilization and customs," has attained "a new era, having overcome various difficulties over the past millennium in defense of her integrity and freedom." The negus advised that "it requires time and people who can do the job for a country to develop," and that schools and education lay at the heart of growth. He volunteered that nobody could deny that during his reign, "We have devoted Our utmost efforts to ensuring that Ethiopian boys and girls grow in education." He pledged that "We shall pursue the same goal," and underlined his commitment to education by reminding Ethiopians that he had introduced modern studies long before the Italian invasion, "at a time when the fruits of education were not well comprehended in Our country, and by the vast majority of Our people." Survivors of the early educated class were currently in positions of great responsibility and power, "assisting Us in Our efforts for the growth of Our country and the welfare of Our people." After return from exile in 1941, however, he had become his own minister "to start all over again and build that which had been destroyed [by the Fascists] in the field of education."

Over the years, he had appropriated at least one-fifth of the total cumulative budget for education, opened schools far and wide, and had ensured that graduates could continue higher studies in Ethiopia or abroad; all in all, "the number of those whom We have trained . . . and who are serving the people in the various fields of the nation's life is bigger now than at any other time." Nonetheless, more technicians, managers, civil servants, and policymakers were necessary, and the emperor promised to expand education, just as he committed himself to continue improving health services.

He cited his record: "We have opened hospitals and clinics and We have established organizations for the control of malaria, tuberculosis, small-pox and other contagious diseases in the whole of

Our Empire." Although much had been accomplished, "We shall labour unceasingly till the desired goal is achieved in this field." Turning next to the economy, Haile Sellassie modestly declared that "there is no need to elaborate on the tremendous improvements in the economic and industrial field during the last few years." The emperor believed that "the basic requirements" for development, "such as various industries and factories, electricity, cement and textile factories, have been established"; he pointed to his achievements as a road-builder and proudly described the progress of Ethiopian Airlines and the recent decision to purchase jet liners. Modern communications, in his view, would tie Ethiopia more firmly to Africa and the world.

Referring to international relations, Haile Sellassie stressed his commitment to collective security and proudly recapitulated that he had brought Ethiopia into the League of Nations and that the country therefore had been a founding member of the United Nations and a participant in the Paris Peace Conferences; she also had taken part in the Bandung meetings and the Accra Conference of Independent African nations, and thus could no longer be considered isolated from either the world or the African continent. The emperor therefore could explain his trips abroad as representational, to establish relations with various countries and to introduce "the people and the history of Ethiopia to them." All told, his policies had retained Ethiopia's independence, and had "won back her territories, [and] her ports and outlets which [had been] taken from her." It was *he* who finally had broken Ethiopia's historic confinement.

While he valued education above all, his accomplishments had taught him also to treasure "age and experience." He had learned that haste only led to the confusion, degradation, and disloyalty so characteristic of the recent coup. This senseless event had retarded development and shed blood needlessly, though he did not wish to dwell upon these facts, nor on the events of the rebellion. Instead, he admonished his subjects to return to their daily activities with a renewed sense of mission and with forgiveness in their hearts for those who had acted so malevolently against king and country. For his part, Haile Sellassie swore "to serve Our people and Our country in accordance with the projects which We have initiated." He declared his belief "that we have done Our best to assist Our people in promoting their welfare, in freeing them from subjection and in making them the owners of their possessions and properties."[24] Broadly speaking, the emperor proclaimed his devotion to policies originally innovated in the less complicated times before World War II, then interrupted by the brief Italian occupation, and undertaken again in 1941.[25]

He confirmed his fixation on the past by naming a new government that was completely reminiscent of the precoup political order. Beginning on 6 February 1961, the emperor made fifty-eight appointments, transfers, and promotions, including those of seven new cabinet ministers and four high military leaders. Although a number of able young officials received recognition, one observer reported that "the top positions of power remain almost entirely in the hands of members of aristocratic families and high military officers, whose appointments stem from their personal loyalty to the emperor." The nominees could be seen to reflect continuity of political tradition, "and they will do little to quell the discontent among the young educated class in Addis Ababa whose frustration at the inefficiency of the government continues to grow." The emperor appeared to have given no recognition to the forces which had shaped and inspired the recent crisis. Moreover, the appointments clearly demonstrated that "the emperor is retaining his absolute control of the government." By mid-March, Haile Sellassie had not named a prime minister, underscoring the fact that cabinet and other officials were his personal appointees, and "quite obviously directly responsible to him." Moreover, there was not the slightest sign that the negus was willing to permit ministers enough authority to implement programs "without constant recourse to him for approval." It was clear to one and all that, like the Bourbon kings, Haile Sellassie had neither forgotten anything, nor learned anything new.[26] To clarify this point, it is necessary to detail the emperor's appointments and changes.

Haile Sellassie first honored the four leading military figures who countered the coup. Major Gen. Merid Mengesha, related by marriage to the imperial family, was elevated to lieutenant general and

24. "A Clarion Call to the Youth of the Land . . ." *Voice of Ethiopia*, 9 (Jan. 1961).

25. For a discussion of the unforeseen effects of these early policies, see my "Infrastructure of the Italo-Ethiopian Crisis," in *Proceedings of the Fifth International Conference on Ethiopian Studies*.

26. Holmes memo on changes in the Ethiopian Government, Addis Ababa, 14 March 1961, SD 775.02/3-1461.

named minister of defense, replacing Ras Abebe Aregai. Major Gen. Kebede Gebre was also promoted to lieutenant general and appointed chief of staff in Merid's stead. Brig. Gen. Issayas Gebre Sellassie, former special chief of staff in the emperor's private cabinet, became major general and commander of the ground forces, Kebede's old post. Finally, Brig. Gen. Assefa Ayene was made major general and commander of the air force, in lieu of Brig. Gen. K. Lindahl, a Swedish national who would return home. In subsequent appointment lists, Col. Debebe Haile Mariam, former senior aide-de-camp to the emperor, was promoted to brigadier general and nominated commander of the bodyguard; his replacement was Col. Assefa Demissie, former military governor of the Addis Ababa district.

Two other military men were prominent cabinet appointees. Brig. Gen. Abiye Abebe was elevated to the rank of lieutenant general and designated minister of the interior, while retaining, for the time being, his post as the emperor's personal representative in Eritrea. The other soldier in the cabinet was Col. Tamrat Yigezu, who was named minister of community development. He had previously been deputy governor general of Kaffa, and, immediately upon the emperor's return, he had been called to Addis Ababa to chair a committee investigating those suspected of complicity in the uprising.

Other establishment appointees came from the aristocracy. Balambaras Mahteme-Sellassie Wolde-Maskal, a bookish man, became minister of public works; Lij Michael Imru, son of the ras, became minister of foreign affairs for a short time; and Dej. Zewdie Gebre Sellassie, a great-great grandson of Yohannis IV (r. 1872–1889) and the crown prince's stepson, was named minister of justice. Other nominees were just as safe: Haddis Alemayehu, lately minister of state for foreign affairs, was placed in charge of the Ministry of Education, acting for the emperor, who retained the portfolio. Emanual Abraham was designated minister of posts, telephones, and telegraphs. He had been chief of political affairs in the emperor's private cabinet and ambassador to London, among other jobs. Dropped from the cabinet was Ras Andargatchew Massai, who had been the powerful and allegedly corrupt minister of the interior. He was named governor of Sidamo, a serious demotion, which he reportedly suffered because of "the discovery of certain financial irregularities [and] suspicion in some quarters of a possibly sympathetic attitude towards the rebels during the early hours of the coup." Also leaving the cabinet, was Dej. (later Ras) Mangasha Seyoum, the minister of public works, who was appointed governor general of Tigre, to replace his father, Ras Seyoum Mengasha, one of the palace casualties. Also permitted the additional title of *leul* or "highness," Dej. Mangasha was doubtlessly relieved to be able to retain control over Tigre for Emperor Yohannis's descendents. Other provincial appointees were Dej. Amha Aberra, former ambassador to Yugoslavia, as governor general of Begemdir and Semien; and Dej. Kifle Dadi, to be deputy governor general of Kaffa.

Other prominent aristocrats received appointments or promotions: Dej. Asrate Kassa (later ras), who played such an important role in rallying loyalist forces, was elevated to the presidency of the Senate; Blatta Tirfie Shoumye, a relative unknown, was made vice-president. Dej. Asfaha Mikail, the chief executive of Eritrea, was given the title, *bitwodded,* or "beloved." Fit. Workneh Wolde Amanuel, former vice-minister of Addis Ababa, was made vice-minister of the Imperial Court. Ras Mesfin, who had held on to Shoa tightly, was promoted to lieutenant general, one of five Ethiopians holding that rank. Two other generals received recognition: the severely wounded Brig. Gen. Makonnan Deneke, former vice-minister of the Imperial Court, became minister of state for security in the Ministry of the Interior; and Brig. Gen. Diressie Dubale, former commander of the third division, was made commissioner of police. Beyond these placements, there were a number of subsidiary appointments for directors-general, assistant ministers, and vice-ministers, as well as some ambassadorial shifts, among them some educated, skilled, and younger people: Yodit Imru, daughter of the ras, became assistant minister of foreign affairs; Salah Hirut, assistant minister of public works and communications; Assefa Demissie, assistant minister of interior; Seyoum Bekele, director in the Ministry of Public Health; Kifle Wodajo, assistant to the resident representative to the United Nations; and Admassu Mehret, director general in the Ministry of Agriculture.[27]

The message of the various appointments was retention of the status quo. The emperor had placed aristocrats, proved partisans, and political hacks in positions of ultimate authority, even if on some lower levels there were scattered excellent choices. The pat-

---

27. Enclosures 1–5 in ibid.

tern was reminiscent of the way Haile Sellassie had ordered government in prewar Ethiopia, when educated individuals returned from
schools abroad ready to work for the nation. He had placed them
in subordinate executive positions, as if he feared their subversion,
while consistently selecting safe and old-fashioned men for policy
positions.[28] Such a juxtaposition did little for government
efficiency—even if it made fine political sense for an autocratic
politician—and led to the chronic frustrations which, in part, un-
derlaid the abortive 1960 coup and the later crisis of 1974. Since the
emperor invariably saw everything in terms of *his* political survival,
his field of maneuver, and *his* governmental security, "he managed
to equate Ethiopia's needs with his own political requirements."[29]
One can therefore easily agree with Edward Holmes's assessment at
that time: "Whatever words the Emperor may see fit to pronounce,
the unchanged character of the regime and of its personnel has
clearly been demonstrated by appointments made thus far."[30]

Meanwhile, pressures were mounting in Addis Ababa. On 10
February, the government opened its case against Mengistu Neway,
in a trial that attracted international attention. The hearings continued off and on for about six weeks, with the main portion after
27 February. It was obvious to all that Mengistu would be con-
victed, even if an observer sent by the International Commission of
Jurists was reasonably impressed by the proceedings he witnessed.
He concluded that:

> a real effort had been made to conduct the trial as fairly as possible and
> this had been achieved to the extent possible in a country with an
> autocratic government, and in the absence of an independent judiciary
> and a strong and well-organized bar.[31]

As expected, on 28 March, the three judges of the High Court of
Addis Ababa unanimously rendered a guilty verdict and condemned

28. The emperor wrote that for development to succeed, "it is necessary to
accustom [the people], through education, to abandon habits by which they have for
long been living, to make them accept new ways—yet not by hasty or cruel methods,
but by patience and study, gradually and over a prolonged period." See Haile
Sellassie I, *My Life and Ethiopia's Progress,* ed. and annot. Edward Ullendorff
(Oxford, 1976), p. 5.
29. On this point, I definitely agree with Patrick Gilkes, *The Dying Lion* (London,
1975), p. 257.
30. Holmes Memo., Addis Ababa, 14 March 1961, SD 775.02/3-1461.
31. Observer, "The Rebellion Trials in Ethiopia," *Bulletin of the International
Commission of Jurists* (April 1963):32.

Mengistu to be hung in a public place, a sentence executed in the early morning of 30 March 1961.[32]

The atmosphere in the capital intensified when army rankers moved to obtain the pay raises which Gen. Merid had promised to match a rebel ploy. The emperor did announce a relatively small increase for all ranks up to colonel, to be effective on 10 March, but the men remained generally dissatisfied. During the week of 20 March, the situation came to a head; by then, at least one vitriolic handbill had appeared, and there had been a mass meeting in Addis Ababa where senior officers, including several generals, had failed to convince the troops that their demands were excessive in national terms. Apprehension grew when it was learned that the soldiers had marched to the palace and presented the emperor with a forty-eight-hour ultimatum. By 22 March, it was evident that Haile Sellassie would have to defer to the enlisted men, and the press began to condition the public for the imperial concession. That afternoon, Haile Sellassie broadcast to the nation that soldiers would receive an additional sixteen Ethiopian dollars per month, with funds supposedly coming from salary cuts to be administered to civil servants.[33] It was the first bold demonstration of the power that unity of purpose brought to the armed forces.[34]

Thus, the institution of the monarchy had been considerably weakened by the attempted coup and Haile Sellassie's concession to the military. By using the soldiers as his basic prop, and following a line of traditional political orthodoxy, he destroyed his ability to reconcile competing interests. No longer could he act as Ethiopia's honest broker, and his policies had alienated the educated bureaucratic elite, which could not, therefore, be relied upon to neutralize or balance the power of others. Moreover, the students, as a group, became so frustrated with the status quo that they moved toward civil insurrection to attain their ends, instead of using the good offices of the emperor. Unable, therefore, to act as the balancer of power, the emperor was increasingly driven to depend upon the army for power, and on the aristocrats and landlords for adminis-

32. Richard Greenfield, *Ethiopia, A New Political History* (London, 1965), pp. 450-52.

33. Ibid., pp. 446-50; the emperor never managed to reduce civilian salaries.

34. The lesson was not lost on the emperor, and he contrived to keep the military off balance thereafter, until his political strategy succumbed to senility in 1973.

trative support. Thereafter, the monarch could not impose reforms
on Ethiopia's political economy for fear of losing his partisans.[35]

The U.S. government never truly understood the workings of the
Ethiopian state, but, as good liberals, Washington's men pushed for
reforms which were in complete contradiction to everything the
emperor and government represented. They overlooked the fact
that Haile Sellassie was a traditional figure and that Ethiopia was
not party to the Western liberal universe. Perversely, however, the
monarch was willing to take on a guise of modernity, to hang paper,
to replaster, to do anything that would keep the addictive American
aid coming without making the fundamental changes Ethiopia
needed. Since the U.S. State Department was neither willing to call
attention to the emperor's "new clothes" nor completely to reoutfit
Ethiopia with a Rostowian wardrobe, U.S. policy towards Addis
Ababa remained essentially unprincipled, even amoral, in its pragmatic opportunism. Survival of an important American facility was
the priority.

35. Thomas E. Dow Jr., and Peter Schwab, "Imperial Leadership in Contemporary Ethiopia," *Genève-Afrique,* 12 (1973):58-59.

7. Prognosis, 1961 and Thereafter

Washington had neither the moral will nor the practical need to pressure the Ethiopian government into becoming a constitutional monarchy. The State Department's basic concern remained geopolitics, an overriding interest reflected in a revised National Security Council statement on "U.S. Policy in the Horn of Africa," issued only two weeks after the emperor's return to Addis Ababa. The NSC expressed anxieties about the irredentism of the Somali government, independent since 1 July 1960, but within the context of policies which sought to prevent Ethiopia "from any kind of connection, relationship, [and] dependency on the Sino-Soviet bloc." Again showing its fascination with the East-West struggle, the NSC directed the embassy to influence Haile Sellassie not only to respond "effectively to 'modernist' aspirations and pressures," but also "effectively to counter the subversive efforts of the Communists." Above all, the White House sought in Ethiopia an "orderly political, economic, and social evolution" that would contain revolutionary pressures in the Horn.[1]

One of the emperor's American advisers, Donald E. Paradis, believed that his employer could foster orderly change by transforming the way Ethiopia was governed. Immediately after the coup, Paradis sent to Haile Sellassie a memo which argued that the empire was now too modern and therefore too complex for one man to govern. Yet, the emperor was called upon to determine even small matters, when Ethiopia's development necessitated the dispersal of decision making. Paradis exhorted his employer to devolve authority and responsibility and to permit ministers to originate and

1. National Security Council, "U.S. Policy in the Horn of Africa," NSC 6028 (30 Dec. 1960), approved without change on 18 Jan. 1961.

execute programs. Like so many experts before and after his time, Paradis misunderstood that the emperor had built his politics on precisely the opposite bases: no power and sanction for the ministers, only jurisdictions. Haile Sellassie alone established all priorities and made all decisions, not only as government coordinator but also as its essential center.

Nevertheless, Paradis assumed that the emperor would do the impossible and delegate power, after which he foresaw that "all else—land reform, modernization of the judiciary, an effective planning and development program—all this and more can follow." He admitted no need to alter the existing structure of government, to amend the administration, or to pass new laws. He warned, however: "The change must come from within. And unless power is delegated and willingness to accept and exercise it exists, even major changes in the constitutional framework would be meaningless." Blaming the symptoms and not the cause for ministerial irresolution was hardly courageous, yet, to be fair to Paradis, he could not point out that the monarch himself was the fault. Instead, he could only threaten "disaster and catastrophe" if reform were not undertaken, and the emperor was an old hand at coping successfully with those old saws.

He probably listened but could not comprehend Paradis's warning that unless Ethiopia changed fundamentally, the educated classes inevitably would turn to revolution "against a system which has created obstacles and frustrations at every turn, which has inhibited and prevented progress." The adviser conjured a new insurrection with consequences "even more horrible" than the recent rebellion. There would be chaos, bloodshed, mayhem, and the emperor's achievements and name would be classified with Gog and Magog: "The forces of history are in motion, and while they may be halted temporarily, they can never be repulsed permanently. We must either move with them or be overwhelmed by them."

Modernity required the monarch to refrain from direct intervention in governmental operations, "even when they are going badly," and to make the imperial will felt through the intermediary of the prime minister. Only when the latter could not solve specific problems should the sovereign interject himself in administration; indeed, Paradis even suggested abolition of the custom of waiting on the emperor daily at the palace. Once more reflecting confusion about cause and effect, the American saw the tradition as a ministerial device for shirking responsibility, for forcing the emperor to make decisions, and for prolonged absences from offices crammed with work and responsibility. Paradis also considered that ministers should operate within the limits of their budgets and refrain from running to the emperor for extraordinary allocations, which would have been unnecessary had there been better planning and foresight. Here the adviser again revealed his ignorance (or total knowledge) of government in Addis Ababa: he failed to appreciate (or clearly understood) that abrogation of supplemental allowances would reduce the emperor's political maneuverability. All in all, the American suggested nothing less than a transition of authority and power.[2]

G. Mennen Williams, ex-governor of Michigan and newly appointed assistant secretary of state for Africa, quickly arrived at the same conclusions when he visited Ethiopia in late February 1961. He was struck by the emperor's inertia, the apparent paralysis of government, obvious unrest, and continuing support for the aims of the coup as revealed by widely circulated handbills. From their tone and style, these documents appeared to have been written by members of the intelligentsia, and they displayed "an undertone of irritation at popular apathy and the lack of popular support for the coup which was so apparent during its progress." The sheets were distributed at night from moving vehicles, and stacks of them were placed near schools, hospitals, and other public buildings.[3]

One broadside was addressed to "Dear Ethiopian Fathers, Mothers, Brothers, Sisters, and Children," and beseeched them to "Rise! Rise! Rise! Raise your arms." It advised that those who fought for "freedom and rights" have not all been killed: "soon your children will rise determined to free you from a 3000-year-old slavery, oppression, illiteracy, and misrule." A second handbill asked Ethiopians "to rise up in arms . . . in unity and get rid of the man whom you call an Emperor, but who actually is a small cock and magician who has no humanity within him." The strong language of a third gave the abortive coup "an honored place in Ethiopian history . . . remembered forever." If Mengistu and Germame had succeeded, "the Ethiopian people would have been freed from the

2. Paradis memo for His Imperial Majesty, Addis Ababa, 16 Jan. 1961, in Richards to Secretary of State, Addis Ababa, 18 Jan. 1961, SD 775.00/1-1861; Memo for His Imperial Majesty, Addis Ababa, 18 Jan. 1961, in Richards to Secretary of State, Addis Ababa, 23 Jan. 1961, SD 775.00/1-2361.

3. Holmes to Secretary of State, Addis Ababa, 31 Jan. 1961, SD 775.00/1-3161.

chains of poverty, ignorance, slavery, and an artificial life." Even though the plot failed, "we should not despair for even one minute for this was the first attempt and not the last chance." The anonymous author believed that a torch had been lit in Ethiopia, to be passed along "until such a time as the desired goal is achieved. Our spirit must burn with ambition!" The sheet extolled the rebel leaders as men who had selflessly "risked their honor and wealth for our sake." Someday monuments would be raised in their honor, whereas "the glittering and decorated statues of our dictator ruler will . . . fall and be smashed on the ground."[4]

Williams agreed that the imperial regime would fall if Haile Sellassie kept educated Ethiopians out of power, particularly since the coup had taught progressives that others shared their thoughts about reform. They could now unite to expose imperial modernity as a facade for feudalism, to free themselves from the "dead hand of the past," and to obtain "a voice in government commensurate with their brains and education." The assistant secretary believed that the emperor could co-opt the educated elite and save the monarchy if he moved "fast and courageously to delegate authority to his ministers, to permit parliament reasonable latitude, to crack down on corruption in high places, and . . . to spread wealth more widely." He was not optimistic, however, because he judged the emperor too old to change and considered that any or all of the monarch's options "would involve undercutting . . . family . . . friends, and . . . supporters."[5] The accuracy of Williams' assessment was revealed in the emperor's speech to ministers and other high-ranking officials on 14 April 1961, an address the embassy represented to Washington as a victory for democracy and progress.

Having tacked his aged ship of state back against the prevailing currents and tides, the emperor decided that it was time to varnish the vessel's old planks. His glossy and polished words reflected his determination not to change charts, crew, and course. He referred to his record of achievement since 1930, a string of slow and cautious successes which had avoided harming "the fabric of the nation." During his regency, from 1916 to 1930, he had established modern, centralized administration, and, in 1931, as emperor, he had introduced the nation's first modern constitution. After the

4. Enclosures 1–3 in ibid. As of December 1981, the emperor's statues were gone, but none had been raised commemorating the two rebels.

5. Williams to Secretary of State, Addis Ababa, 21 Feb. 1961, SD 775.00/2-2161.

Fascist occupation, he had dispersed governmental responsibility by promulgating Order No. 1 of 1943, defining ministerial duties and the "powers requisite to discharging them"; and by organizing a modern court system, "where our subjects might go to seek redress for wrongs done to them." He proudly cited the revised constitution of 1955, which permitted direct election of parliamentary representatives. He drew attention to the recent publication of modern law codes "covering all aspects of the lives of Our citizens and setting forth . . . the principles which were to guide them in their relationships with others and with the State." He discussed the genesis and implementation of the first five-year plan "in order that the growth of Ethiopia's economy [might] proceed in a planned and co-ordinated manner."

In the emperor's opinion, his accomplishments had so complicated government that it was essential to disperse decision making for "Who, today, can be an expert in all fields? Who, today, can single-handedly make all the decisions necessary to the administration of a Government's program?" Ministers, he announced, must take responsibility for their ministries and their programs. The government must no longer be "overwhelmed and benumbed with details." Duties must not be shirked: "No longer shall We accept your responsibilities, when We have given the power to you." Ministers must administer in accord with the constitution and within the framework of the five-year plan. Dishonesty and incompetency would earn instant dismissal, but genuine problems could be brought to the attention of the prime minister, who, in his turn, might refer the matter "to Us." Nevertheless, Haile Sellassie advised that the ministers were ultimately responsible to the people, "and it is to them that you must answer for your stewardship." On the other hand, each minister retained the privilege of a weekly audience "to report on the progress you have made," but not "to ask or obtain from Us decisions which are rightfully yours to make."[6]

However badly the emperor's stated intentions worked out, he apparently believed in them at first. Richards talked with Haile Sellassie the day after the speech and found him "relaxed, cheerful and in [a] mood [to] reminisce rather than deal with specific problems. He looked and acted alert although he impressed me [as] showing signs of age." The negus remarked that the world was

---

6. Emperor's Speech of 14 April, in Holmes to Secretary of State, Addis Ababa, 14 April 1961, SD 775.11/4-1461.

moving ahead at an "increasingly fast speed and both governments and individuals must adapt themselves to the new tempo," exactly his reason for giving executive responsibilities to his ministers. "It was hard [to] break with tradition and habit but changes must be made and he was determined [to] carry them out." As if to underscore his resolve, and undoubtedly with tongue in cheek, the emperor responded to the ambassador's efforts to review some outstanding diplomatic issues by saying "it [was] his firm intention [that] Cabinet Ministers should handle such matters." If Richards were not successful with the relevant official, Haile Sellassie advised approaching the prime minister, and only if the latter could not handle the problems, "did he wish [to] be consulted."[7] On its face, the apparent devolution of power seemed consequential, even if it did not address the socio-economic problems plaguing Ethiopia.

Washington was, of course, fundamentally unconcerned about the country's internal situation and continued its programs in Ethiopia without attempting to force basic reforms. The decision, in the breach, to support the status quo—albeit with some progressive window dressing—harmonized with the primacy of safeguarding the U.S. position in the Red Sea, Arabia, and the eastern Mediterranean. As usual, however, embassy officials were fully aware of Ethiopia's real situation, best stated in two informed and well-written reports which amplified thoughts and ideas already expressed by various ambassadors and even by Assistant Secretary Williams.

The first was a "Politico-Economic Assessment" written by the embassy's highly competent economics officer, W. D. Fisher. He opened by complaining that central government fiscal practices hindered economic development by constricting the supply of capital. Lack of growth "contributes to [the] frustrations and political discontent that is the dominant factor in the current Ethiopian scene, with questionable implications for the future." The coup was not merely an elitist response to Ethiopia's very limited economic and social progress but also involved dissatisfaction "to a degree, among the masses." Although Fisher believed the latter to be "strongly loyal" to the emperor, they were showing "signs of awakening to the economic and social injustices prevalent in the still-feudal regime." Without developing this intriguing theme, he returned to the plight of the educated elite whose ideas and expertise were frus-

7. Richards to Secretary of State, Addis Ababa, 15 April 1961, SD 775.11/4-1561.

trated at every turn by the "ignorance and ineptitude in top levels of government." The relatively few young people in this category had now come to realize that they were merely part of a facade "behind which backwardness prevails."

The economics officer was therefore pessimistic about the achievement of fundamental change, either "with the present regime . . . [or with] one that might take its place by military take-over or other form of coup d'état or revolution." While the social motivation of new rulers might be high, they would waste important resources on more soldiers and more equipment, to safeguard Ethiopia's unity, as they defined it, "against real or imagined external threats ('Greater Somalia', 'Moslem encirclement')." After making that uncannily accurate prophecy, Fisher rehearsed the standard view that the armed forces of the Haile Sellassie regime were "in excess of real requirements," and that recently granted pay rates compounded the already excessive costs of the defense establishment and took valuable resources away from the civilian sector. Moreover, if it were not for U.S. military assistance ("to assure exclusion of the Soviet bloc from this field"), which provided virtually all outlay for equipment, the Ethiopians would be in great financial difficulty. Yet, the economics officer warned that the "operation and maintenance of the equipment provided constitutes a growing charge on the budget, further limiting resources that can be devoted in the future to economic and social development."

While the cost of upkeep was not yet an important restrictive factor, the lack of a real development program was. The current five-year scheme, "aside from avoiding unpleasant requirements such as land and tax reforms, is more a statement of aspirations than a plan, and even so has been given scant consideration by the individual operating ministries." Moreover, the criteria applied to projects were "prestige; Imperial desire, [and] foreign policy, [with] the facade concept frequently playing a greater role than sound economics." Even the modern agricultural schemes were designed for display, and were just as effective in raising standards as were the "handsome schools" so prominently placed in Addis Ababa. In reality, only 2.8 percent of the school-age population was in school, and Ethiopia spent more of its education budget on administration than any other country in Africa, with the same being true of public health. Fisher charged that "a disproportionate amount of public funds go into ostentatious buildings of various kinds in Addis Ababa and a few other cities that contribute to the facade [of Ethiopia's modernity]."

While reprehensible, this penchant for show was not so serious a hindrance to development as Ethiopia's "complicated and largely feudal system of land tenure." Reform was absolutely necessary, even if significant vested interests such as the church might be threatened. The land question was intricate for other reasons:

> Many areas of the country are virtually inaccessible with present transport. Cadastral surveys have never been made; land titles are unclear and inadequately registered; there are ancient tribal land tenure practises; the illiterate peasant population is loath to leave traditional areas for promised, more fertile lands; there is limited confidence in the central government; and law, as it is customarily applied, gives little land title or tenure security to the small peasant.

Even with a very well-intentioned government, Fisher warned that land reform would be a most difficult undertaking. A competent civil service was needed, and such an institution would not be a reality until great educational progress had occurred. Even then, there would have to be basic attitudinal changes among officials, who must be made to separate self-interest from national policy.

Despite his own implicit pessimism, the economics officer could not bring himself to recommend the discontinuance of American aid efforts in Ethiopia. From 1950 to 1960, the United States had expended fifty million dollars in grants, a like amount in military aid, and was committed to forty-three million dollars in credits from the Development Loan Fund and the Import-Export Bank, as well as to the outright grant of a similar sum for the military, over the next five years. The cessation of ongoing technical assistance programs would not only be wasteful but would also result in "serious retrogression" and "remove a constructive force for change." Furthermore, in light of the global competition between East and West, the American diplomat saw no alternative since "the vacuum created by an abrupt cessation [of U.S. aid] might well be filled by the Soviet Bloc and any drastic action on our part might jeopardize vital military communications facilities at Kagnew Station, Asmara." Still, there were great dangers inherent in proceeding with a complex aid program in Ethiopia.

Fisher rehearsed the view that the present political order would not survive much longer. "If this is true, we run the risk that our assistance programs, especially military assistance, have identified us to a disturbing degree as supporters of an archaic regime." Thus the problem was "how to protect our future position without jeopardizing our present position and our military facilities at Kagnew." This Janus-like maneuver involved "a progressive identification with the forces of change in Ethiopia" and a reduction of American visibility in Addis Ababa. He advised that Washington and the embassy make clear to Ethiopian officialdom and "to those elements that constitute informed public opinion, that we really believe in the principles and ideas involved in announced AID concepts." Such enlightenment "may require that we specifically indicate that Ethiopia should undertake social and economic reforms, and comprehensive planning," even on threat of reconsideration of policy and program.[8]

If Fisher was of two minds about the possibility of stimulating reform, Edward Holmes, the embassy's political officer, argued that Ethiopia would not change under Haile Sellassie. As for the coup, "there is little doubt that it would have introduced a vastly altered power situation in the country." Even in its failure, "it has hastened the day of radical change," notwithstanding the emperor's efforts to recreate the political *status quo ante.* The few appointments of younger people to important positions "were generally . . . window dressing." The monarch's delegation-of-authority speech was greeted by "largely justified [and] widespread cynicism." In Holmes's opinion, "nine months after the revolt the government has returned very much to what it was before December." Haile Sellassie had reinstituted "the traditional game of musical chairs whereby he undermines potential opposition and consolidates his own rule by constant shifts of personnel."

Over the longer run, however, tradition could not withstand the pressure from below, particularly among the younger educated group, whose members occupied important second-echelon positions and also were influential "by virtue of their family connections." Since, however, the educated elite were not organized and lacked a clear idea of Ethiopia's future, "for the time-being, the young educated group represents a potential rather than an immedi-

8. Fisher memo, "Politico-Economic Assessment," Addis Ababa, 18 July 1961, SD 775.00/7-1861. In August 1961, Fisher was killed in a plane crash.

ate threat to the present regime." Holmes nonetheless cleverly connected this elite to the many educated junior- and middle-grade military officers who also sought "radical changes." While it was impossible to judge the determination and cohesiveness of the soldiers, their opposition "may be of vital importance in the days to come."

Another source of antipathy was already present among separatists in Eritrea, Ogaden, and in southern Oromo areas, who collectively scorned the Amhara- and Christian-dominated central government. A more democratic regime or ruler might end their alienation and thereby win important support. The American did not foresee that a weakening of Amhara hegemony and a disruption of the tightfisted monarchy might have the opposite effect of strengthening and stimulating the various subnational movements. Yet, Holmes correctly understood that Amhara domination had evoked many liberation movements opposed to the emperor's continued rule.

For now, however, Haile Sellassie appeared quite strong, if reactionary: "He has reverted to the same techniques of divide and conquer which served him so well in the past, and has given no sign that he understands the new forces gradually changing the face of Ethiopia." The monarch, Holmes argued, was too old at sixty-nine to alter his manner of governing, but the coup had reduced his majestic charisma, and "Ethiopians of all classes now feel free to criticize [his] shortcomings . . . to an extent undreamed of before December." Many even believed in Haile Sellassie's deposition, by which "the reforms they insist are necessary" might be achieved. Since the emperor's critics included the educated, ethnic minorities, the younger military officers, students, and many middling bureaucrats, "the Embassy does not believe the present situation can go on much longer . . . a radical change will take place relatively soon."

Holmes was clearly wrong about the imminence of Haile Sellassie's political demise. The old emperor was more immanent and craftier than anyone imagined him to be. In most essentials, however, the political officer correctly analyzed the factors tending toward revolution in Ethiopia and offered the following scenario:

> Present discontent, although growing, appears uncoordinated and lacking in any effective organization. It is possible that at some point an "Ethiopian Colonel Nasser" will arise who possesses the drive, the ability, and the popular appeal to galvanize the discontent into an effective

instrument of power. Young educated Ethiopians would play a leading role in such a movement, but to have any real prospects of success it would also need support from within the Army. *At the present time, no such leader can be identified.*[9]

Thus, just a few months after the 1960 crisis, the elements which composed the creeping coup of 1974 were present. First, the army had flexed its muscles, admittedly this time in favor of Haile Sellassie, but it was an obvious fact, if not a foregone conclusion, that the military represented the political power of the future. During the inter-coup years, most observers foresaw the armed forces as the real rulers of Ethiopia, with Asfa Wossen as a figurehead.[10] U.S. Embassy officials hoped that the soldiers would be conditioned to American ways after using U.S. equipment, and after having been trained by MAAG or educated in stateside military schools.[11] As it turned out, this possibility was eroded by the student attack on Haile Sellassie, which in part concentrated on his powerful external supporter, the United States Government. For the students, the university with its many American personnel and its John F. Kennedy library came to represent the sham of democratic American liberalism allied to despotic Ethiopian feudalism,[12] a humbug whose existence they publicized far and wide.

Although the history of modern Ethiopian radicalism has only begun to be written, its collective authorship will necessarily acknowledge the students' seminal role in its development. Their support of the 1960 coup was the first manifestation of the forward position which Ethiopia's young educated were prepared to take in face of apparently increasing corruption, profiteering, and exploitation in high places. Combining patriotic idealism with bookish theories, the students unceasingly challenged the policies and personnel of the Imperial Ethiopian Government. Confrontation brought repression, jailing, even martyrdom, which substantiated

9. Holmes memo, "The Attempted Coup d'Etat—Nine Months Later," Addis Ababa, 15 August 1961, SD 775.00/1-1561; italics mine.

10. See, for instance, Marina and David Ottoway, *Ethiopia: Empire in Revolution* (New York, 1978), p. 1.

11. Ironically, some Ethiopians, including Mengistu Haile Mariam, experienced degrading racial incidents while training in the United States and came to abhore American society.

12. It became fashionable to attack U.S. involvement in Ethiopia, whenever one wanted to criticize the Addis Ababa government or its head of state. See, for example, *Challenge,* the organ of the Ethiopian Students' Organization in North America, for the years 1962–1968.

and gave notoriety to the student movement within and without the country.[13]

Ethiopians studying abroad enjoyed freedom of movement and organization, and were deeply influenced by the Marxist-Leninist thought sweeping through the world in the sixties and seventies. Many were able to study socialism in its various guises in North Africa, Europe, and Asia. They began to view the world and its problems increasingly in terms of the struggle of progressive forces against world imperialism, led by the United States. Logically, therefore, Haile Sellassie was an agent of reaction, and his supporters, the country's oligarchs, were compradors and running dogs that exploited Ethiopia for the benefit of the United States and its allies. For young Ethiopians, such a situation was appalling, since it meant the country's chronic underdevelopment.[14] In their eyes Washington was again the enemy, right behind Haile Sellassie, and student propaganda stridently connected the internal reaction of one with the international position of the other.

Their analysis was rational: the United States was less concerned with Ethiopia's political soul than with geopolitics. Though the 1960 coup had weakened the monarchy, Haile Sellassie's favor was to be courted, at least until the Asmara listening post became unnecessary in the satellite age. Nevertheless, the White House would have supported any government which agreed to the American presence. Washington's policy boiled down to an amoral—if not unreasonable—opportunism that ensured Kagnew Station's survival, and was expressed in terms of banal and jejune rationales for sustaining a regime whose inaction frustrated and disgusted most serious observers.[15]

U.S. Embassy personnel and private citizens clearly defined the wellspring of Ethiopia's problems but failed to convince their superiors to apply pressure to sponsor desirable programs and changes on the Addis Ababa government, as a matter of policy. Quite probably, the imperial government could not have responded productively, given the bases of its political support, and Washington

13. Legesse Lemma, "The Ethiopian Student Movement, 1960–1974: A Challenge to the Monarchy and Imperialism in Ethiopia," *Northeast African Studies* 1 (1979): passim.

14. Michael Ståhl, *Ethiopia: Political Contradictions in Agricultural Development* (Stockholm, 1974), pp. 75–77.

15. Tom J. Farer, *War Clouds on the Horn of Africa: A Crisis for Detente* (New York, 1976), p. 143.

remained, therefore, in the ironic position of doing nothing to impede developments that led to the social chain reaction of 1974. The abortive coup of 1960 thus had little effect upon the workings of the Ethiopian state and political economy.

The realization of the 1950s, that the country was backward, developed into the scandal of the sixties. Ethiopia's students became increasingly militant, and its bureaucratic and officer classes chafed under the weight of the Solomonic Empire's pretentions, which consumed a disproportionate amount of the poor nation's wealth.[16] The growing bourgeoisie was denied access to political power, and the masses were exploited to impoverishment. Those who directed the coup of 1960 clearly had appreciated the reactionary nature of Haile Sellassie's state, and imagined themselves as representing the people, even if they really were acting in the interests of the elites of which they were a part. Germame's pseudosocialism was no more than liberalism and reformism, but his ideas might have provided a satisfactory basis for a new and progressive government, had the coup not been so badly botched.

Although the emperor won a new lease on his reign, the crisis taught him little, and his subsequent actions, particularly the formation of a new government, revealed that he was unable to provide the direction necessary to transform Ethiopia into even a bourgeois state. Instead, he looked backward towards the glorious days of the thirties, when everything was possible and every small act an achievement. After World War II, however, the world had become a more complicated place, and the technology born of the maelstrom required a trained mind to understand and use it. Haile Sellassie's lacked the modern education to penetrate economics, public administration, and, finally, mass politics. Thus, during the last fifteen years of his reign, Haile Sellassie could not provide the leadership necessary to a country entering the modern age.[17]

Meanwhile, external events and serious domestic crises fostered increasing social strife in Ethiopia. First, the long closure of the Suez Canal after 1967 had a negative effect on the Ethiopian balance of payments and stimulated an inflation which ultimately spurred the embryonic working class, the urban bourgeoisie, and salaried military personnel in Addis Ababa and elsewhere to take direct action

16. "La Revolution en Ethiopie," *Missions . . . Messages . . !* (April 1976): 10–11.
17. Editorial, *Combat* 11 (1974):7.

against the regime. Second, the Arab-Israeli conflict added to the general economic crisis and also stimulated Islamic and separatist movements in Somali-inhabited areas and in Eritrea. The latter posed a mortal danger, since secession threatened the loss of Ethiopia's coast and Assab and Massawa, its two ports. Consequently, during the penultimate stages of Haile Sellassie's reign, Ethiopia was forced to allocate increasingly more of its resources for military efforts, at the expense of necessary civilian programs or relief.[18]

The emperor, given his supporters, could not manage serious land reform. His failure to convince parliament to vote against its own class interests opened the way for hitherto absentee owners and others, mainly of the bureaucratic and military elites, to undertake capitalistic agriculture, often with the support of foreign-financed programs. These developments were accompanied by enclosures of common pasture lands, limitations on access to water, and evictions. Even when property owners did not foreclose tenants, they raised rents to exorbitant rates in terms of money or shares. While these phenomena were not widespread, their incidence was increasing, causing still untrammeled cultivators to worry about the future. Moreover, as most southern peasants were generally beholden to Amhara overlords and to a Shoan-dominated administration, they already had experienced deep frustration in their powerlessness to confront and withstand inimical measures and policies.[19]

Thus, by 1974, there were sufficient grievances available to unite a congeries of Ethiopians. The students were obdurate in their disapproval of what they now termed Ethiopia's semifeudal, semicapitalistic state. The workers, the soldiery, and the bureaucrats were greatly distressed by runaway inflation. Peasant anxiety about land dispossession was widespread in the south, where farmers also

18. Colin Legum, *Ethiopia: The Fall of Haile Selassie's Empire* (London, 1975), p. 2.
19. For a review of the land tenure problems of the 1960s and the reforms that were proposed by the government, see John M. Cohen and Dov Weintraub, *Land and Peasants in Imperial Ethiopia: The Social Background to a Revolution* (Assen, 1975), pp. 76-104; H. C. Dunning, "Land Reform in Ethiopia: A Case Study in Non-Development," *UCLA Law Review* 2 (1970):277-81; Gene Ellis, "Land Tenancy Reform in Ethiopia: A Retrospective Analysis," *Economic Development and Cultural Change* 28 (1980):523-45. Also see Negga Belew, "The Unfolding Class Struggle in Ethiopia," *Pan African Notes* 4-5 (1975); Gadaa Melbaa, *Oromia* (Finfine, 1980):55-58.

complained about high taxation and rents.[20] There was also considerable ethnic and religious factionalism, particularly in the Ogaden and in Eritrea. Haile Sellassie, who, in 1960, was able to surmount crisis and suppress opposition, was by now eighty-two years old, appeared enfeebled, and was by all reports sliding toward senility and to the apparent end of his reign. He nonetheless lingered stubbornly in power, he refrained from naming a successor for the crown prince who had suffered a stroke, and he continued his refusal to allow his own cabinet and prime minister to exercise discretionary power. He also clung religiously to his belief that the United States would solve the nation's problems.[21] He was, of course, wrong: the changing world situation had alienated the State Department from Ethiopia, a disengagement which became perceptible after the Somali-Ethiopian hostilities of October and November 1963.

Initially, the imperial army fared badly against the Somali infiltrators, but advantages in numbers and especially in airpower won the day for Addis Ababa, which, however, was plunged into gloom by the poor performance of its soldiers. The emperor immediately sought massive U.S. infusions of matériel and a large augmentation of MAAG. Gen. Merid Mengesha, the Minister of Defense, told Ambassador William Korry that the "time had come for [America to] choose who its friends were [in] this part of the world. Either [the] U.S. would come to Ethiopia's assistance [to] save it from [its] 'Greatest threat in recent history' or Ethiopia might have to 'deal with [the] devil itself' to save [the] country." Merid informed Korry that his government had decided to recall its contingent in the Congo, since Ethiopia, he explained, came first in its hour of "great danger." The ambassador commented sourly that the projected withdrawal was a scarcely subtle attempt to "blackmail us into agreeing [to] furnish equipment requested."[22]

Already in the first throes of the Vietnam War, Washington advised Korry that it could not afford to expand its military assistance

20. Jan Valdelin, "Ethiopia 1974-7: From Anti-Feudal Revolution to Consolidation of the Bourgeois State," *Race and Class* 19 (1978):379; John M. Cohen, "Effects of Green Revolution Strategies of the Tenants and Small Scale Landowners of the Chilalo Region of Ethiopia," *Journal of Developing Areas* 9 (1975):335-58.

21. John H. Spencer, "Haile Sellassie: Leadership and Statesmanship," *Ethiopianist Notes* 2 (1978):33-36.

22. Korry to Secretary of State, Addis Ababa, 25 Nov. 1963, no decimal classification (hereafter ndc).

effort in Ethiopia; that it did not believe the country's economy could bear the internal expenses of an enlarged military program; and that the Ogaden problem could only be solved through socio-economic development and by granting autonomy to the population.[23] In reply, Korry asked the department to assess "very objectively" Ethiopia's importance to the United States in terms of Kagnew Station and the emperor's "leadership role in Africa and in the non-aligned world." The ambassador thought both were significant enough to warrant supplementary aid programs for Ethiopia,[24] and the State Department convinced the Pentagon to agree to provide increased logistical and training support for counterinsurgency warfare.[25] The Ethiopians complained that the aid was insufficient to combat the threat of a Somali army trained and supplied by the Russians.[26]

Whatever the justice of that charge, Washington had not yet shipped the Ethiopians equipment promised years before. Annual "sharp funding ceilings" had delayed deliveries by three or four years in many cases, and some major items had been postponed until "FY-1974 repeat FY-1974." Ethiopia's ceiling of $9.5 million in military aid was too low to meet the Imperial Government's demands for advanced jet planes to counter the Somali buildup in MIGs.[27] By May 1964, Addis Ababa's complaints that Washington was "not keeping [its] commitment" had become "a very serious irritant [in] US-IEG relations."[28]

By then, a U.S. Army survey team had been sent out to investigate, and its conclusions were of major importance to the subsequent development of Ethio-American relations. First, it acknowledged that the U.S. was not fulfilling its pledge of 1960 to provide support for an Ethiopian army of 40,000, "in light of delivery performance to date [and] the outlook for coming years under the current programs." Second, it found that "the communications and tracking facilities at Kagnew Station [were] of major importance, *if not actually vital*, to U.S. national security." Third, it advised that the Ethiopian failure had little to do with shortages of men or equipment, as the Addis Ababa government asserted.

23. Ball to Embassy, Washington, 15(?) Dec. 1963, ndc.
24. Korry to Secretary of State, Addis Ababa, 18 Dec. 1963, ndc.
25. Rusk to Embassy, Washington, 29 Feb. 1964, ndc.
26. Korry to Secretary of State, Addis Ababa, 30 April 1964, ndc.
27. Vance to Secretary of State, Addis Ababa, 9 May 1964 ndc.
28. Korry to Secretary of State, Addis Ababa, 21 May 1964, ndc.

It was "due, in a large part, to the lack of combat capability of the Ethiopian ground forces, traceable to training deficiencies." The Ethiopian request for heavy weapons obscured homegrown weaknesses in logistics and administration "which would exist regardless of the quality of equipment possessed." Therefore, "assuming that a thorough reexamination of Kagnew Station confirms the value attached to it," the army team recommended a new, six-year military assistance program for the fiscal years 1965 to 1970, in order to bring in more MAAG personnel to advise higher staff echelons in training, logistics, and administration and to assist "in massively retraining . . . the Ethiopian armed forces in the shortest time practicable." Beyond better training, the report recommended an additional $33.7 million through fiscal year 1970, to permit the acquisition of twelve F-5s and to bring the Ethiopian army to its promised strength of forty thousand men.[29] In other words, the team recommended against a massive infusion of equipment but rather suggested a program to improve the battle readiness of the army and the air force, the latter already considered the best small force in the Middle East.

Because of its financial problems, the United States government could not agree to the recommended program. Secretary of State Dean Rusk explained to the embassy that shortfalls throughout the entire military assistance program, an expected congressional cut, "plus unexpected demands for Congo, Vietnam, Laos, and other crisis situations," did not permit an increase in military assistance for Ethiopia, now set at $9.9 million a year. Both the Defense and State Departments were "fully aware" of the impact on Ethiopia which a diminished American military program would have, and they therefore had decided to supply three F-5s in fiscal year 1965 and to accelerate other deliveries. Rusk closed by suggesting that, "If IEG indicates willingness [to] cooperate in African collective security measures to stabilize Congo situation, to include possible re-entry IEG forces, USG would most definitely consider resultant requirements."[30] In other words, Kagnew Station was not enough; given the global situation, Washington sought Ethiopia's active participation in its geopolitical program. Korry commented bitterly that there was simply not enough money available to fulfill past and

29. USTRICOM to JCS and to Secretaries of State and Defense, n.p., 29 May 1964, ndc; italics mine.
30. Rusk to Embassy, Chief MAAG, and USCINCMEAFSA, Washington, 13 Aug. 1964, ndc.

present commitments "much less [to] give us any flexibility [to] meet sound new demands even when required politically. We simply keep digging ourselves deeper in [the] hole at [the] cost [of] our policy goals."[31]

Washington tried to keep the policy damage to a minimum, but the increase in the funding ceiling for the period of 1966 to 1971 to $13.5 million was not enough to satisfy the Ethiopian High Command because it immediately spent the additional monies on such expensive items as the F-5 jets and the HMS *Ethiopia,* a refitted seaplane tender, "depleting or deferring more urgent needs for vehicles, ammunition, and spare parts."[32] The Ethiopians, however, remained convinced that the country's biggest threat came from Somalia, which was being armed by the Russians.[33] The United States tended to believe that the Ethiopians were paranoiac about the danger and were exaggerating the force levels that the Somali army had achieved, but it was a fact that in 1966–67, bands of armed Somalis up to fifty in strength were raiding well into Bale and obtaining the cooperation of the people living there. Moreover, the threat from Eritrea was growing in proportion to the return from military schools in Iraq, Syria, and the United Arab Republic of hundreds of Eritreans who were equipped with mortars, bazookas, modern automatic rifles, even small-caliber artillery.[34] In January 1967, in order to meet Ethiopia's challenges, the minister of defense requested a new five-year program of American assistance which would completely modernize and reequip the Ethiopian army, navy, and air force.

Korry was scandalized. The plan would have cost the United States tens of millions of dollars, over and beyond the current ceiling figure, and would have added thirty million Ethiopian dollars in local support funds to the annual Ethiopian budget. At meetings with ranking officials, he pointed to the extravagance of the scheme in terms of the government's recent request that Washington help feed starving Eritreans, since Addis Ababa could not "afford to ship food from the surplus producing areas of the country because of the heavy transportation costs and could not afford to buy grain for non-reimbursable distribution." He could not understand how the

31. Korry to Secretary of State, Addis Ababa, 14 Nov. 1964, ndc.
32. Rusk to Embassy, Washington, 2(?) May 1967, ndc.
33. Memo of conversation between Gen. E. Eschenburg and HIM, 21 June 1966, in Vance to Department, Addis Ababa, 25 June 1966, ndc.
34. Korry to Secretary of State, Addis Ababa, 19 Jan. 1967, ndc.

government could seriously contemplate adding to its defense costs, when "on the basis of the most objective analysis, there was no need for such military investment." Korry rang the tocsin: "If investment were not made in the productive centers of the economy, it would simply multiply the security problems and lead to chaos and the collapse of the structure of the Empire." The major threats faced by Ethiopia were internal: "there could be no security without development. . . .Who was going to be responsible for all the unkept promises to Ethiopia when funds would not be forthcoming for schools, public health, agricultural and industrial development?" Such projects were particularly important for Eritrea, Hararghe, and Bale provinces, where social and economic programs might retard and finally block the drift toward separatism. Finally, Korry brought to the Ethiopian Government's attention the fact that the United States was fighting a costly war in Vietnam, and that it might be more appropriate for Addis Ababa to ask how it could assist Washington than to request aid at a time when President Lyndon Johnson was asking his countrymen to pay higher taxes.[35]

In a sense, Korry was raising the ante for a game that no self-respecting African power could play, and a year later, it became clear that the United States was winding down its military involvement in Ethiopia. The embassy was informed that assistance would continue "as long as US interests require but we do not have a legal commitment for indefinite support." The ambassador was instructed not to use the term "support commitment" in discussions with Ethiopian officials, and to "give no indication that we accept any obligation to replace worn out equipment for [an] indefinite period of time."[36] The embassy immediately asked if the new "policy [is] in part based on new developments reducing [the] importance [of] Kagnew," or did it have anything to do with "question [of] student riots?"[37] Rusk answered much later and ambiguously, although the meaning was without doubt: he reported that the

35. Memo of conversation between Lt. Gen. Kebede Gebre, Minister of Defense; Lt. Gen. Iyassu Mengesha, Chief of Staff, Ethiopian Armed Forces; Robert Sonhauser, Deputy Chief of Mission; Brig. Gen. E. Eschenburg, Chief MAAG; and Ambassador Korry, Addis Ababa, 18 Jan. 1967, enclosure in ibid.; and Korry to Secretary of State, Addis Ababa, 21 Jan. 1967, ndc.

36. Rusk to Embassy, Washington, 20 April 1968, ndc.

37. Hall to Secretary of State, Addis Ababa, 26 April 1968, ndc. Communications satellites increasingly took over Kagnew's functions, and one author has written that by 1972, the station was redundant. See Steven David, "Realignment in the Horn: The Soviet Advantage," *International Security* 4 (1979):89-90.

military assistance ceiling had been cut back to twelve million dollars for fiscal years 1969 and 1970, but that the reduction "should not suggest any lessening of interest or withdrawal of support for Ethiopia. There had been no change in our policy or objectives."[38] But there had been, and the import of the shift was clear: the United States would not help Ethiopia to develop an offensive military capability; it would assist Addis Ababa in counterinsurgency, but it would also urge socio-economic change to decrease internal dissidence.[39] The Agency for International Development made great efforts from the late 1960s through 1974 to sponsor economic change, but most programs failed to reach the masses. On the contrary, the reactionary nature of Ethiopia's political economy led to disaster.

The crisis attendant upon the famine of 1973–74 revealed that the Imperial Ethiopian Government was incompetent and oblivious to the obvious need of hundreds of thousands of its subjects. Addis Ababa's inaction became an international scandal which strongly aroused latent hostilities among dissidents and stimulated others, particularly in the army, to become socially conscious. As it became clear that Haile Sellassie's monarchy could not respond to domestic and international obloquy, and that the government was paralyzed because of the emperor's senility, the military intervened, at first indirectly and then openly.[40] I believe that it was during the period of growing military political involvement that Washington made ready to abandon Ethiopia: Kagnew Station was no longer at issue; Egypt was in the process of changing the geopolitics of the Middle East; U.S. public opinion would not support any adventures in the Red Sea area, either for or against Ethiopia; nor would official U.S. policies permit providing Ethiopia with an offensive capability. Moreover, given Washington's inherent distaste for radical change and its predilection for liberal democracy, there was no reason to remain involved in a country that was taking a revolutionary road. Since the United States was no longer willing to protect Ethiopia from aggression and dismemberment, the new government realized that a new savior was required. A star was perceived in the east, a

---

38. Rusk to Embassy, Washington, 17 Jan. 1969, ndc.

39. Embassy/MAAG to Secretary of State and Secretary of Defense, Addis Ababa, 16 Sept. 1969, ndc.

40. Fred Halliday and Maxine Molyneux, *The Ethiopian Revolution* (London, 1981), chapter 2.

new religion was received, and with it, totems powerful enough to shield both state and revolution. While Moscow's advent signalled the end of American primacy in the Horn of Africa, Washington continues to watch from Egypt, Somalia, and Sudan with an oversight that may be a form of foresight.

Bibliography

Books

Addis Hiwet.* *Ethiopia, From Autocracy to Revolution*. London, 1975.
———. *From Autocracy to Bourgeois Dictatorship*. London (?), 1976.
Ambrose, Stephen E. *Rise to Globalism*. rev. ed. New York, 1976.
Baram, Philip J. *The Department of State in the Middle East, 1919–1945*. Philadelphia, 1978.
Bentwich, Norman. *Ethiopia, Eritrea and Somaliland*. London, 1945.
Churchill, Winston S. *Triumph and Tragedy*. The Second World War, Vol. 6, Boston, 1953.
Clapham, Christopher. *Haile Selassié's Government*. London, 1969.
Cohen, John M., and Koehn, Peter. *Ethiopian Provincial and Municipal Government: Imperial Patterns and Post-Revolutionary Changes*. East Lansing, 1979.
Cohen, John M., and Weintraub, Dov. *Land and Peasants in Imperial Ethiopia: The Social Background to Revolution*. Assen, 1975.
de Juniac, Gontran. *Le Dernier Roi des Rois: l'Ethiopie de Hailé Séllassié*. Paris, 1979.
Drysdale, John. *The Somali Dispute*. New York, 1964.
Farer, Tom J. *War Clouds on the Horn of Africa: A Crisis for Detente*. New York, 1976.
Gilkes, Patrick. *The Dying Lion*. London, 1975.
Greenfield, Richard. *Ethiopia, A New Political History*. London, 1965.
Haile Sellassie I. *My Life and Ethiopia's Progress*. Edited and annotated by Edward Ullendorff. Oxford, 1976.
Halliday, Fred, and Molyneux, Maxine. *The Ethiopian Revolution*. London, 1981.
Hoopes, Townsend. *The Devil and John Foster Dulles*. Boston, 1973.
Howard, William E. H. *Public Administration in Ethiopia*. Groningen, 1956.

*Ethiopians use their praenomens to identify themselves, since the second appellation is their father's first name. Hence, Addis Hiwet is Mr. Addis, not Mr. Hiwet. Consequently, I shall render the names of Ethiopian authors as given and will alphabetize them by praenomen.

Huffnagel, H. F. *Agriculture in Ethiopia*. Rome, 1961.

Konovaloff, Col. Th. *Con le Armate del Negus, Un Bianco Fra i Neri*. Bologna, 1938.

Legum, Colin. *Ethiopia: The Fall of Haile Selassie's Empire*. London, 1975.

Lewis, I. M. *The Modern History of Somaliland*. New York, 1965.

Louis, W. H. *Imperialism at Bay*. Oxford, 1977.

Marcus, H. G. *The Life and Times of Menelik II: Ethiopia, 1844–1913*. Oxford, 1975.

Markakis, John, and Nega Ayele. *Class and Revolution in Ethiopia*. Nottingham, 1978.

Melbaa Gadaa. *Oromia*. Finfine, 1980.

Mitchell, Sir Philip. *African Afterthoughts*. London, 1954.

Norberg, Viveca Halldin. *Swedes in Haile Selassie's Ethiopia, 1924–1952*. Uppsala, 1977.

Ottoway, Marina and David. *Ethiopia: Empire in Revolution*. New York, 1978.

Pankhurst, E. Sylvia. *British Policy in Eritrea and Northern Ethiopia*. Essex, 1946.

Pausewang, S. *Peasants and Local Society in Ethiopia*. Bergen, 1978.

Perham, Margery. *The Government of Ethiopia*. New York, 1948.

Sabby, Othman Saleh. *The History of Eritrea*. Beirut, 1975.

Scholler, Heinrich, and Brietzke, Paul. *Ethiopia: Revolution, Law and Politics*. Munich, 1976.

Spencer, John H. *Ethiopia, the Horn of Africa, and U.S. Policy*. Cambridge, Mass., 1977.

Ståhl, Michael. *Ethiopia: Political Contradictions in Agricultural Development*. Stockholm, 1974.

Stephen, Robert. *Nasser, A Political Biography*. London, 1971.

Thorne, Christopher. *Allies of a Kind*. New York, 1978.

Touval, Saadia. *Somali Nationalism*. Cambridge, Mass., 1963.

Wilmington, Martin W. *The Middle East Supply Centre*. Albany, N.Y., 1971.

Zervos, A. *L'empire d'Ethiopie: Le Miroir de l'Ethiopie moderne*. Alexandria, 1935.

Articles

Amin, Samir. "Underdevelopment and Dependence in Black Africa, Origins and Contemporary Forms." *Journal of Modern African Studies* 10 (1972).

Assefa Bequele. "The Ethiopian Elite and Intelligentsia." *Dialogue* 1:1 (1967).

Bereket Habte Selassie. "From British Rule to Federation and Annexation." In *Behind the War in Eritrea*, edited by Basil Davidson, Lionel Cliffe, and Bereket Habte Selassie. Nottingham, 1980.

Campbell, John Franklin. "Background to the Eritrean Conflict." *Africa Report* 16:5 (1971).

Caporaso, James. "Dependence, Dependency, and Power in the Global System, A Structural and Behavioral Analysis." *International Organization* 32:1 (1978).

Clapham, Christopher. "Imperial Leadership in Ethiopia." *African Affairs* 68 (April 1969).

Cohen, John M. "Effects of Green Revolution Strategies on the Tenants and Small Scale Landowners of the Chilalo Region of Ethiopia." *Journal of Developing Areas* 9 (1975).

Comhaire, Jean. "Urban Growth in Relation to Ethiopian Development." *Cultures et développement* 1:1 (1968).

Cooper, Adi, et al. "Class, State and the World Economy: A Case Study of Ethiopia." Conference paper, Sussex University, 1975.

Coquery-Vidrovitch, Catherine. "Recherches sur une mode de Production Africain." *La Pensée*, n. 144 (1969).

———. "La Mise en Dépendance de l'Afrique noire: essai de periodisation, 1800–1970." *Cahiers d'etudes Africaines* 16 (1976).

Cumming, Sir Duncan. "The U.N. Disposal of Eritrea." *African Affairs* 52 (1953).

David, Steven. "Realignment in the Horn: The Soviet Advantage." *International Security* 4:2 (1979).

Diamond, Robert A., and Fouquet, David. "American Military Aid to Ethiopia and Eritrean Insurgency." *Africa Today* 19:1 (1972).

dos Santos, Theotonio. "The Structure of Dependence." *The American Economic Review* 60:2 (1970).

Dow, Thomas E. Jr., and Schwab, Peter, "Imperial Leadership in Contemporary Ethiopia." *Genève-Afrique* 12 (1973).

Dunning, H. C. "Land Reform in Ethiopia: A Case Study in Non-Development." *UCLA Law Review* 2 (1970).

Duri Mohammed. "Private Foreign Investment in Ethiopia." *Journal of Ethiopian Studies* 7 (1969).

Ellingson, Lloyd. "The Emergence of Political Parties in Eritrea." *Journal of African History* 18 (1977).

Ellis, Gene. "Land Tenancy Reform in Ethiopia: A Retrospective Analysis." *Economic Development and Cultural Change* 28 (1980).

Fecadu Gedamu. "Some Thoughts on the Social and Cultural Backgrounds of the Overthrow of the Ethiopian Feudal Regime." Conference paper, Conference on Feudalism, Addis Ababa University, Institute of Ethiopian Studies, 1976.

Foster-Carter, Aidan. "The Modes of Production Debate." *New Left Review*, n. 107 (Jan.–Feb. 1978).

Gamst, Frederick C. "Peasantries and Elites Without Urbanism in the Civilization of Ethiopia." *Comparative Studies in Society and History* 12 (1970).

Greenfield, Richard. "Pre-Colonial and Colonial History." In *Behind the War in Eritrea,* edited by Basil Davidson, Lionel Cliffe and Bereket Habte Selassie. Nottingham, 1980.

Hagos Gebre Yesus. "Land Reform; Plus Ça Change. . . ?" *Challenge* 5:1 (March 1965).

Harbeson, J. W. "Territorial and Development Politics in the Horn of Africa: The Afar of the Awash Valley." *African Affairs* 77 (1978).

Henock Kifle. "Ethiopian Economic Development: An Alternative." *Challenge* 9:2 (1969).

Ianni, Francis A. J. "Ethiopia: A Special Case." In *The Transformation of East Africa,* edited by Stanley Diamond and Fred G. Burke. New York, 1966.

Jandy, Edward C. "Ethiopia Today: A Review of its Changes and Problems." *The Annals of the American Academy of Political and Social Sciences,* n. 306 (1956).

Keyder, Cagler. "The Dissolution of the Asiatic Mode of Production." *Economy and Society* 5:2 (1976).

Legesse Lemma. "The Ethiopian Student Movement, 1960–1974: A Challenge to the Monarchy and Imperialism in Ethiopia." *Northeast African Studies* 1:3 (1979).

Levine, Donald. "Haile Selassie's Ethiopia—Myth or Reality." *Africa Today,* May 1961.

Magdoff, Harry. "Militarism and Imperialism." *American Economic Review* 60:2 (1970).

Marcus, H. G. "The Infrastructure of the Italo-Ethiopian Crisis: Haile Sellassie, The Solomonic Empire, and the World Economy." In *Proceedings of the Fifth International Conference on Ethiopian Studies,* part B (Chicago, 1979).

———. "Ts'hai Negus (Sun King)." In *L'Ethiopie moderne/Modern Ethiopia,* edited by J. Tubiana. Rotterdam, 1980.

Markakis, John, and Asmelesh Beyene. "Representative Institutions in Ethiopia." *Journal of Modern African Studies* 5 (1967).

Mesfin Wolde-Mariam. "The Rural-Urban Split in Ethiopia." *Dialogue* 2:1 (1968).

Negga Belew. "The Unfolding Class Struggle in Ethiopia." *Pan African Notes* 4–5 (1975).

Norberg, Viveca Halldin. "Swedes as a Pawn in Haile Selassie's Foreign Policy, 1924–1952." In *L'Ethiopie moderne/Modern Ethiopia,* edited by J. Tubiana. Rotterdam, 1980.

Papini, Italo. "L'Eritrea ha ragione di esistere." *Affrica* 2:5–6 (15 June 1947).

Pausewang, S. "Peasant Society and Development in Ethiopia." *Sociologia Ruralis* 13 (1973).

Petros Desta. "Le Secret de la Politique étrangère de Hailé Sellassié." *Remarques Africaines*, n. 281 (1967).

"The Rebellion Trials in Ethiopia." *Bulletin of the International Commission of Jurists*, April 1963.

"La Revolution en Ethiopie." *Missions . . . Messages . . .!*, April 1976.

Ricci, Lanfranco. "Organisation de l'Etat et structures sociales en Ethiopie." *Civilisations* 14 (1964).

Schwab, Peter. "Haile Selassie: Leadership in Ethiopia." *Plural Societies* 6:2 (1975).

Scott, James C. "The Analysis of Corruption in Developing Nations." *Comparative Studies in Society and History* 2 (1969).

Siemienski, Zbigniew. "Impact of the Coffee Boom on Ethiopia." *The Middle East Journal* 9 (1955).

Spencer, John H. "Haile Selassie: Triumph and Tragedy." *Orbis* 18 (Winter 1975).

———. "Haile Sellassie: Leadership and Statesmanship." *Ethiopianist Notes* 2:1 (1978).

Sylvain, P. G. "Note sur le café de'Ethiopie." *Zaïre* 9 (1955).

Terray, Emmanuel. "Long Distance Exchange and the Formation of the State: the Case of the Abron Kingdom of Gyaman." *Economy and Society* 3:3 (1974).

Valdelin, Jan. "Ethiopia 1974-7; From Anti-Feudal Revolution to the Consolidation of the Bourgeois State." *Race and Class* 19 (1978).

Watt, D. C. "The 'Decembrists': Russia 1825, Ethiopia 1960." *International Relations* 2:7 (1963).

Newspapers and Magazines (in chronological order)

Groussard, Serge. "Entretien avec Hailé Sellassié Iᵉʳ." *Le Figaro*, 25 March 1959.

[University College of Addis Ababa] *News and Views* 4 (16 Dec. 1960).

"Amnesty Offered to Ethiopian Rebels." *New York Times*, 19 Dec. 1960.

"His Imperial Majesty Pays Tribute to Heroic Ground and Air Forces, Police and People." *The Ethiopian Herald* (19 Dec. 1960).

"Selassie Pledges Unchanged Rule." *New York Times*, 21 Dec. 1960.

"Transition Period Ahead for Ethiopia." *Times* (London), 22 Dec. 1960.

"Ethiopian Rebels Beaten by Hesitation." *Times* (London), 22 Dec. 1960.

Luke, Sir Harry. "Witness of Ethiopian Palace Revolt." *Sunday Times* (London), 30 Dec. 1960.

"Ethiopia, Time for Apologies." *Time*, 2 Jan. 1961.

"A Clarion Call to the Youth of the Land . . ." *Voice of Ethiopia*, 9 Jan. 1961.

Walz, Jay. "The 'Conquering Lion' Still Reigns." *New York Times* [*Sunday*] *Magazine*, 15 Jan. 1961.

Unpublished Government Documents

The Public Record Office, London:

Foreign	371/7365
Office	16994
	20167
	27514
	27518
	27520
	27524
	31593
	31597
	31602
	31603
	31608
	35603
	35633
	35634
	36514
	36527
	41448
	41449
	41450
	41452
	41453
	41454
	41455
	41457
	41460
	41463
	41465
	41491
	46052
	53446
	53461
	53462
	53464
	53467
	53489
	63136
	63141
	63144
	63149
	63158
	63160

6920B
69291
69293
69295
69299
69327
69328
69340
69424
69445
73701
73765
73788
80247
80262
90080
403/255

War   32/9641   193/879   230/99
Office

The National Archives, Washington:

Decimal Files of the State Department, Ethiopia, 1930–1950

865D.01	884.50
884.00	884.50A
884.001 Selassie	884.51
884.014	884.515
884.143	884.555
884.154	884.6363
884.20	884.6363, Soc. Eth.
884.24	884.01A
884.42	

Miscellaneous Documents:

"Eritrea, Port of Assab," *Intelligence Report,* Aden, 1 March 1944, Record Group 226, OSS 64047.

"Ethiopia: Relations with Russia . . . ," *Intelligence Report,* Addis Ababa, Aug. 1944, Record Group 226, OSS 99715.

National Security Council, The Executive Secretary, "Disposition of the Former Italian Colonies in Africa." n. 19, 1949.

State Department, Office of Intelligence Research, Division of Research for the Near East and Africa. "The Capacity of

Eritrea for Independence." *Intelligence Report,* n. 5311, 25 July 1950.

Joint Chiefs of Staff, "Visit to Ethiopia by a Representative of the President," JCS 210.482 (5 Sept. 1951), Record Group 218.

Agency for International Development Reference Center, Washington:

Adams, Dale. "Agricultural Development Strategies in Ethiopia, 1950–1970." typescript, 18 Sept. 1970.

Andrews, Stanley. "Ethiopia." typescript, probably 1961.

Molohon, Albin D. "Report, USOM/E Agricultural Program, 16 July 1956–31 July 1959." typescript, 1959.

Truman Library, Independence, Missouri:

File 85E, Haile Selassie 319, Ethiopia

Special Collections, The Library, Michigan State University:

Deposited here are official U.S. Government documents from 1950 to 1969, released under the Freedom of Information Act.

Decimal Files of the State Department, Ethiopia, 1950–1961

611.75	775.02
711.56	775.11
770.00	775.5-MAP or -MSP
775.00	875.00

Various State Department Documents, 1962–69, with no decimal classifications.

Department of Defense Files

092, Ethiopia (9-26-56), Section 2

National Security Council Reports

"US Policy Toward Ethiopia." Approved 29 May 1957 as NSC 5615/1

"U.S. Policy Toward the Horn of Africa." Approved 2 March 1959 as NSC 5903.

"US Policy in the Horn of Africa." Approved 18 Jan. 1961 as NSC 6028.

Unpublished Private Documentary Sources

Greenfield Collection, Oxford, England:

Written Deposition of Leul Ras Imru, n.d., given to the Commission of Inquiry headed by Col. Tamrat Yigezu.

Written Deposition of Dej. Kebede Tessema, 20/4/53 E.C., given to the Commission of Inquiry headed by Col. Tamrat Yigezu.

The Patriarch's Leaflet

Published Government or Official Documents

Ethiopia, Government of, Press and Information Department. *Eritrea and Benadir*. Addis Ababa, 1945.

——, Ministry of Foreign Affairs. *Memoranda Presented by the Imperial Ethiopian Government to the Council of Ministers in London, Sept. 1945*. revised ed., London, 1946.

——, Ministry of Information. *Selected Speeches of His Imperial Majesty Haile Sellassie First, 1918-1967*. Addis Ababa, 1967.

——, Revolution Information Centre. *Ethiopia in Revolution*. Addis Ababa, 1977.

Four Power Commission (Deputies). *Final Report*. London, 1948.

Oromo Liberation Front, Foreign Relations. *Oromia Shall be Free*. mimeo., West Berlin, 1978.

United States, Government of, U.S. Operations Mission to Ethiopia. *The Point Four Program in Ethiopia*. Addis Ababa, 1954.

——, 91st Congress, Senate, second session. *United States Security Agreements and Commitments Abroad*, part 8 (Ethiopia). Washington, 1970.

Unpublished M.A. Thesis

Germame Neway. "The Impact of White Settlement Policy in Kenya." Columbia University, 1954.

Unpublished Doctoral Dissertations

Balsvik, Randi Rønning. "Haile Selassie's Students — Rise of Social and Political Consciousness." University of Trømso, 1979.

Gebru Tareke. "Rural Protest in Ethiopia, 1941-1970: A Study of Three Rebellions." Syracuse University, 1977.

Hamilton, David Napier. "Ethiopia's Frontiers: The Boundary Agreements and their Demarcations, 1896-1956." Trinity College, Oxford University, 1974.

Index

*See note on Ethiopian names above, p. 191.

Designer:	Barbara Llewellyn/Al Burckhardt
Compositor:	Interactive Composition Corporation
Printer:	Braun-Brumfield, Inc.
Binder:	Braun-Brumfield, Inc.
Text:	10/12 Sabon
Display:	Sabon

DATE DUE